for **Bill Salmon**

Drawings
for
TATTOOS
Volume 4
Kahlil Rintye
Edited by Don Ed Hardy

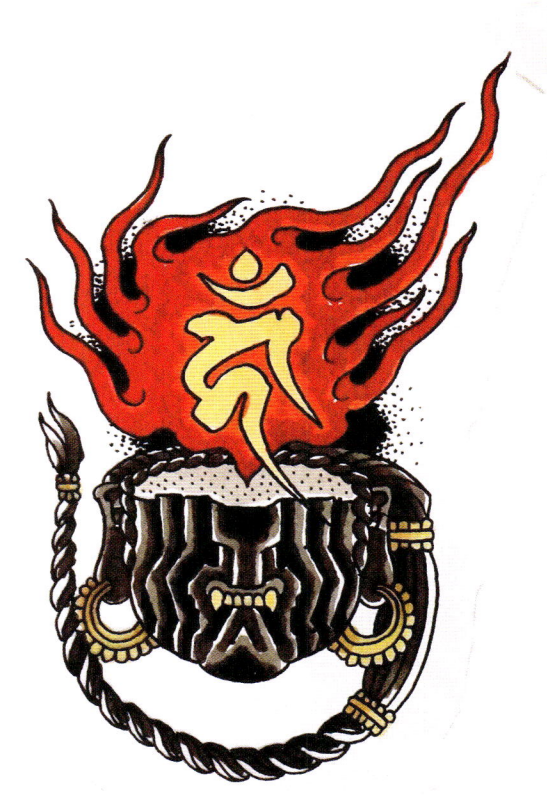

HM

HARDY MARKS PUBLICATIONS

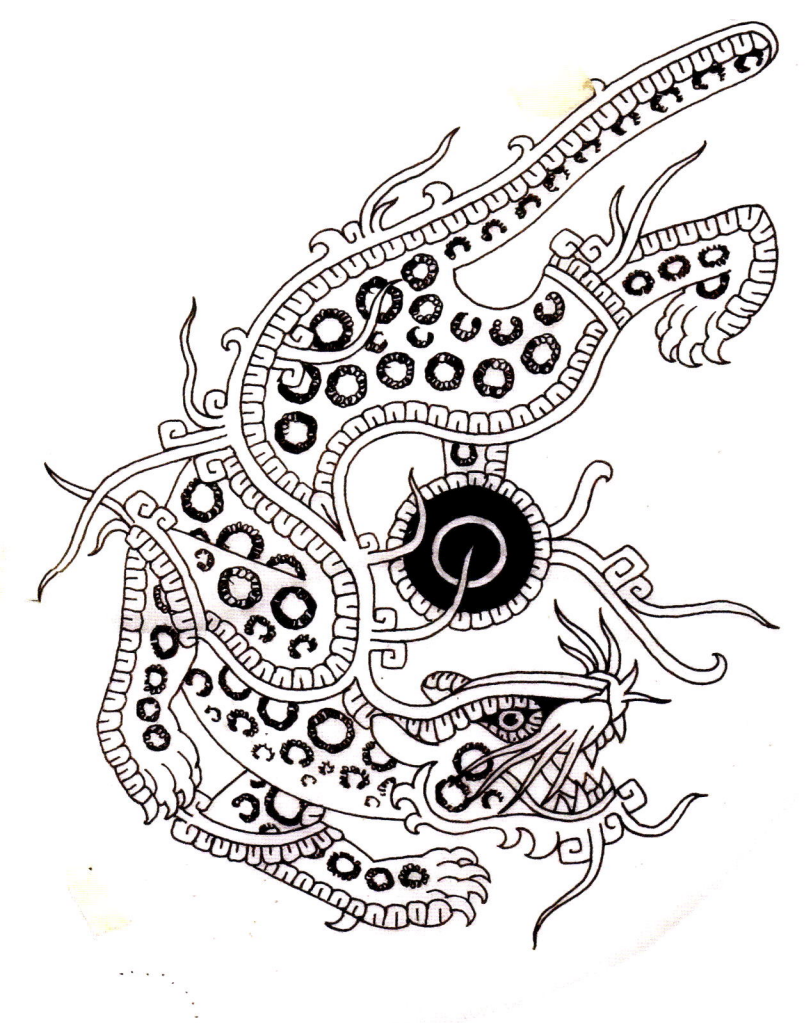

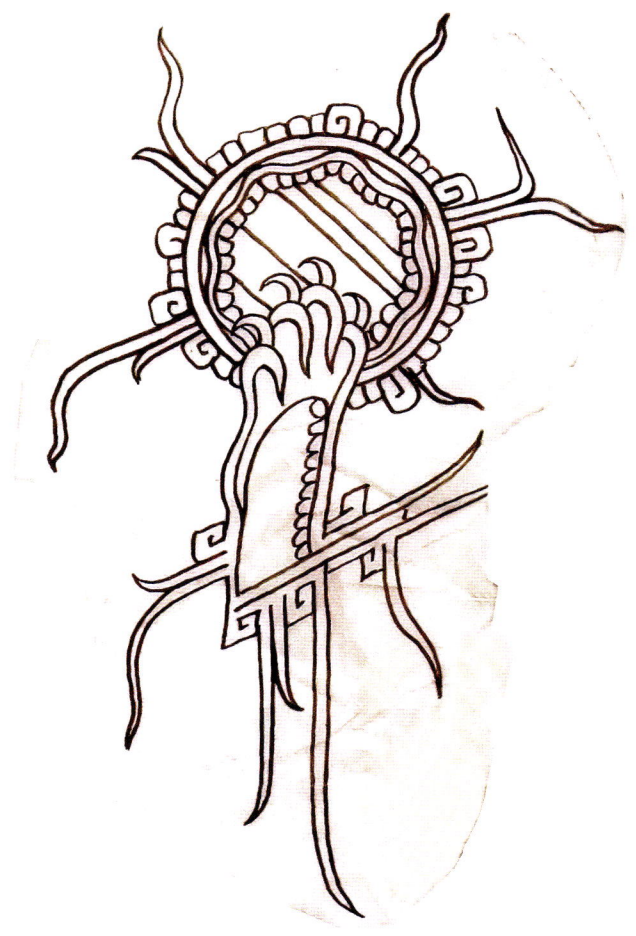

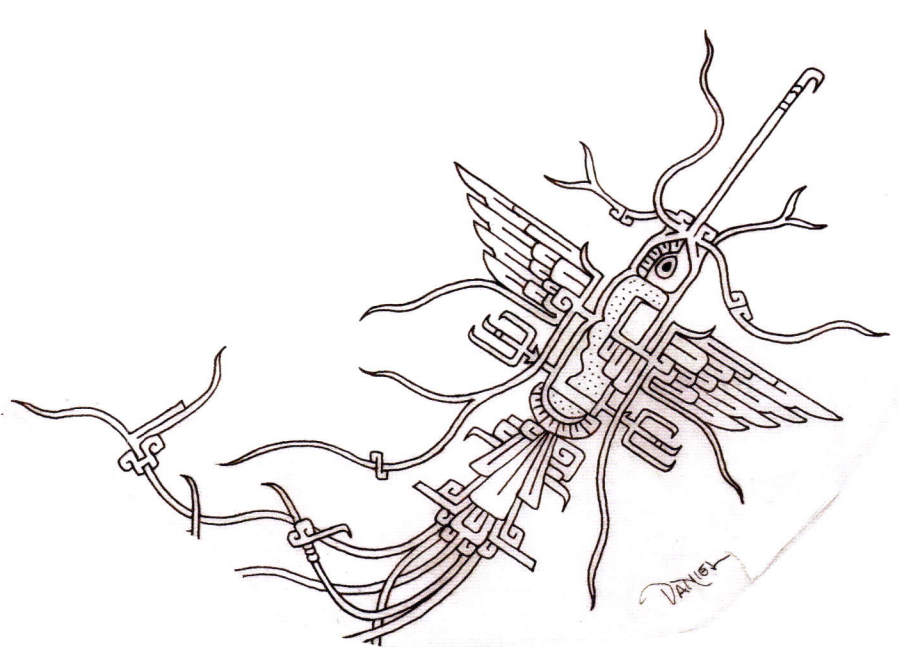

front cover:
GMK Battle Royale
38 x 22

title page:
Fudo Rock Head
7 x 4½

this page (from top):
Jaguar
10½ x 8
Jaguar Paw
7½ x 4½
Hummingbird
10½ x 7½

opposite page:
Koi and Dragon
13½ x 8½

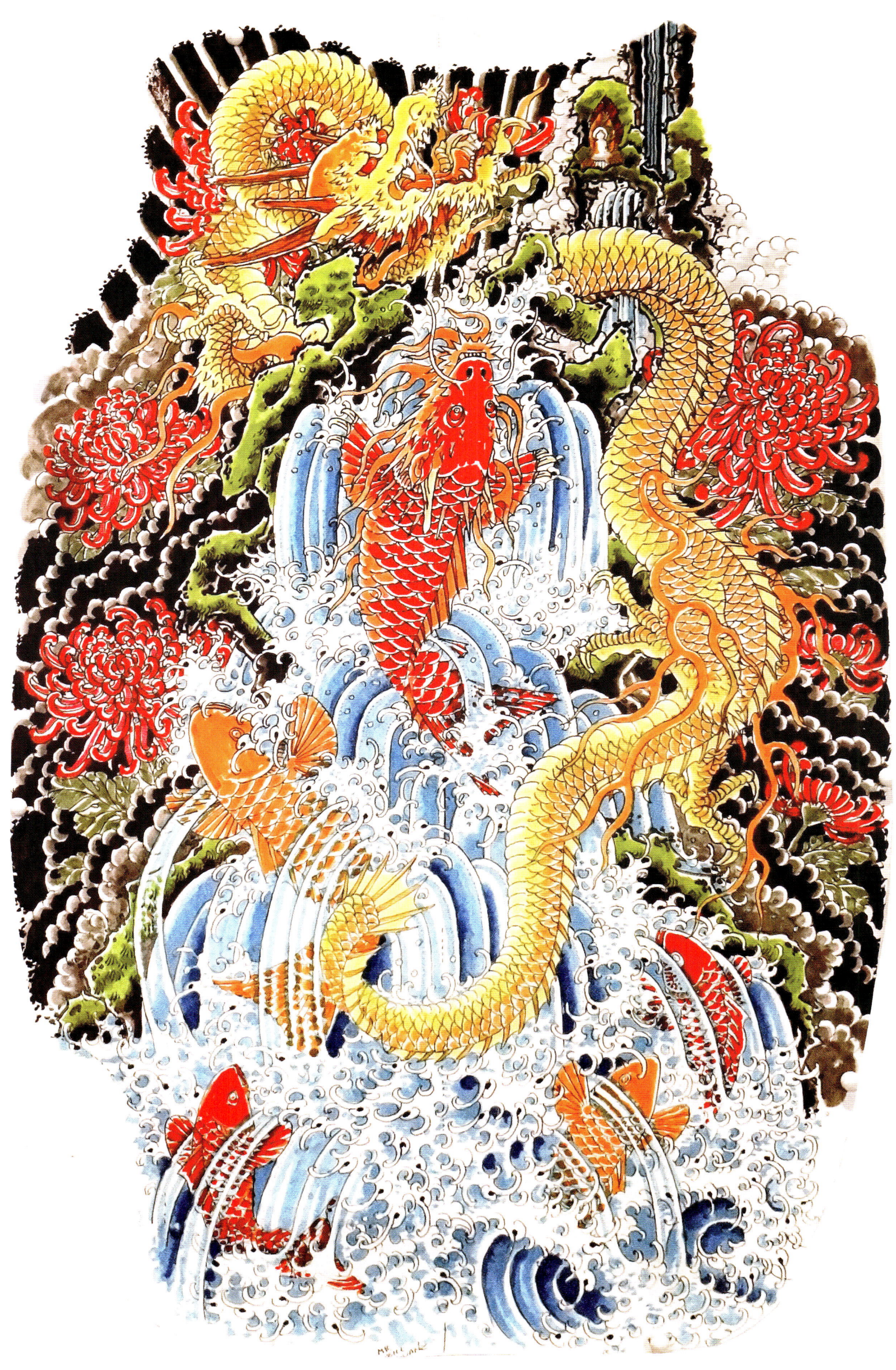

Kahlil Rintye
Drawings for TATTOOS Volume 4

For me, the people that appear in Hardy Marks Publications are the stuff of myth & legend. They fly from caves on misty mountaintops or dwell in surreal alphabet city apartments. They expand my understanding of reality and the things that connect all of us. These people change things.

What in the hell am I doing in a Hardy Marks publication?

When asked by Ed if I was up for making this book, I said "I'll do it!" while thinking of all the other people who would be better subjects for it—this pretty much sums up the way I've approached every tattoo in my career as well. I am one of the lucky few whose tattoos Ed Hardy actually looks at, and to appear in this *Drawings for Tattoos* series next to him is a staggering honor. Out there in the world there are hundreds and hundreds of tattooers, thousands probably, that have truly picked up what Ed was laying down, and any one of them could have been the subject for this book.

The first copy of *Tattootime* I laid hands on (the *Music & Sea Tattoos* issue) had already been read so many times it looked 50 years old. A hallowed document.

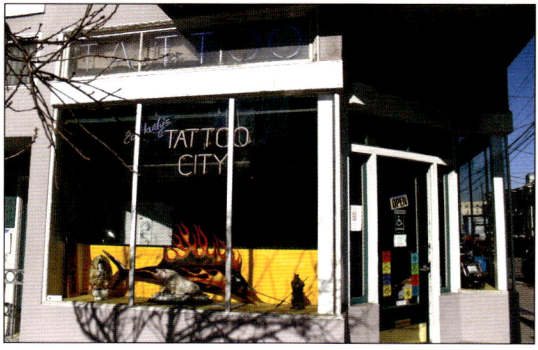

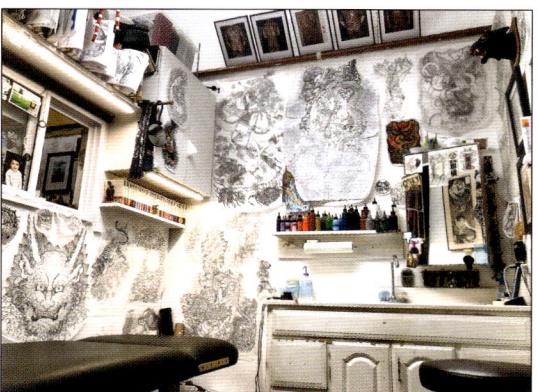

I look at it now...and that's my professional life there, chasing what's in that book. I still find it hard to believe I work at Tattoo City, even after all this time, and that the man who made that book is such a good person in real life. I have found again and again as I have gotten to meet my heroes—the extended tattoo family that together cracked this thing wide open—so many are just great humans.

The changing of the guard happens whether we want it to or not, and that change is now upon us. The ladies & gentlemen continuing this 'new' tradition that Ed started...if we all really are to be the 'new' Old Men, then WE must carry the fire, keep it pure, and pass it on. For those that passed it to us.

Thank you, Ed...for everything. In the galactic sense.

Thank you to my customers for trusting me. I would like to thank Daniel Balderas, who wanted a Quetzalcoatl tattoo that spawned a whole family of drawings that continue today. Also thank you to Nick Hunt, who asked me for the first panther thing. I'm pretty sure those two threads of work are why Ed made this book. Thank you to Mike Martin for letting me in the business, and thank you to Fip Buchanan for putting my name in the mix when it counted the most. Last but not least, thank you to my two favorite people in the world, they know who they are...

Keep your aim true,
Kahlil Rintye
San Francisco
January 23, 2019

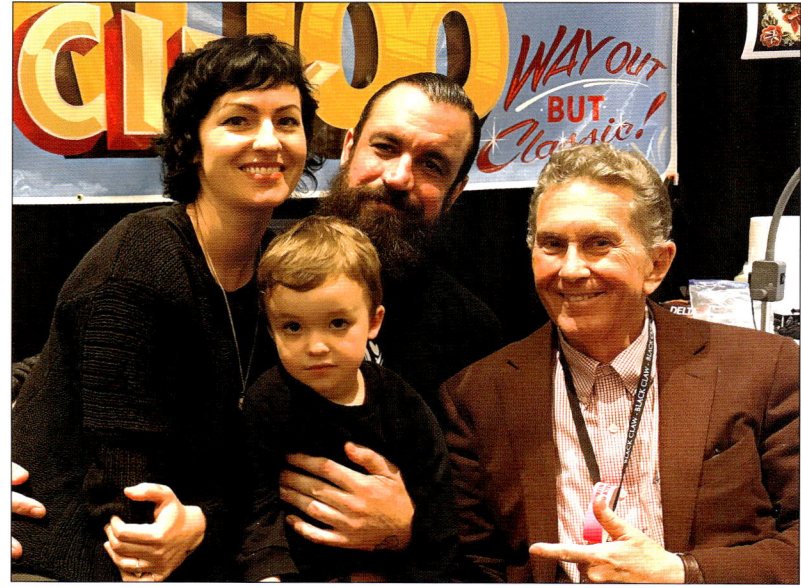

From left: wife Wendy Wagner, son Gus, Kahlil Rintye, Ed Hardy (at the San Francisco Tattoo Convention, 2018)

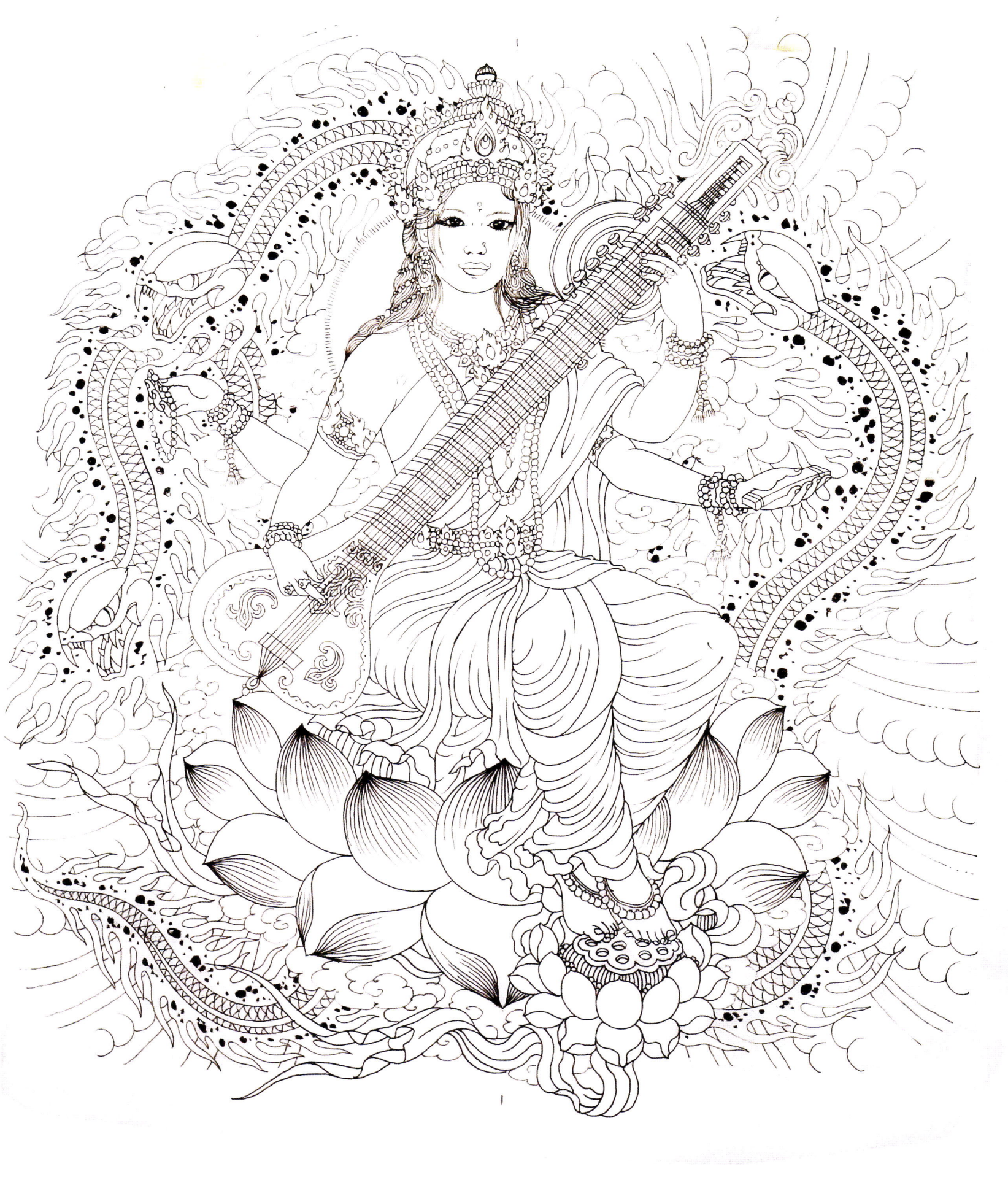

Sarasvati
25 x 21½

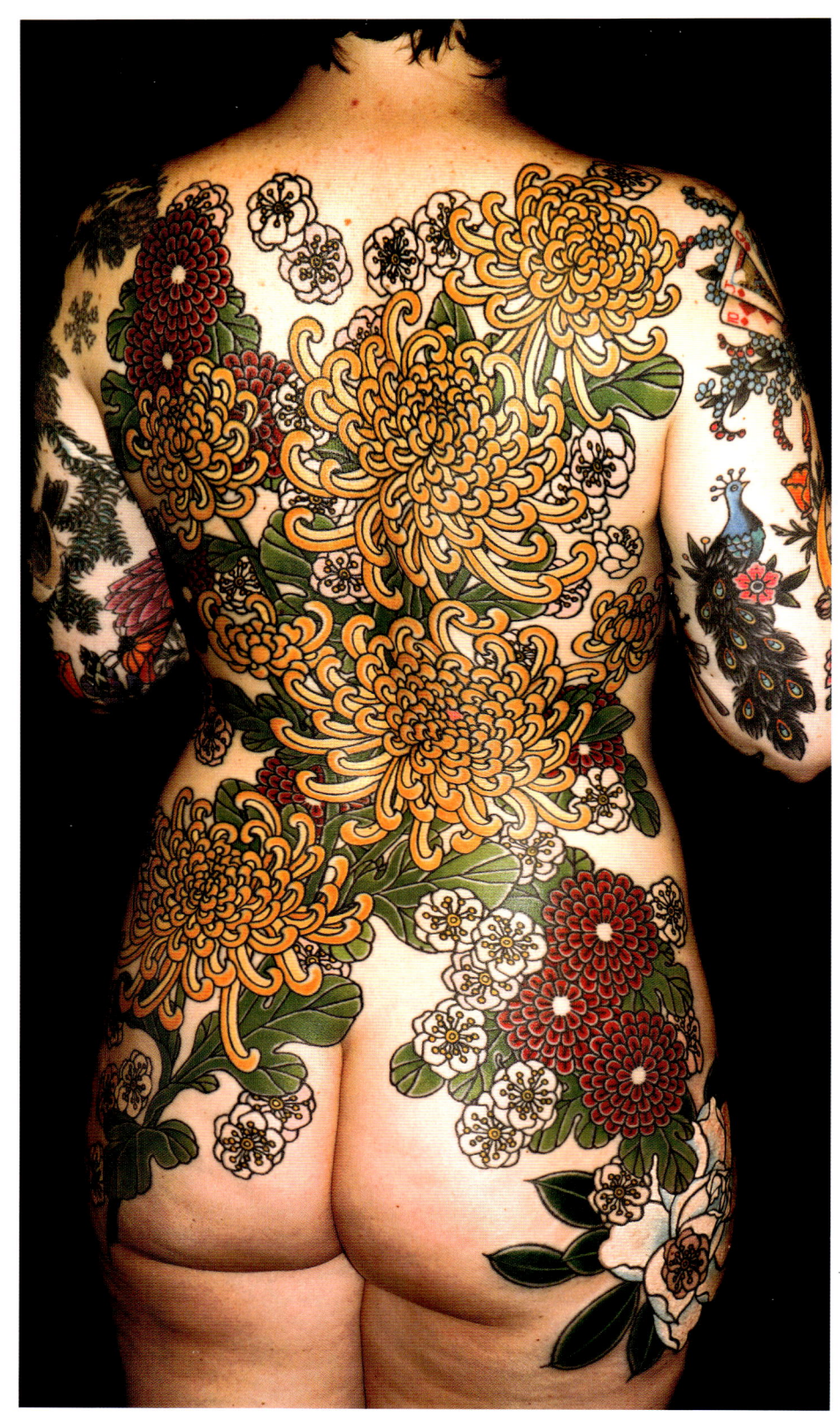

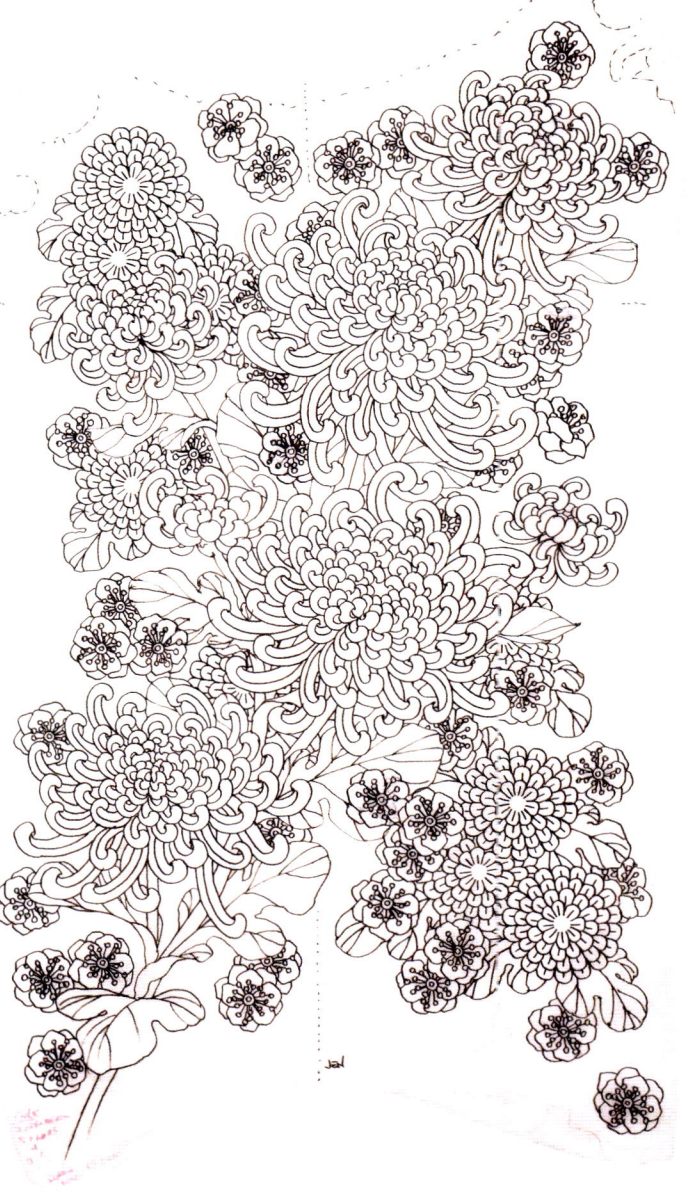

Mum
26¹/₂ x 15¹/₂

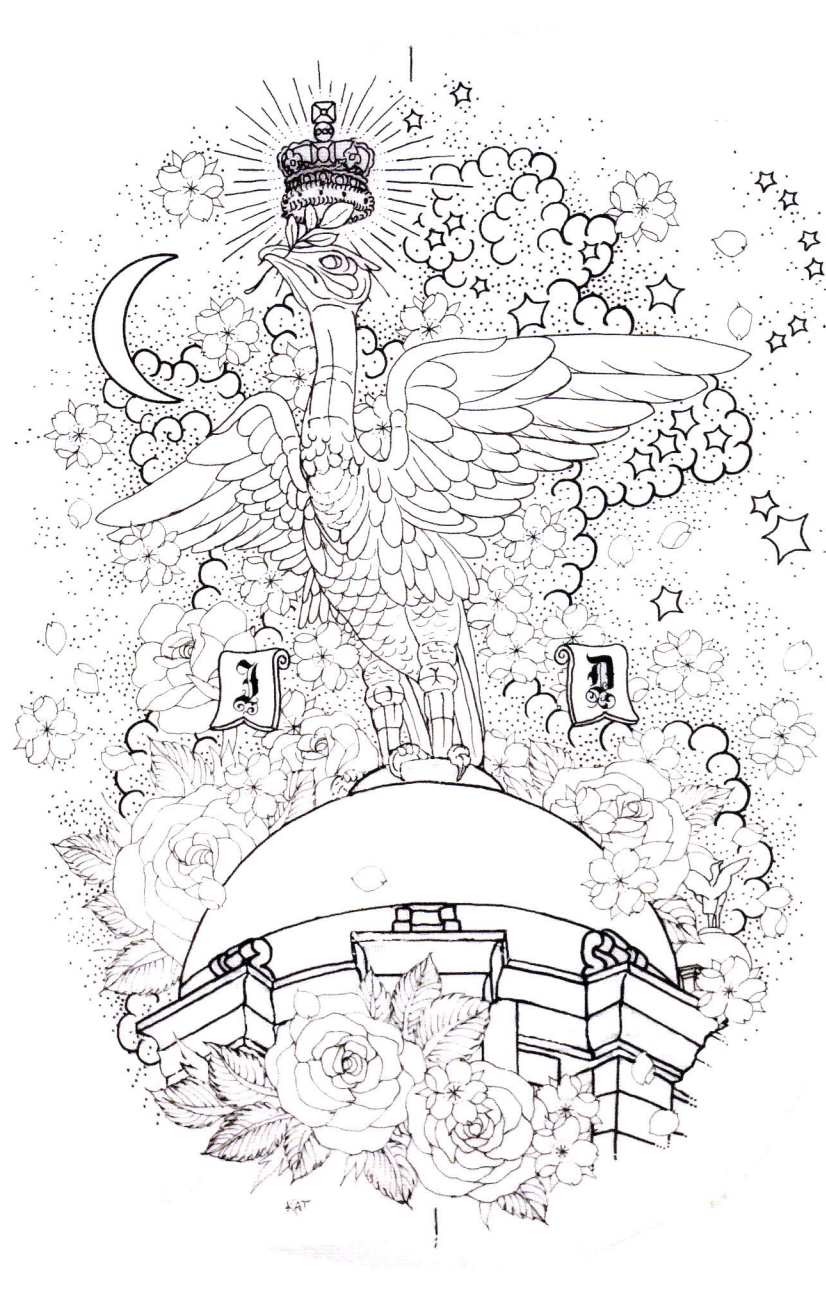

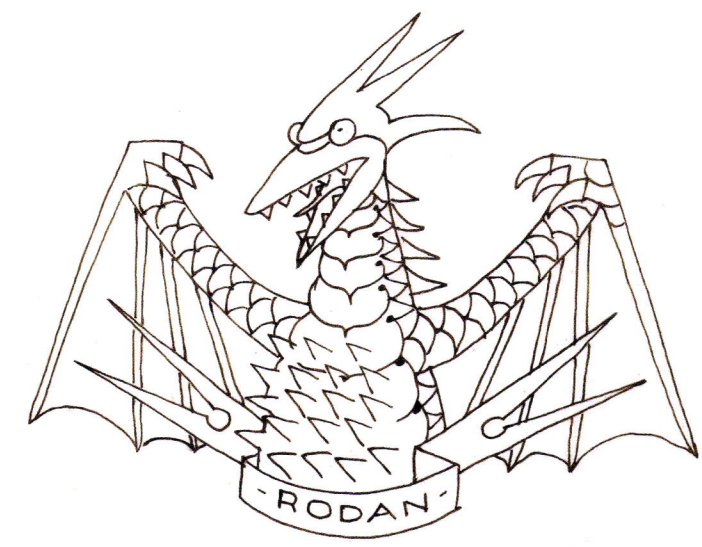

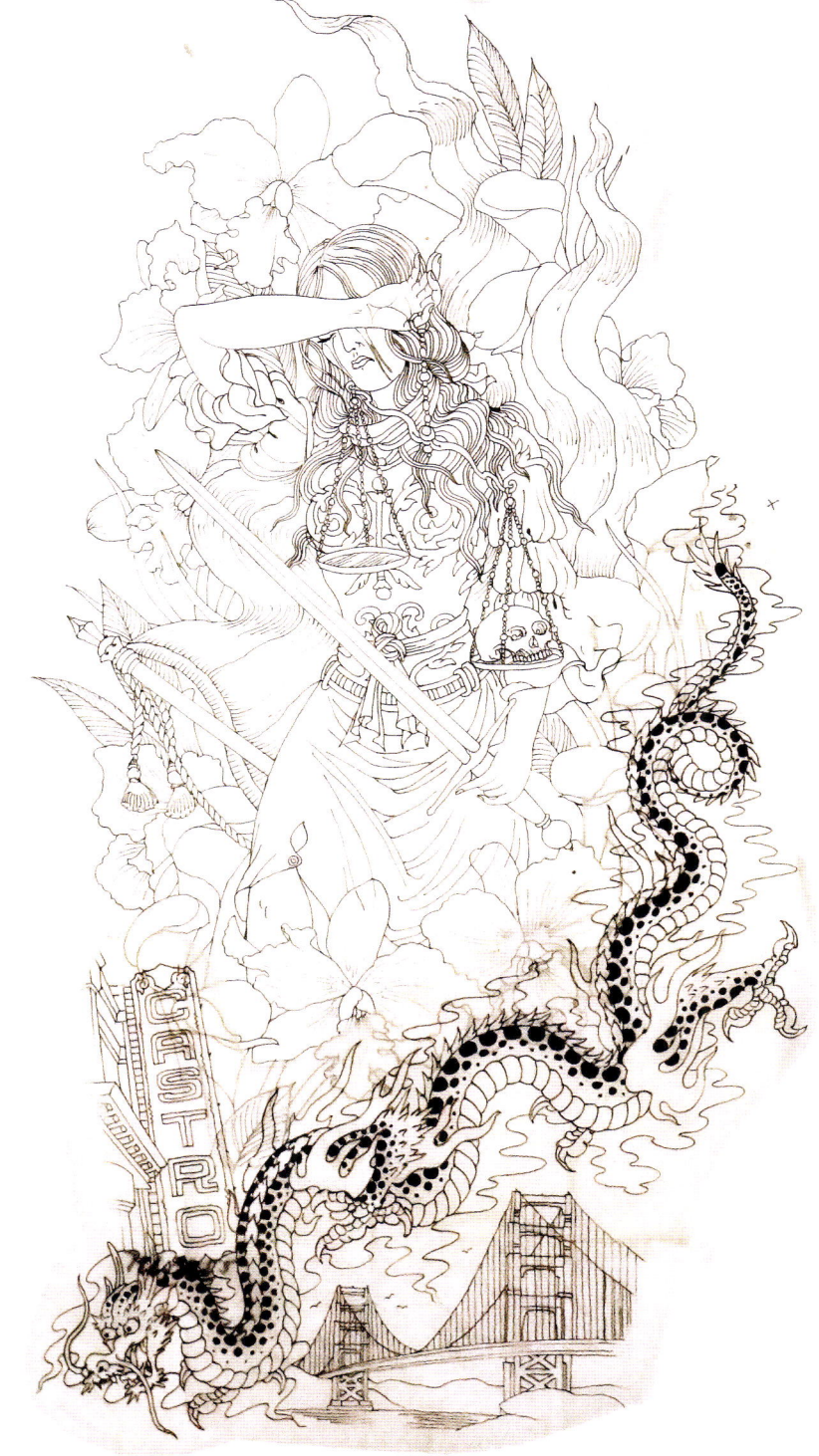

top left:
Liverpool
20 x 14

top right:
Rodan
6 x 5

bottom:
Gay Rights SF
24 x 13

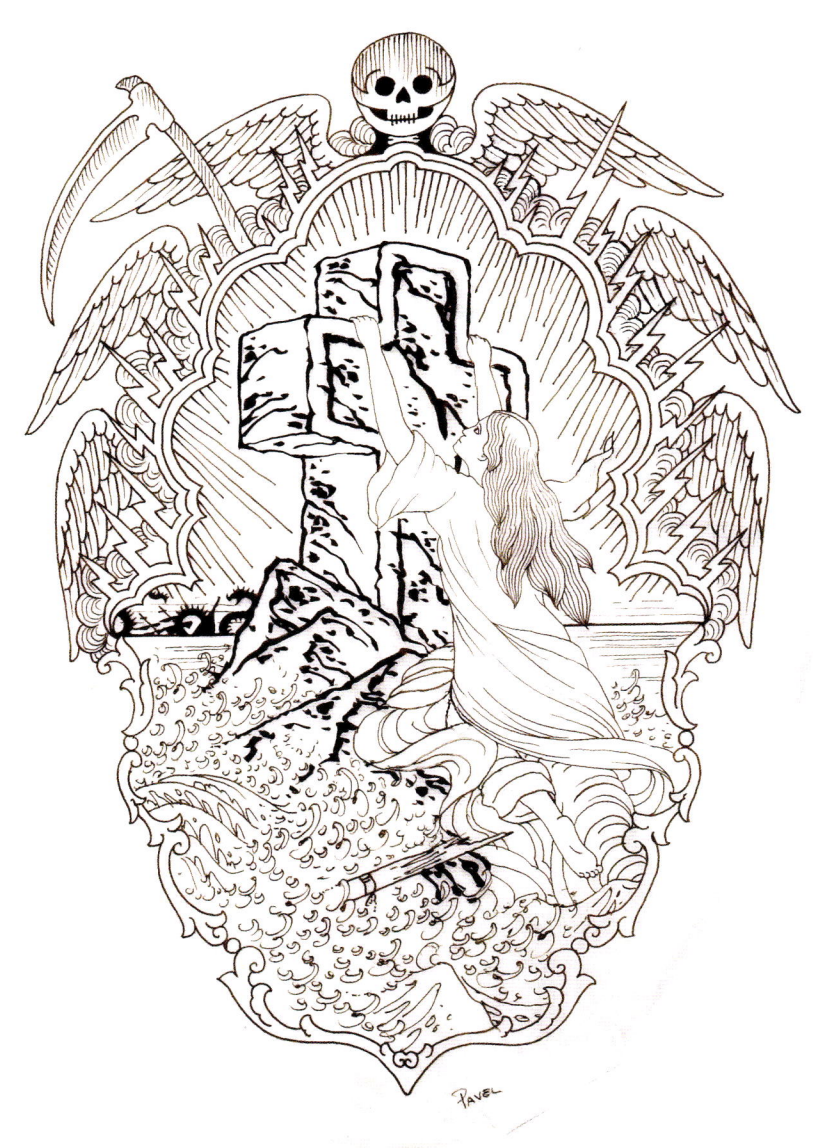

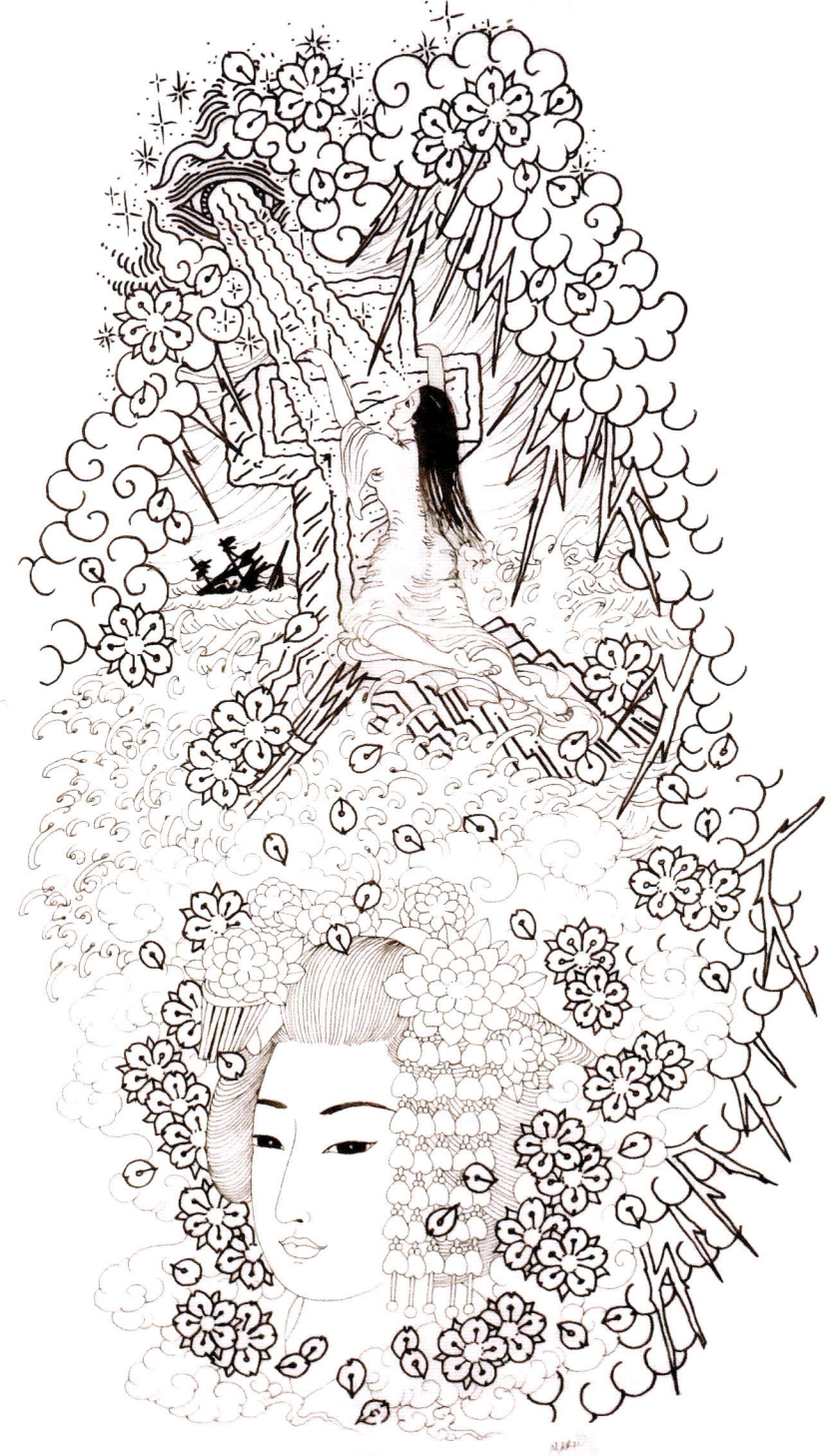

top:
Rock of Ages
25 x 17

bottom:
Rock of Ages and Maiko
24 x 13

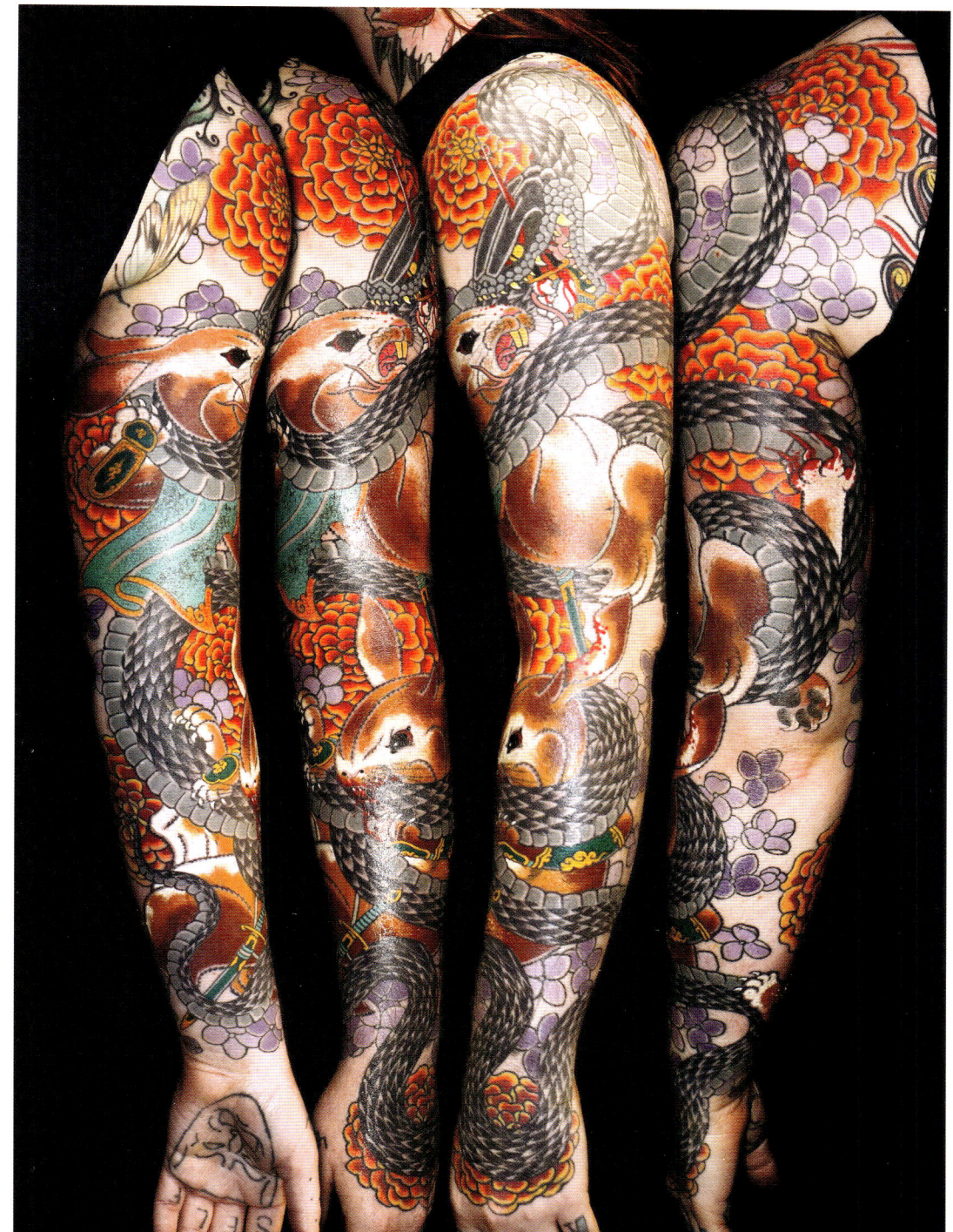

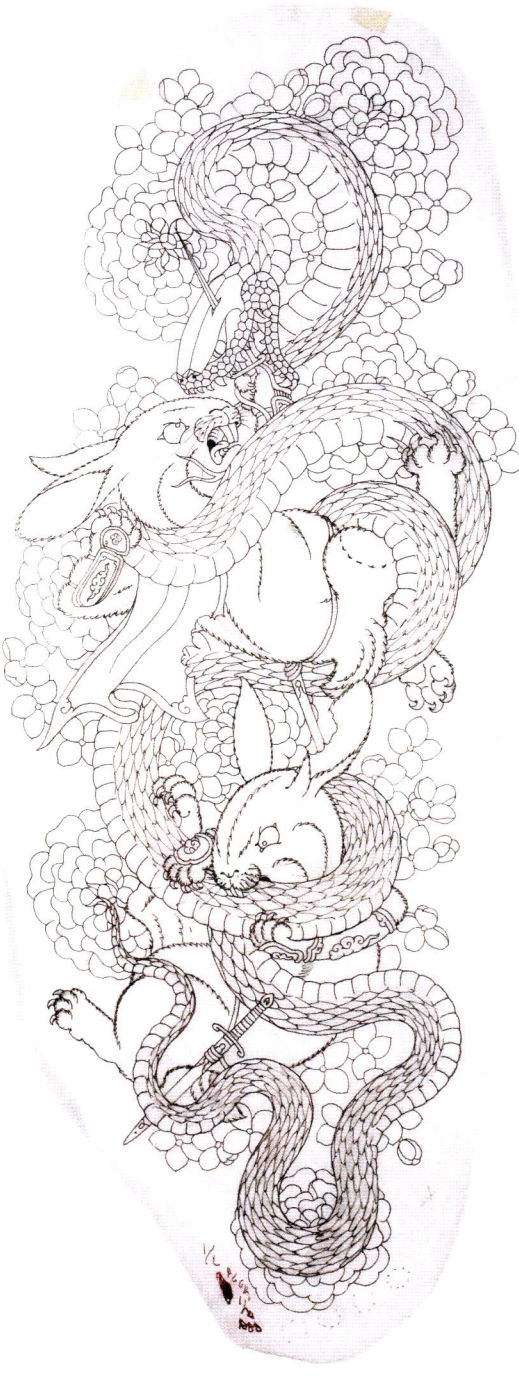

Rabbits Fighting Snake
28 x 11

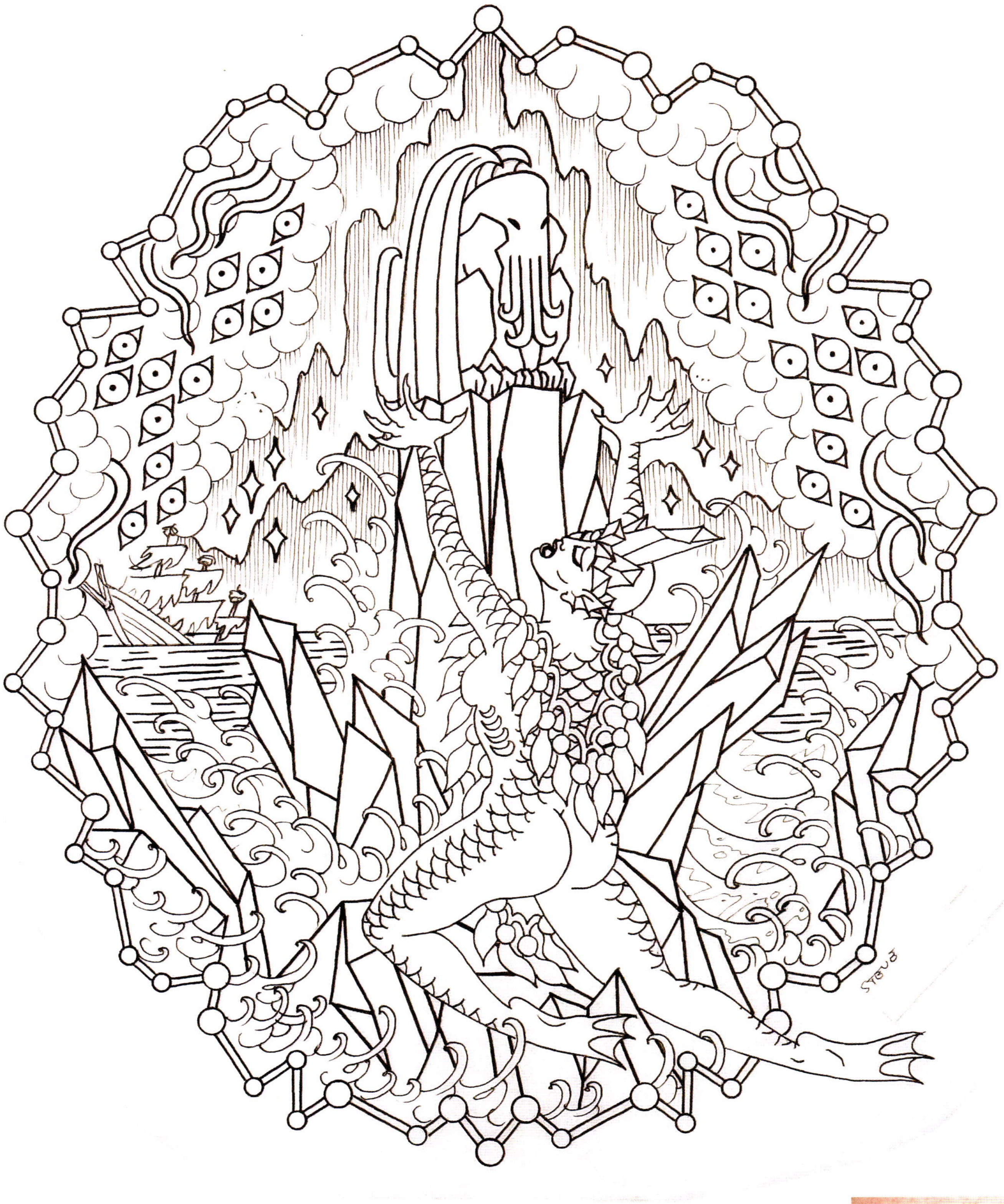

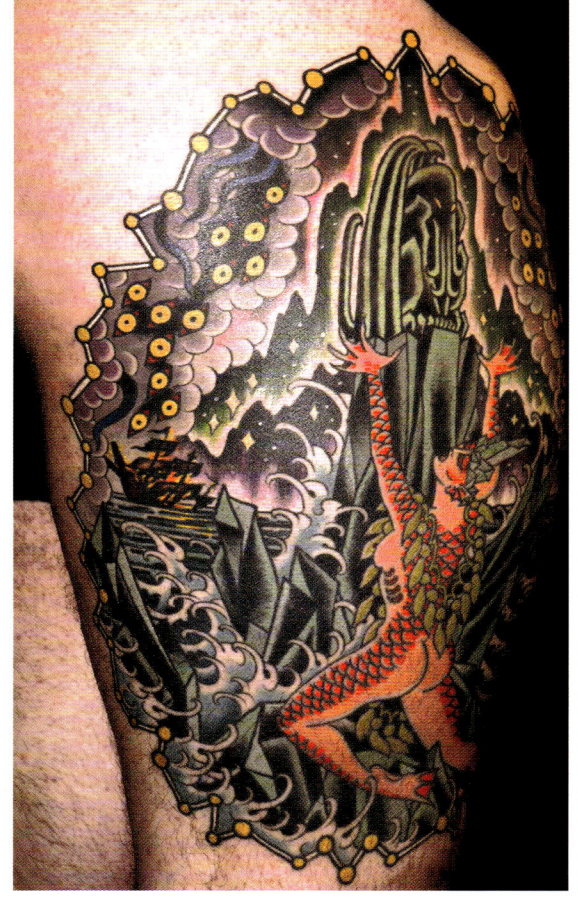

this page:
Rock of Cthulu
15$\frac{1}{2}$ x 13

opposite page top:
Kid Monsters
20 x 14

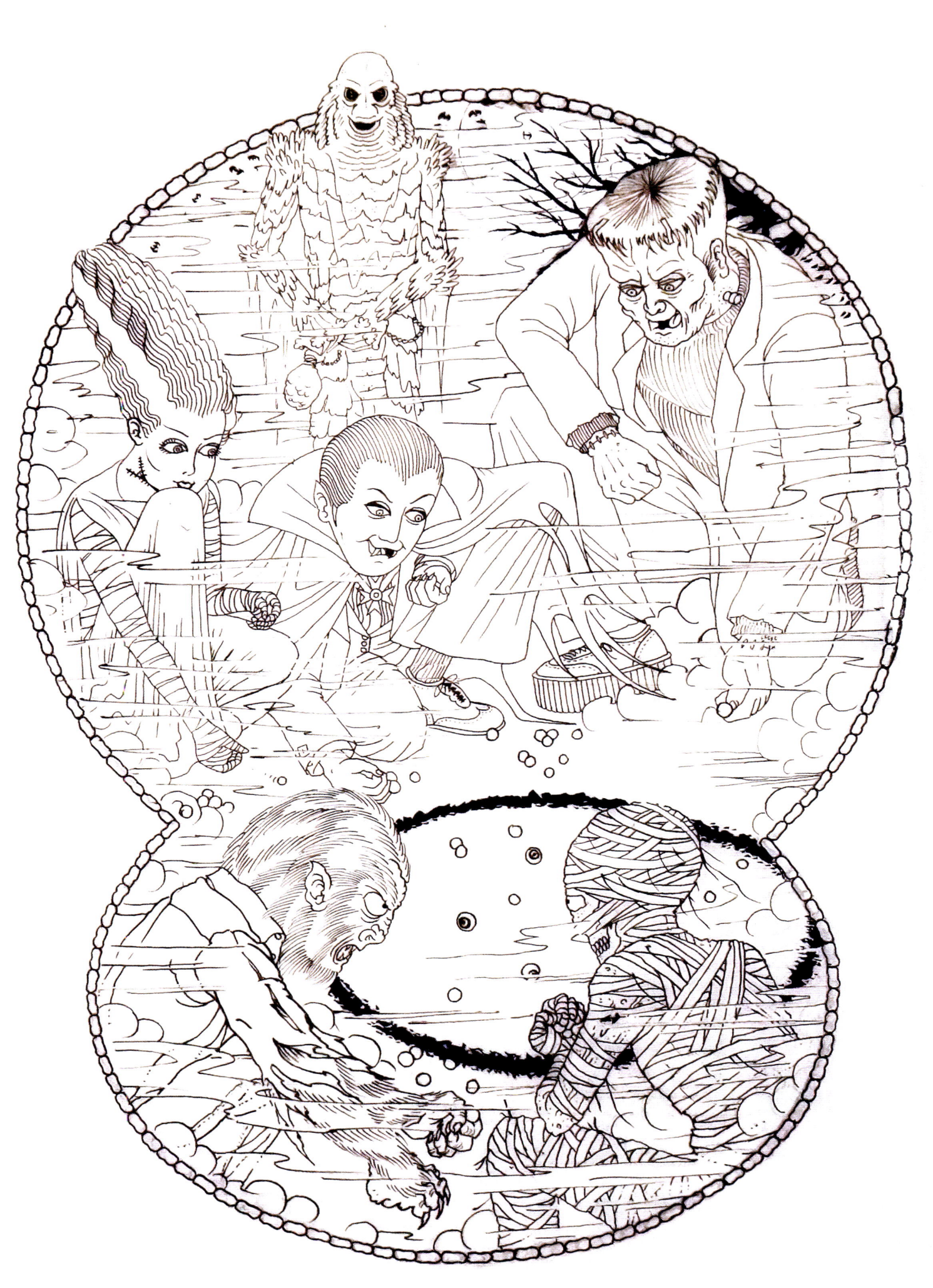

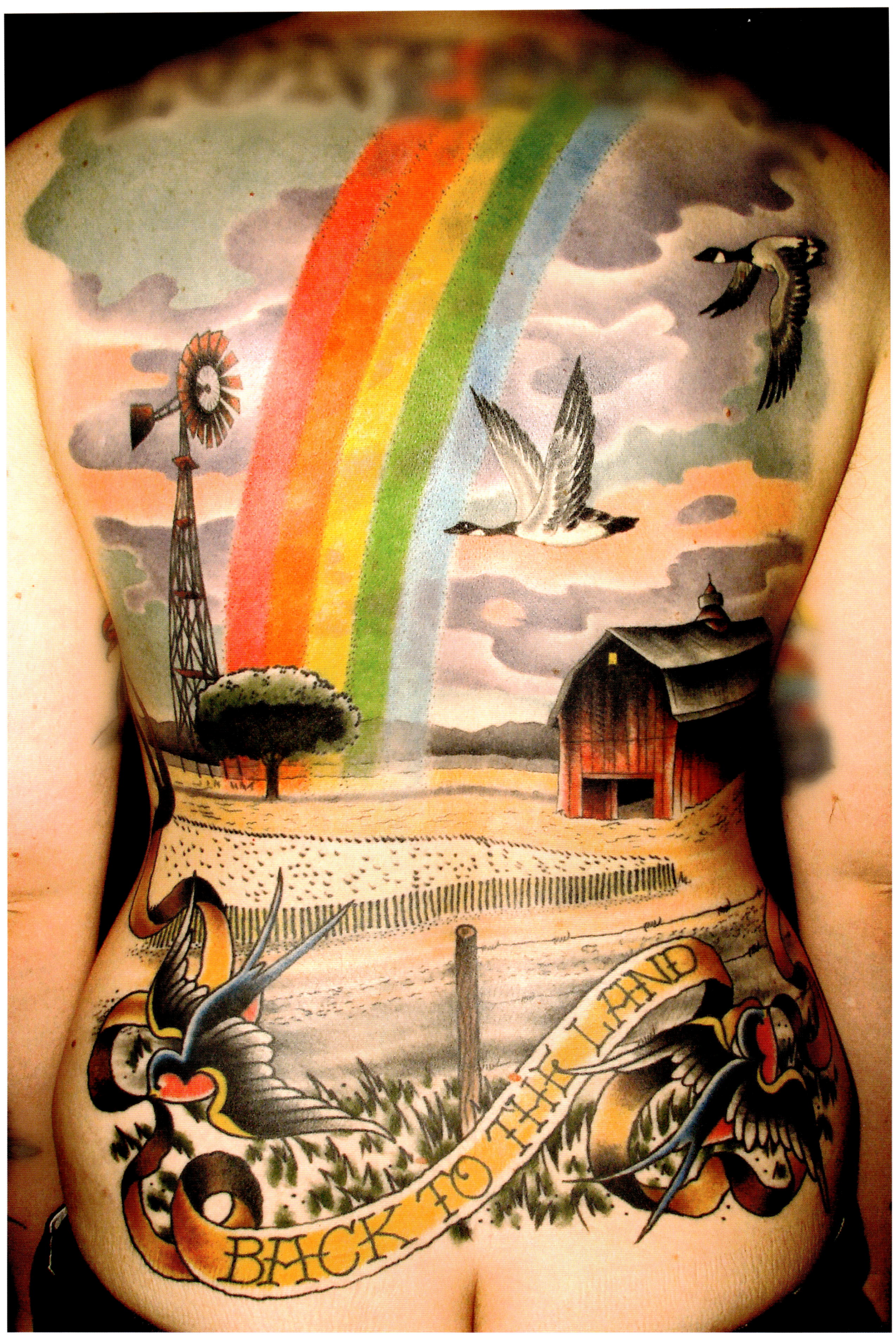

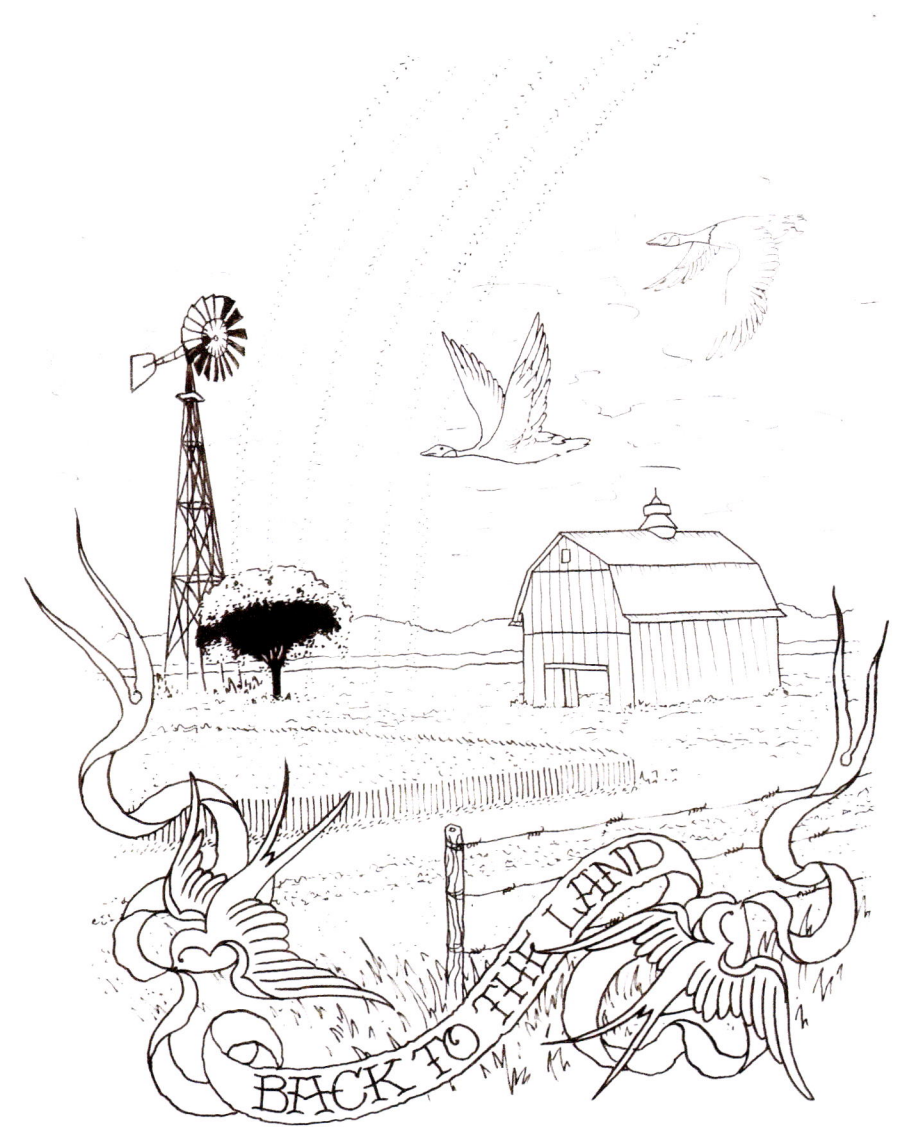

Back to the Land
20 x 15

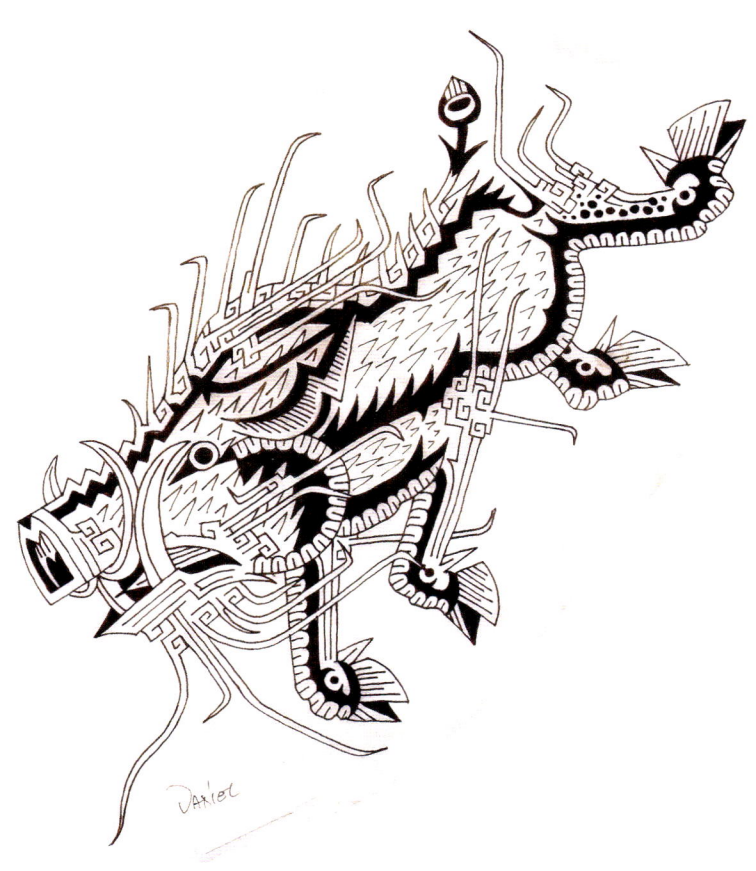

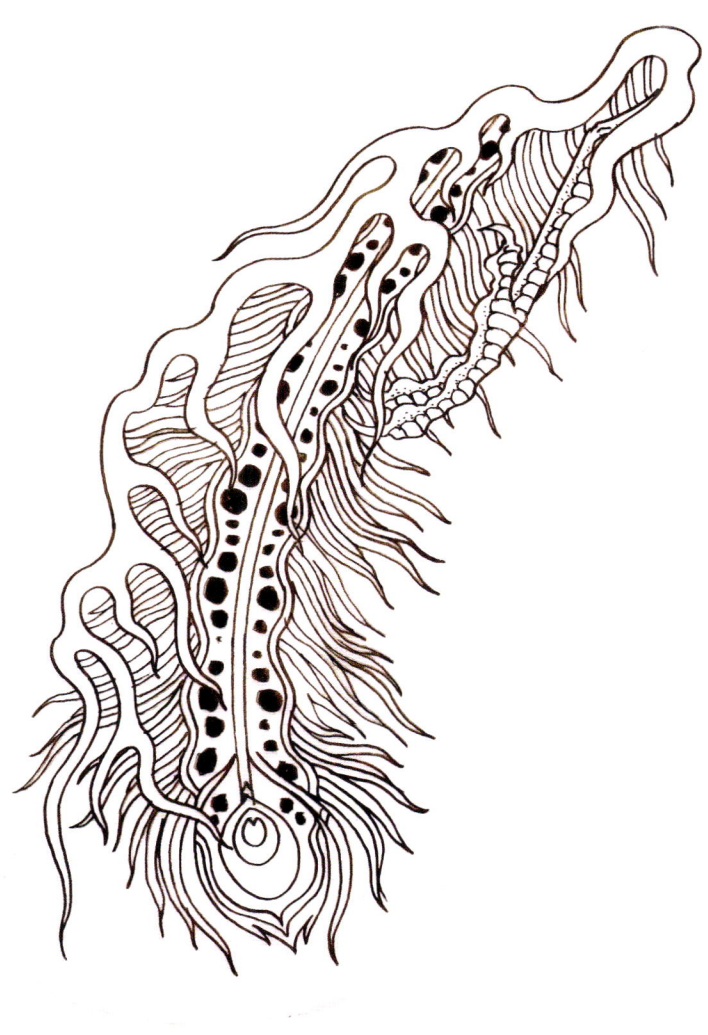

left:
Boar
12 x 10

right:
Bit O Phoenix
15 x 7

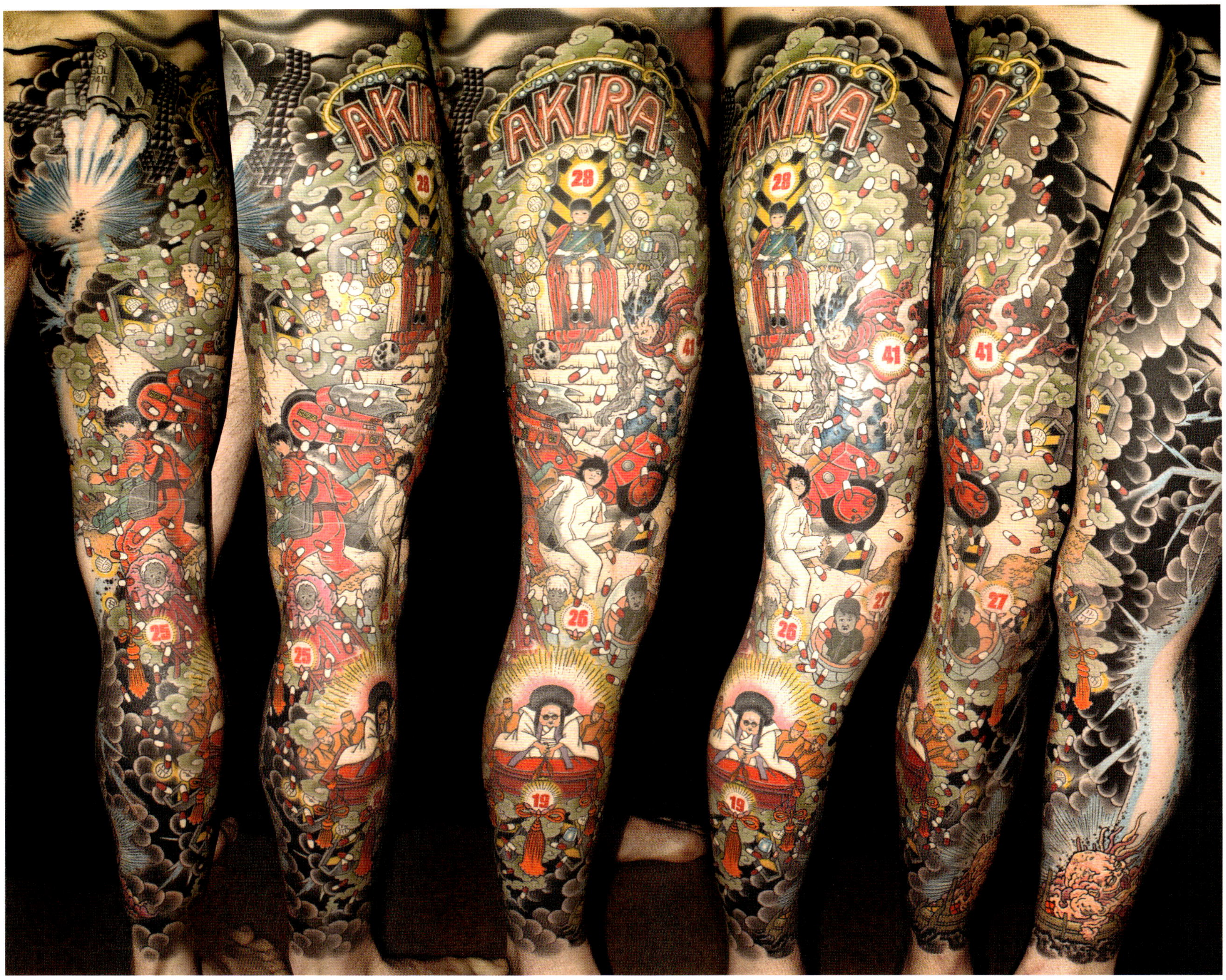

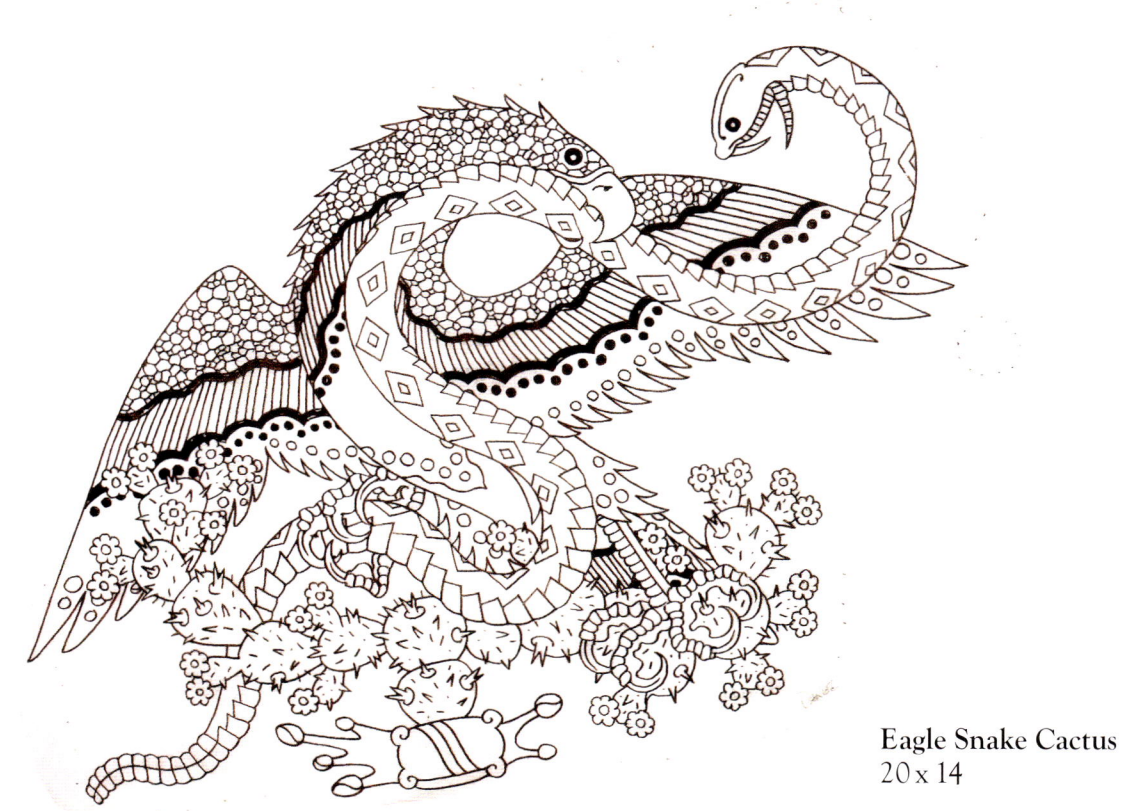

Eagle Snake Cactus
20 x 14

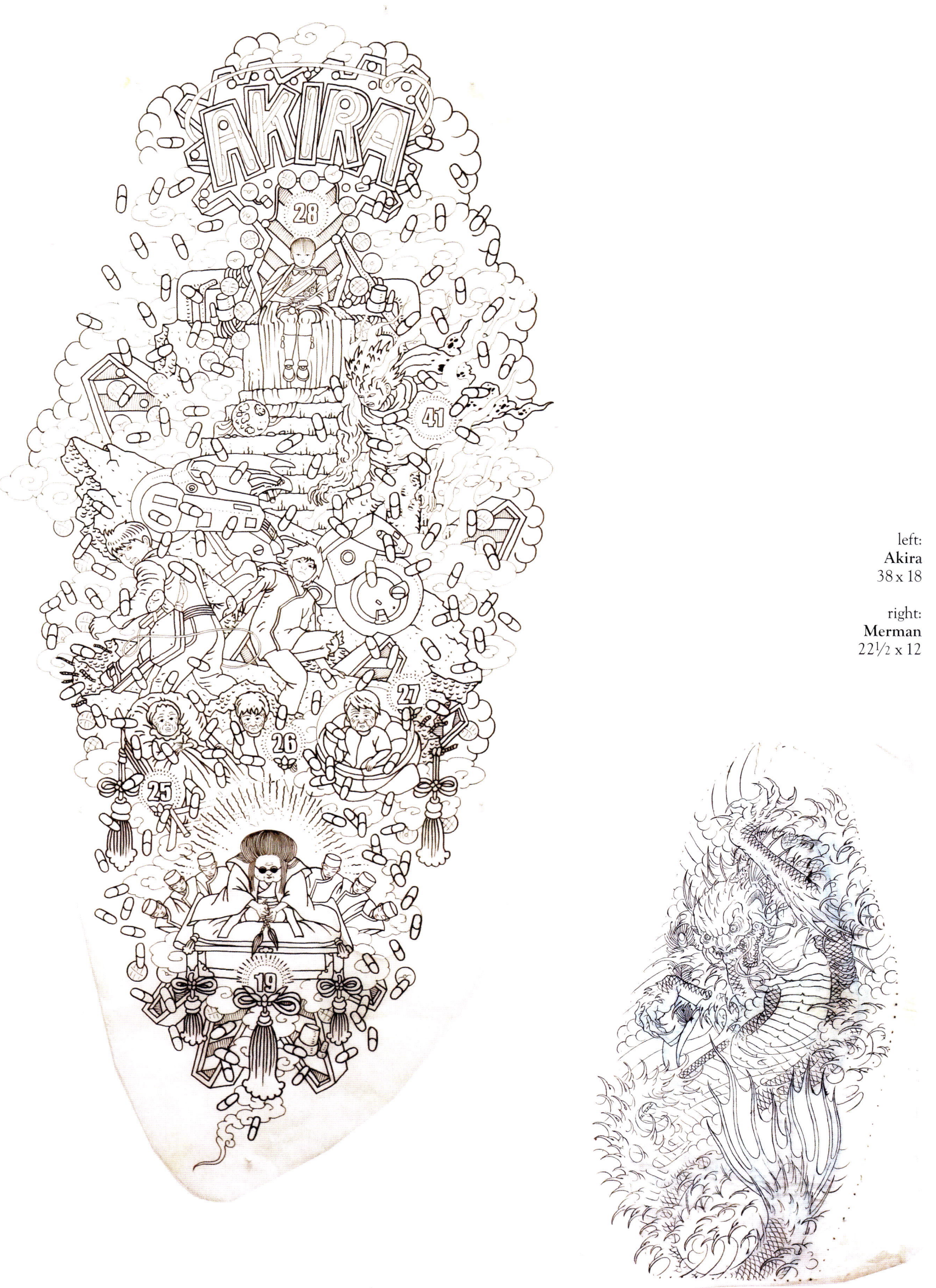

left:
Akira
38 x 18

right:
Merman
22½ x 12

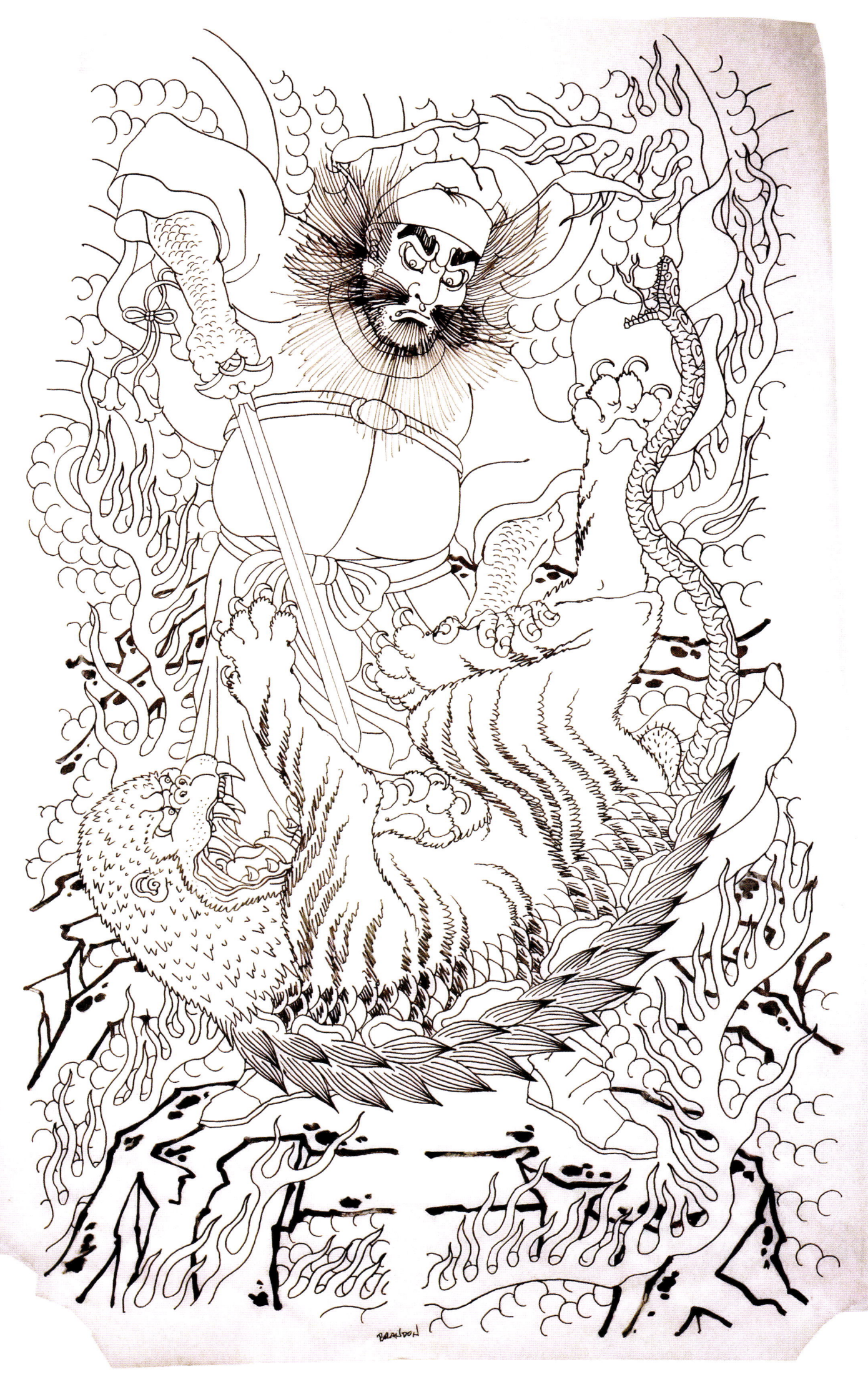

Shoki vs. Nue
34 x 21

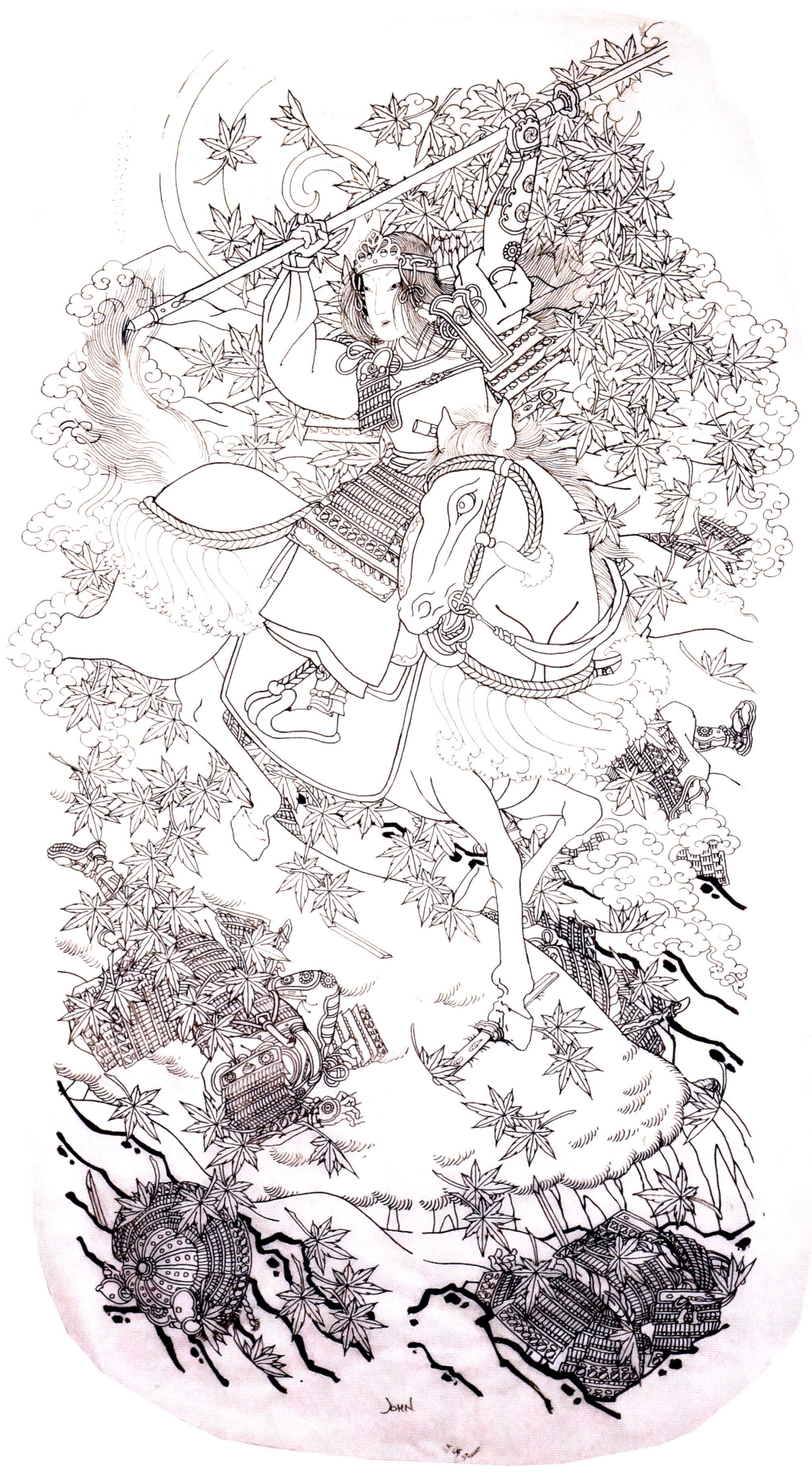

Tomoe Gozen
41 x 23

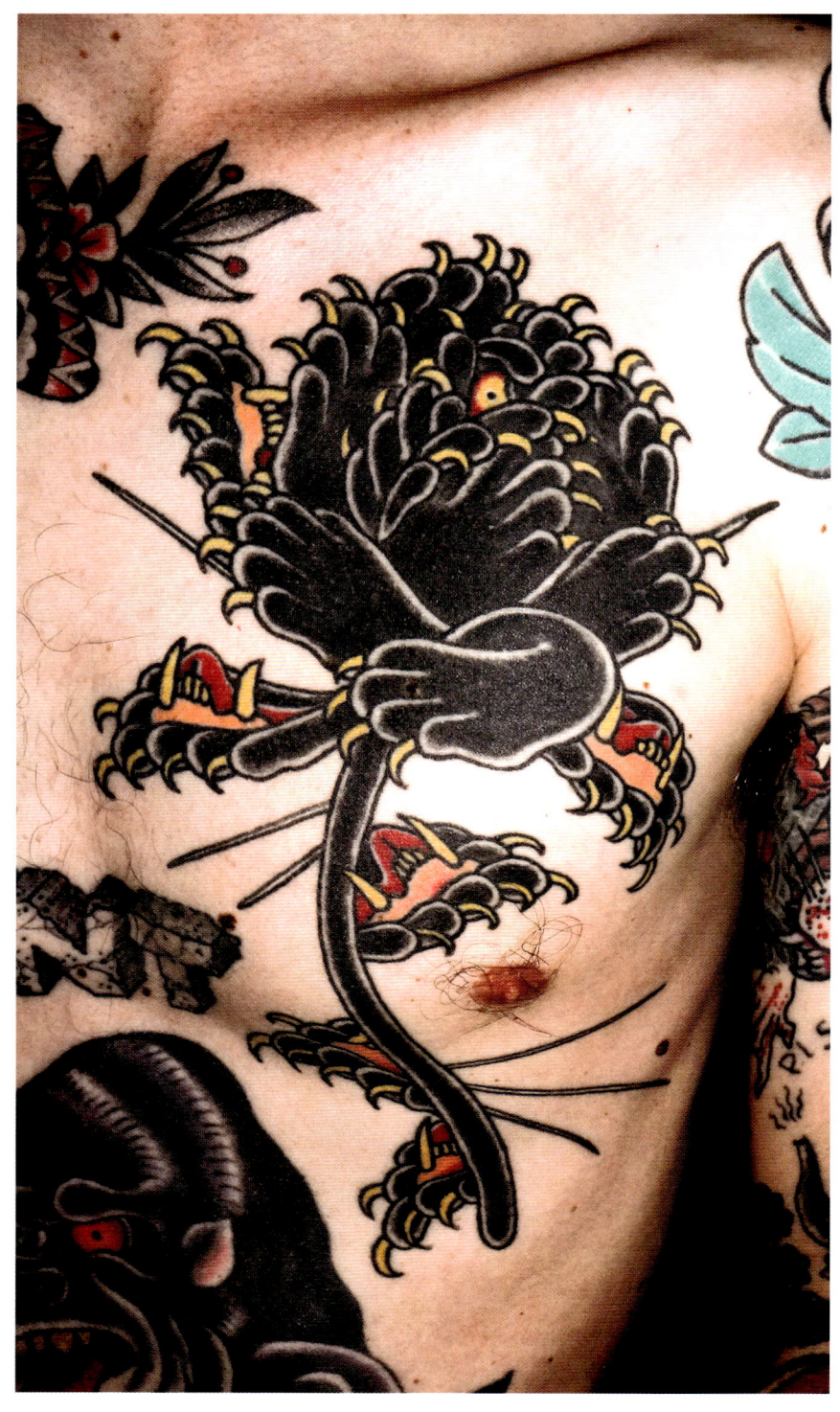

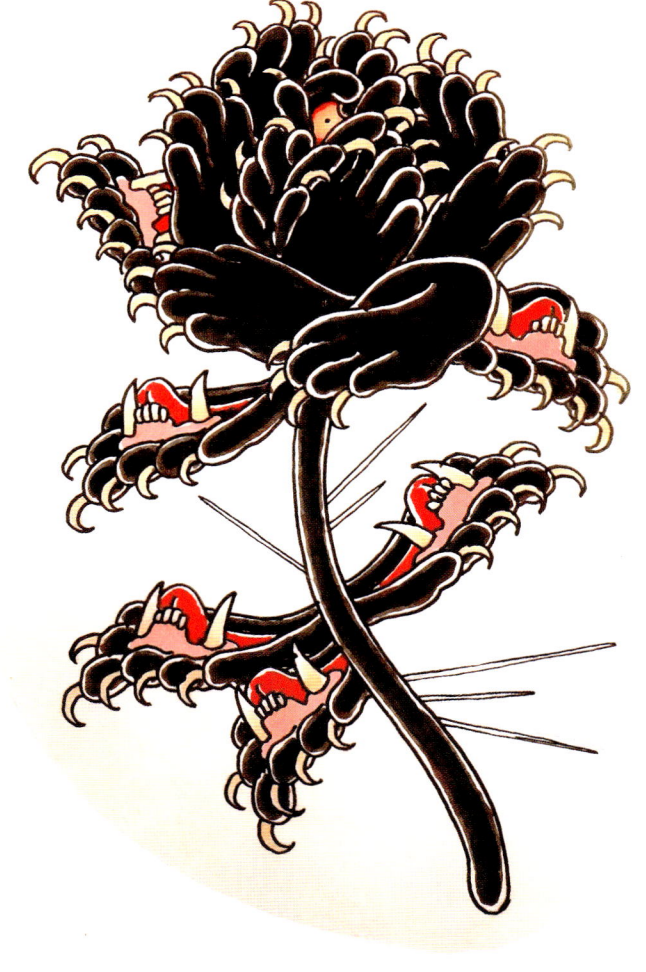

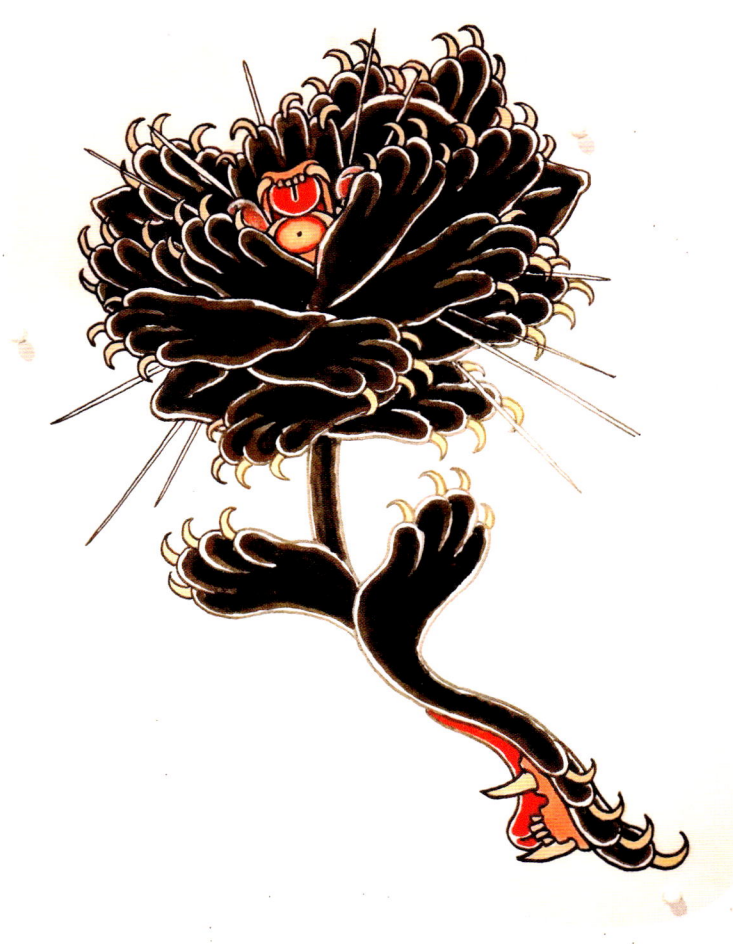

top right:
Panther Rose 1
10 x 6

bottom:
Panther Rose 2
10 x 6

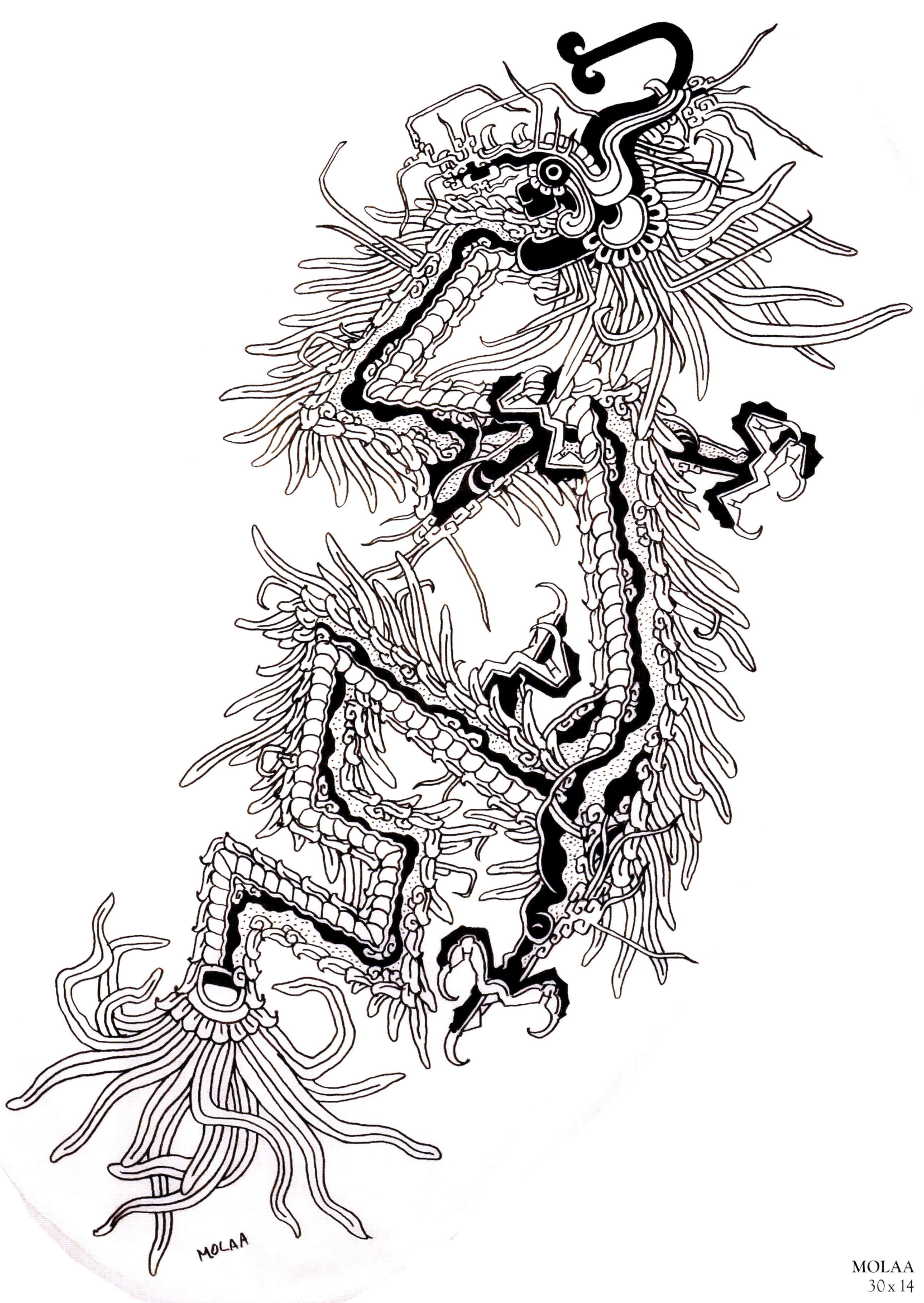

MOLAA
30 x 14

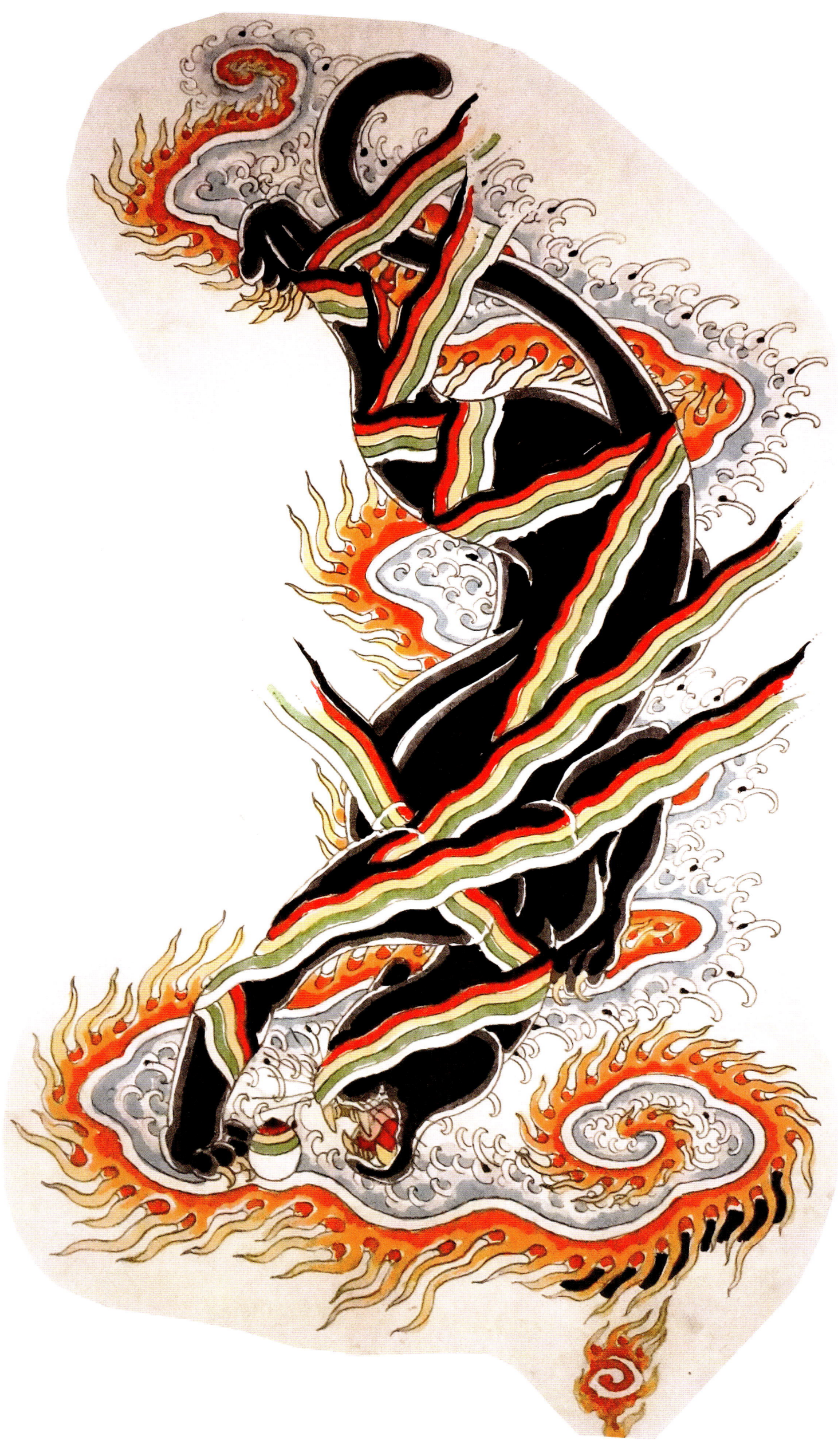

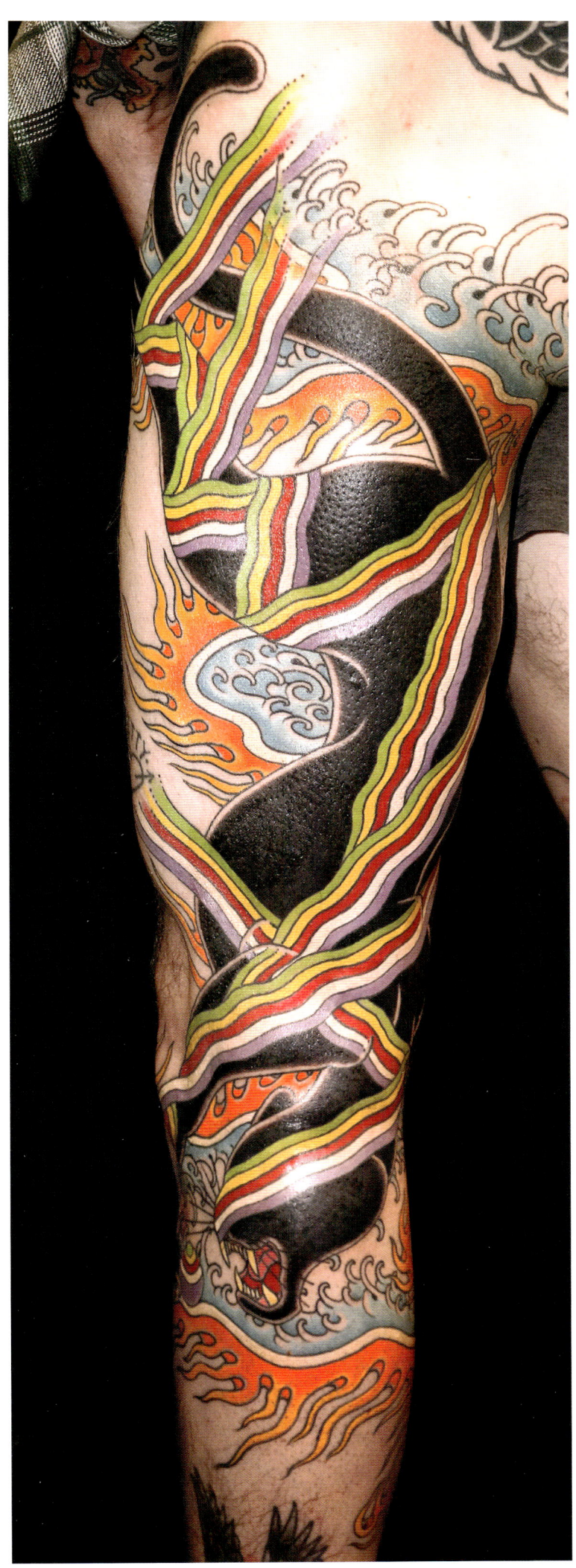

opposite page:
Panther Epiphany
14 x 8

this page right:
Panther Epiphany
29 x 15½

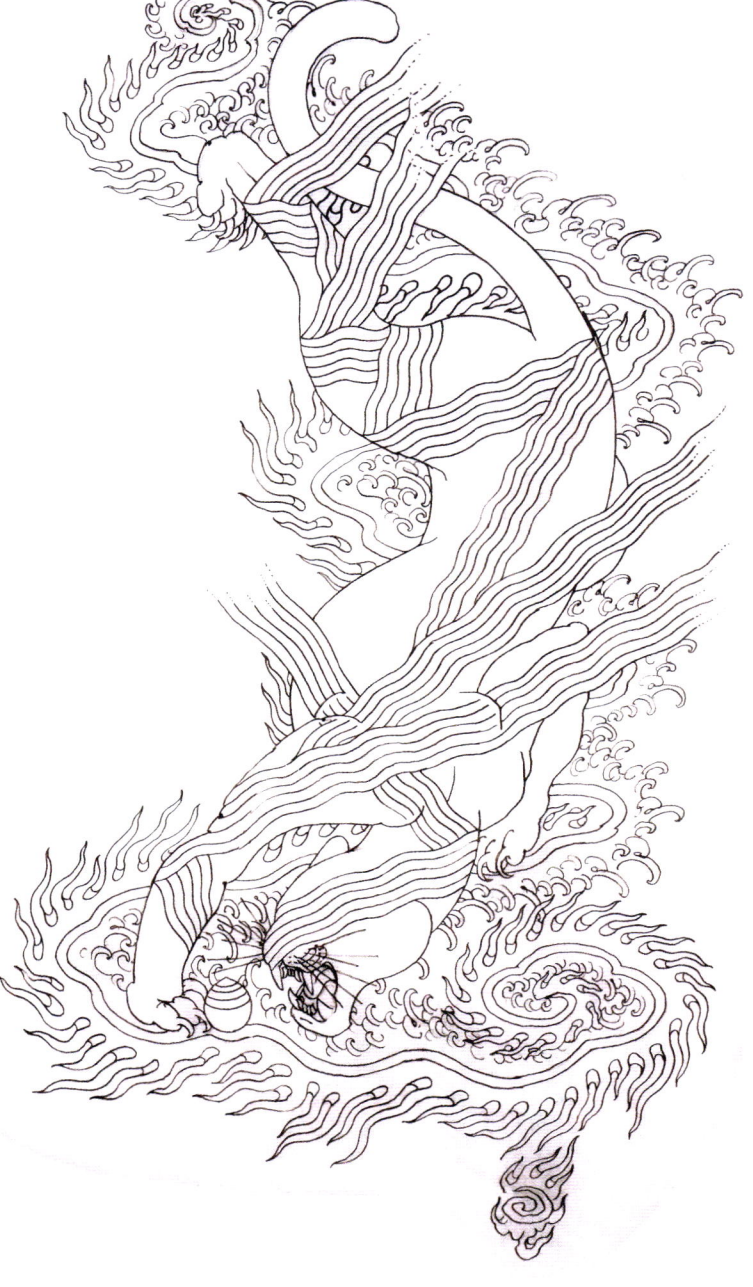

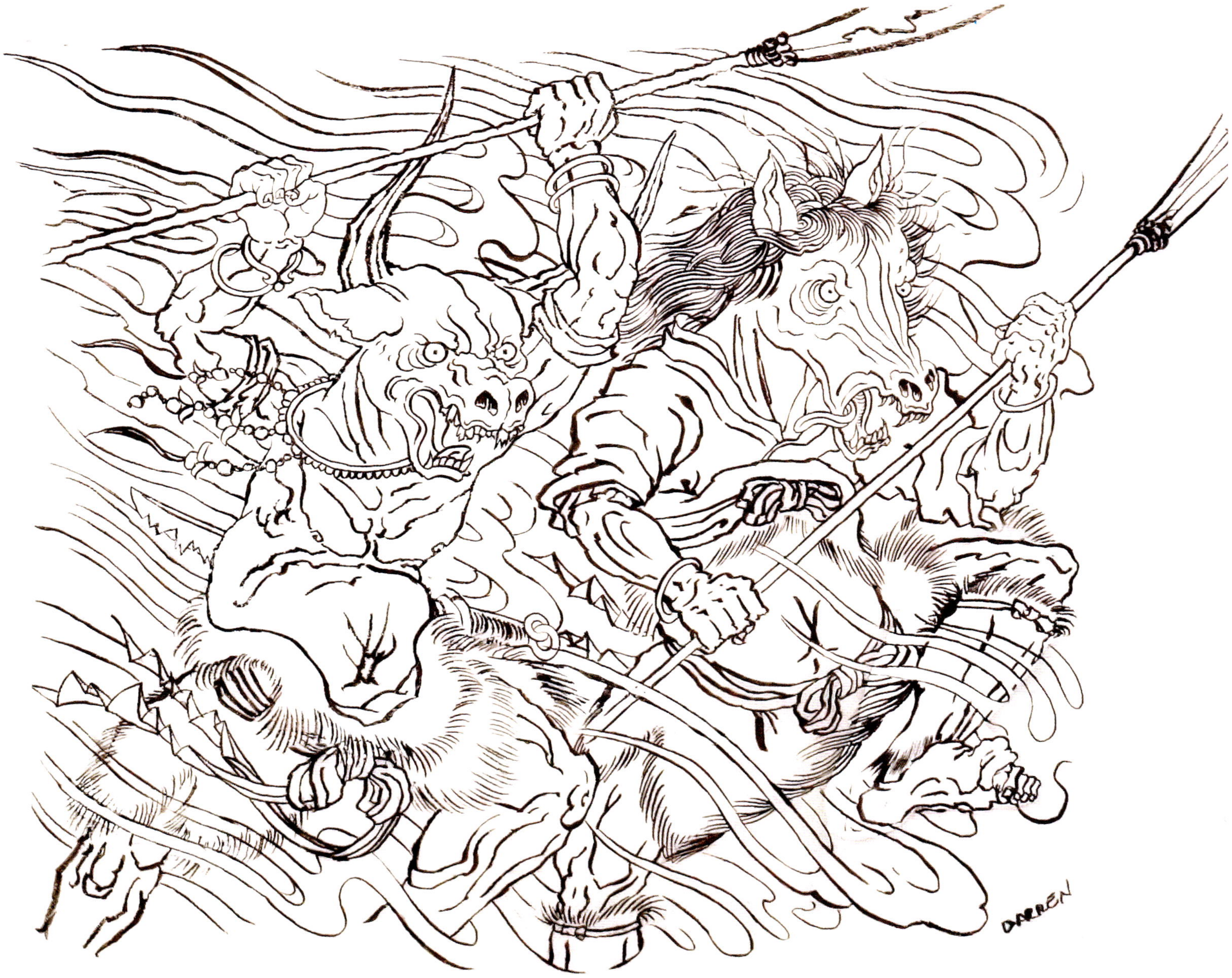

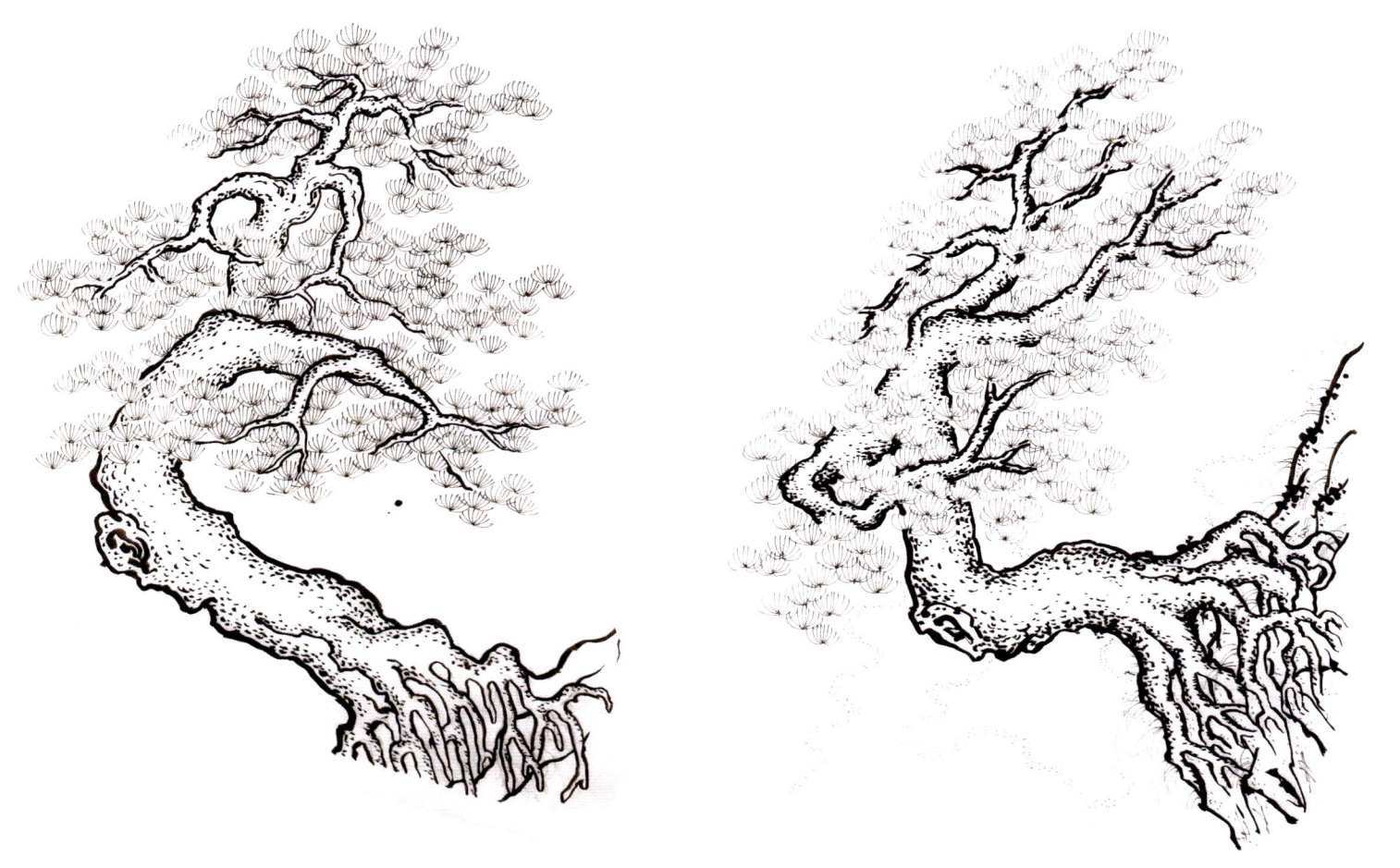

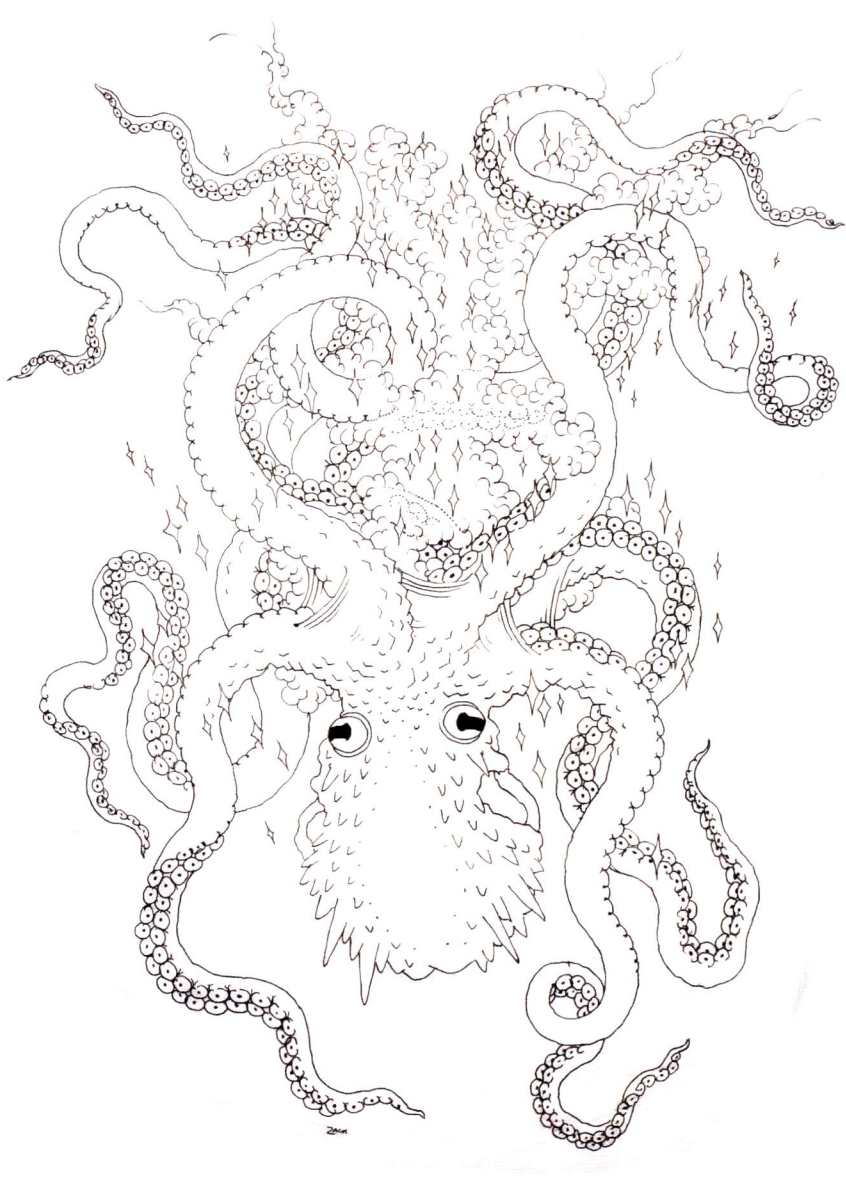

opposite page top:
Meifumado
13 x 14$^{1}/_{2}$

opposite page bottom left:
Tree 1
18 x 13

opposite page bottom right:
Tree 2
19 x 14

this page top left:
Octopus and Ink
21 x 16

this page right:
Peacock
40 x 23

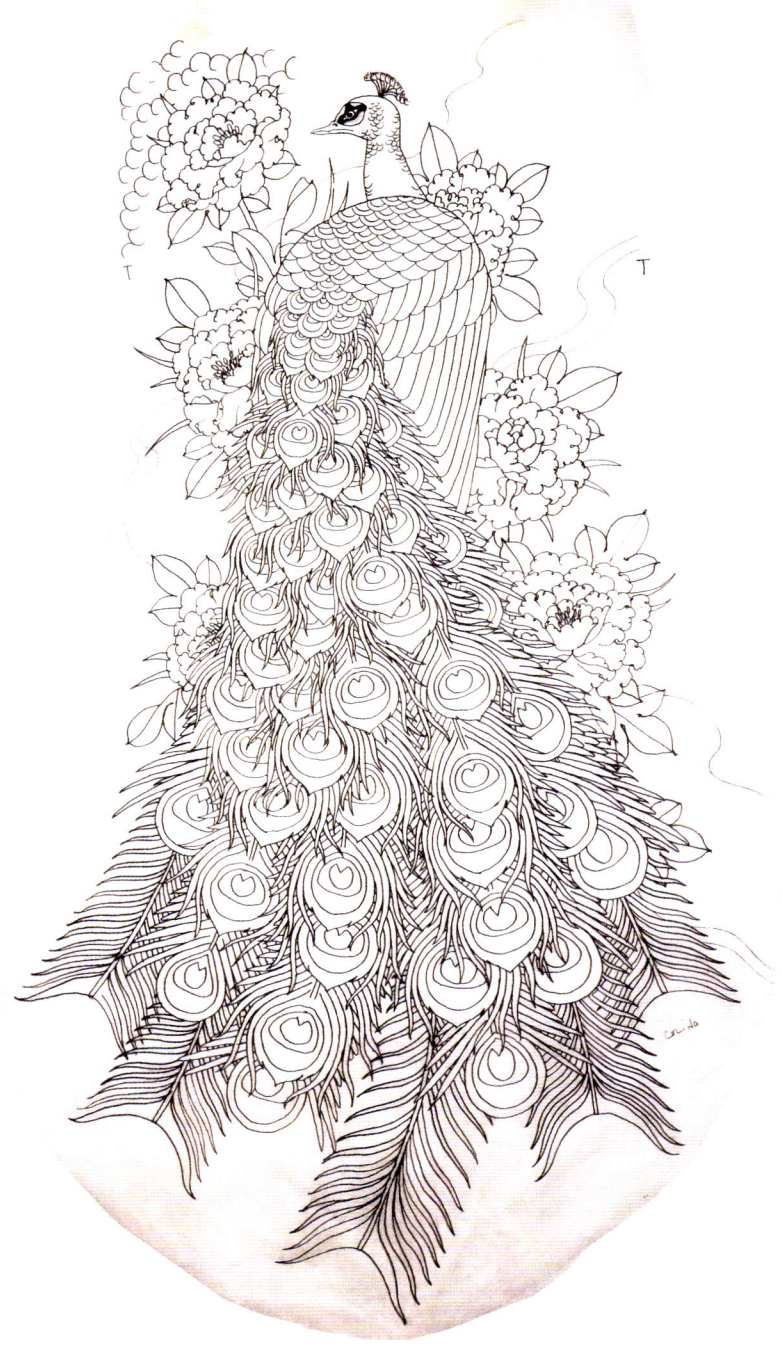

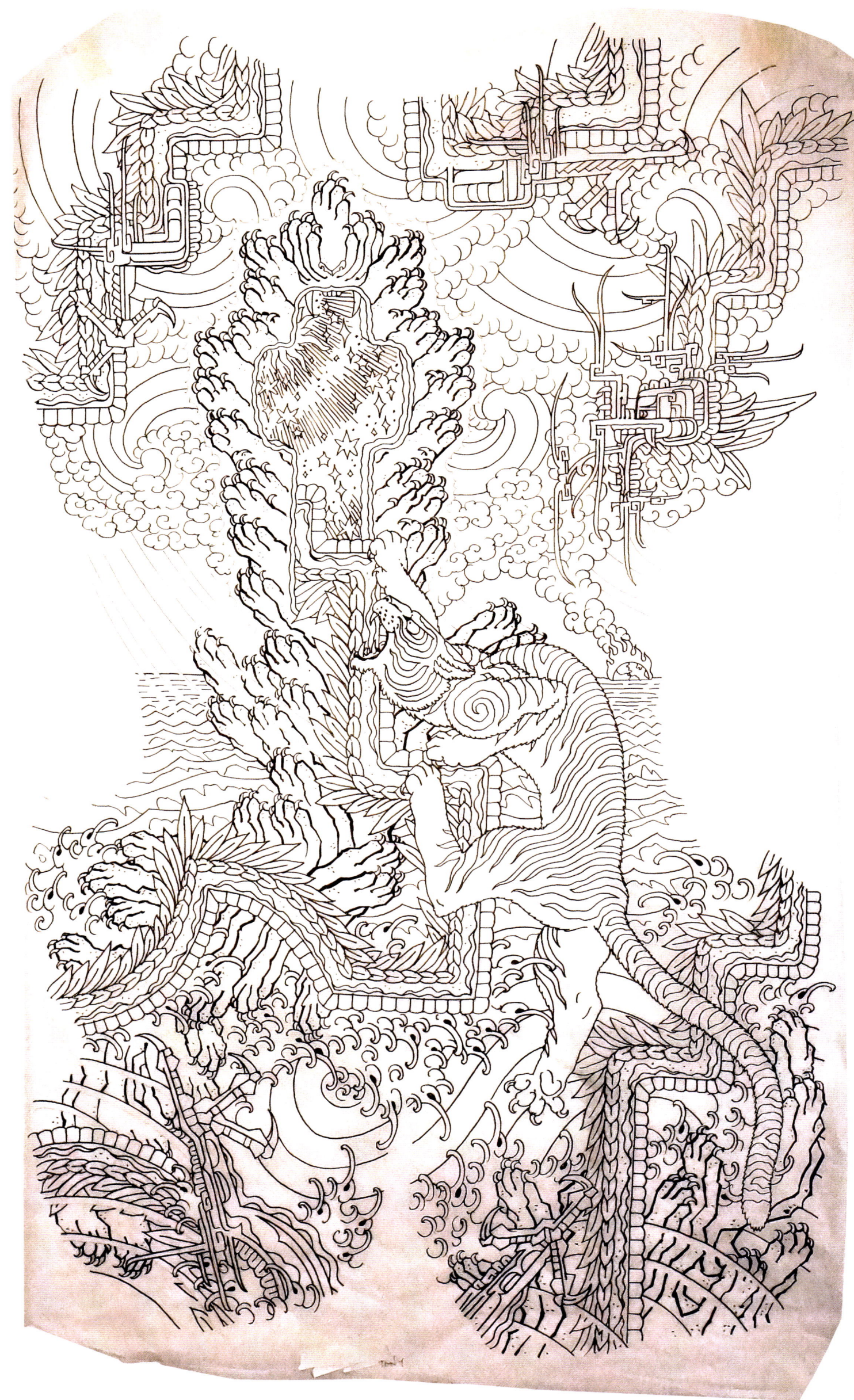

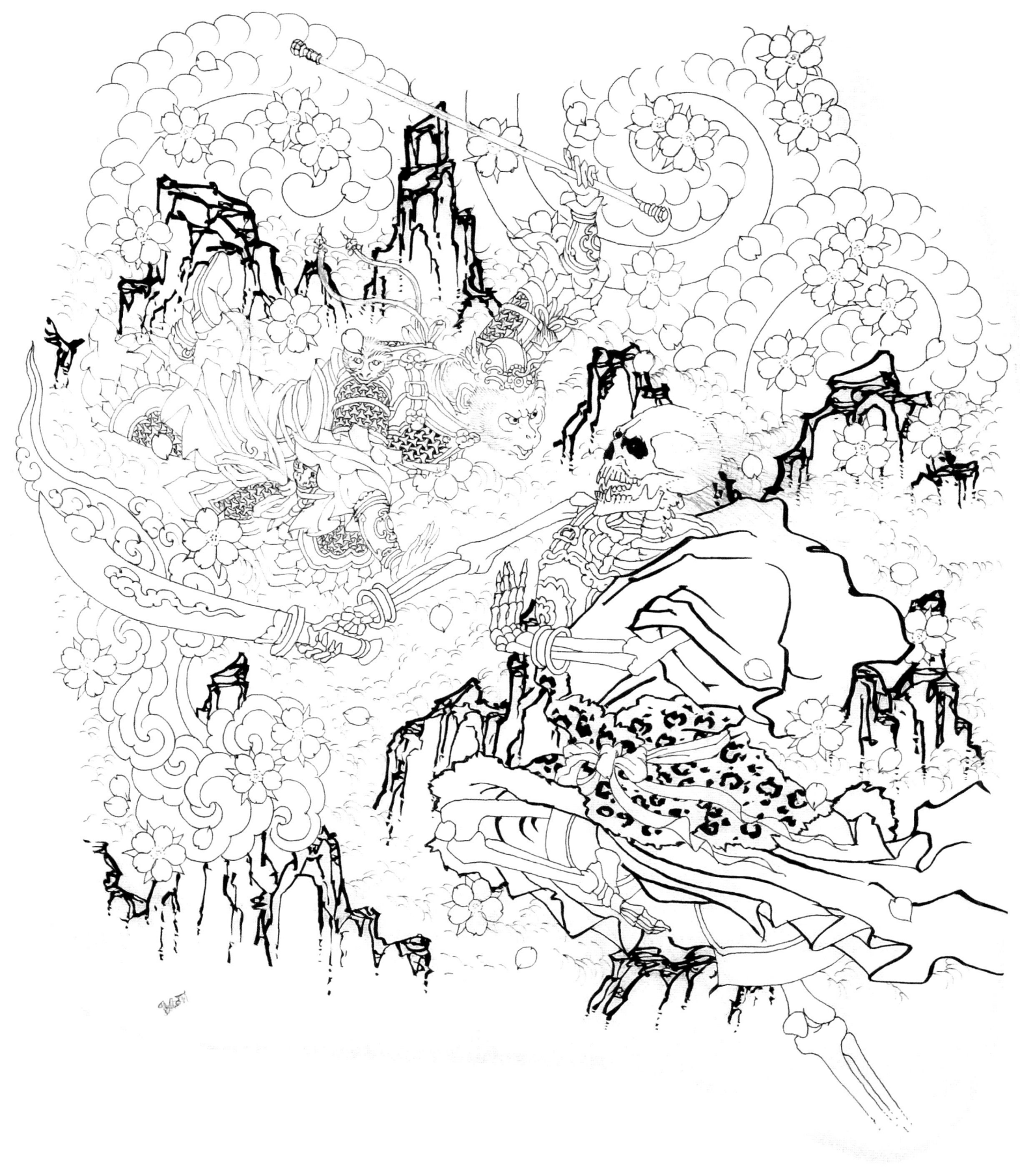

opposite page:
Panther Rock of Ages
36 x 23

this page:
Hanuman
24 x 21

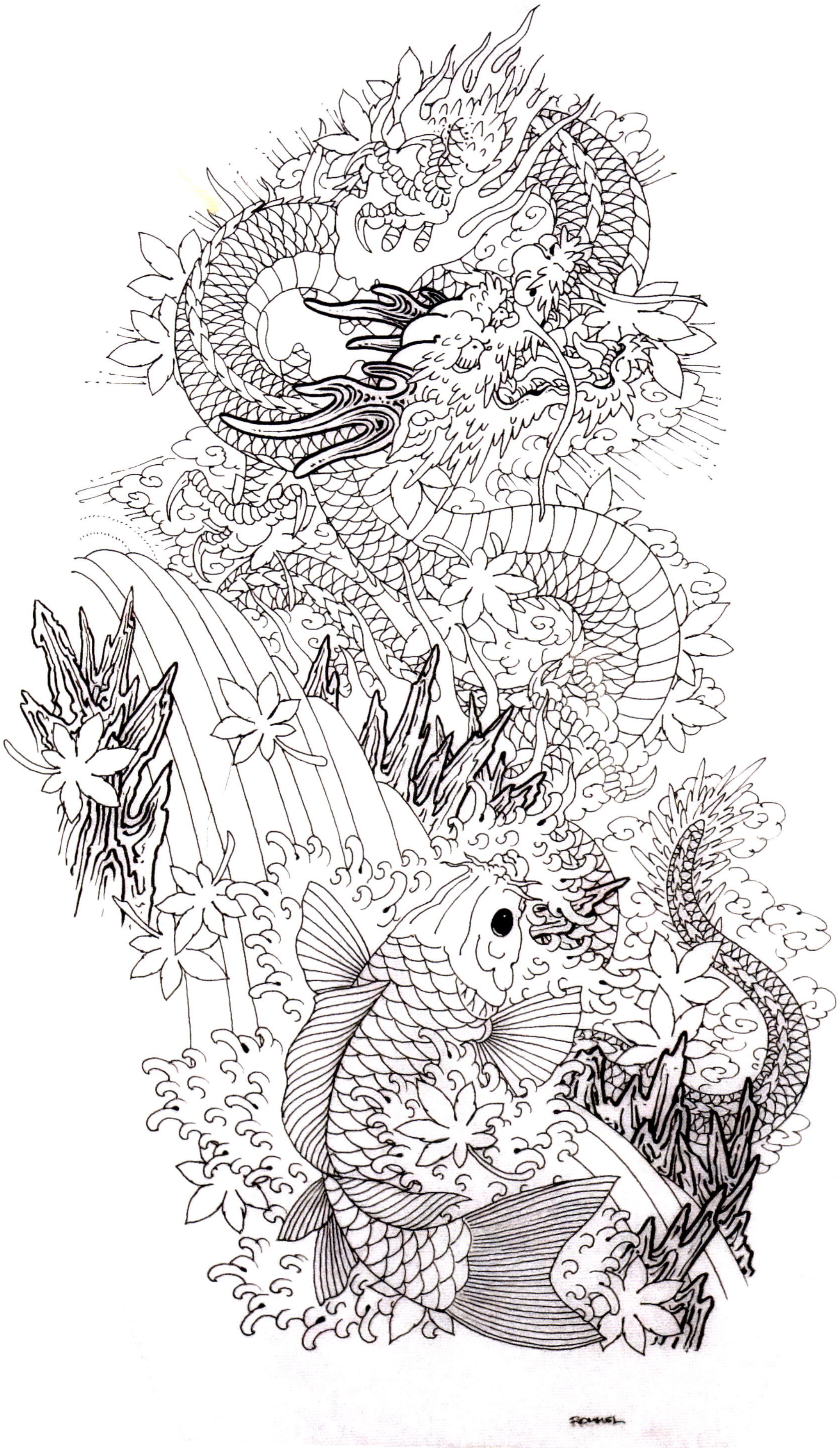

Koi and Dragon
25 x 15

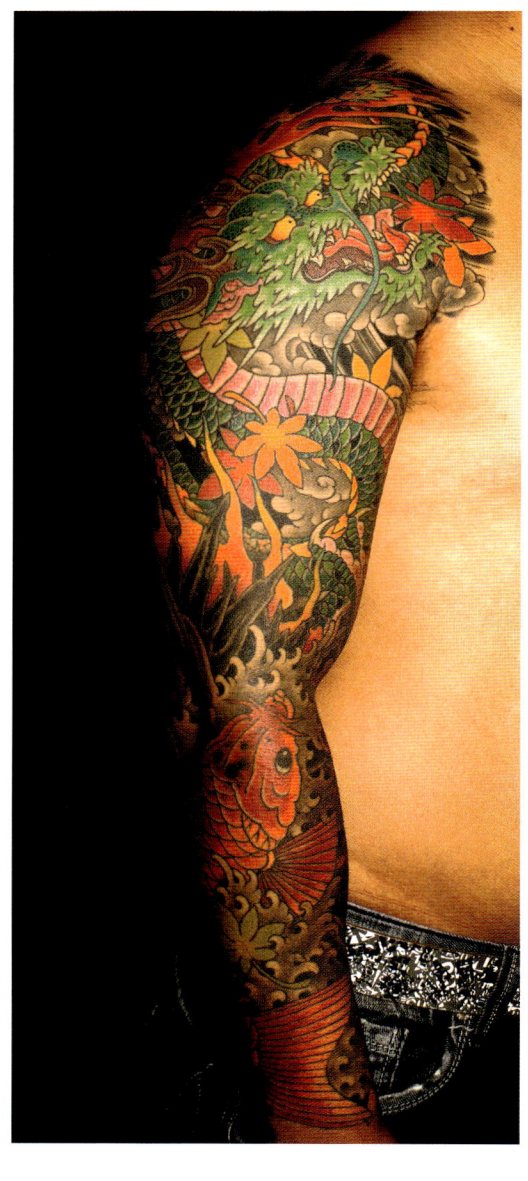

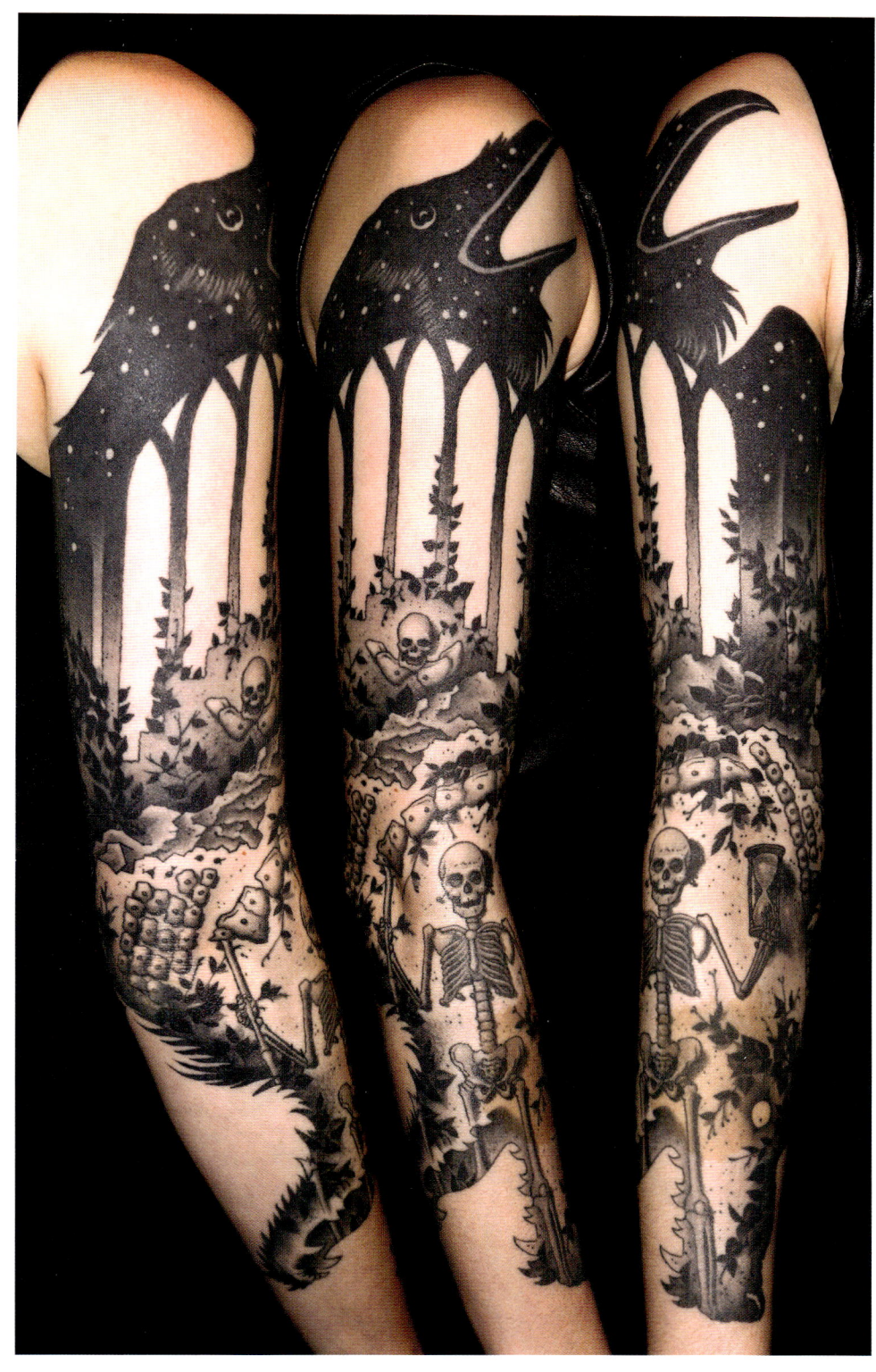

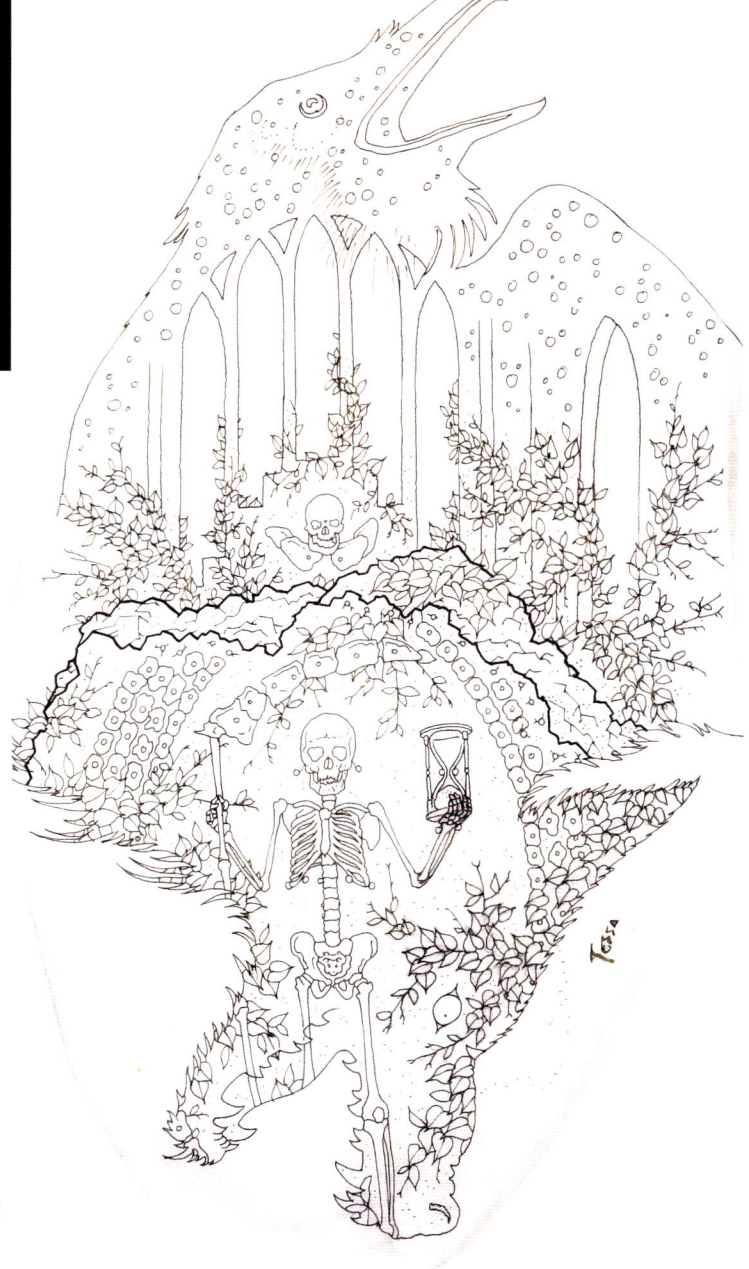

Crow Bones Wolf
19 x 11

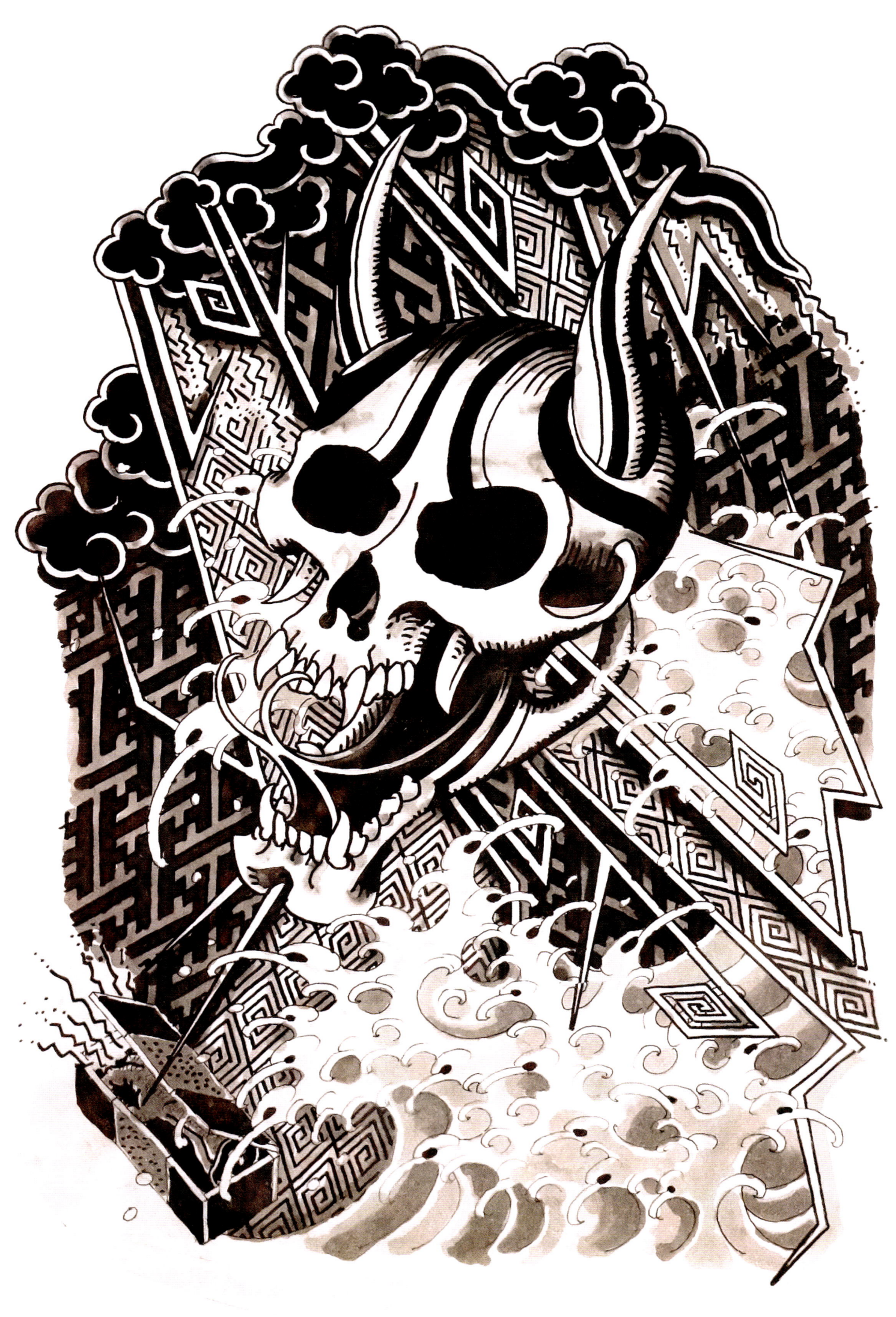

Ibaraki
12 x 7½

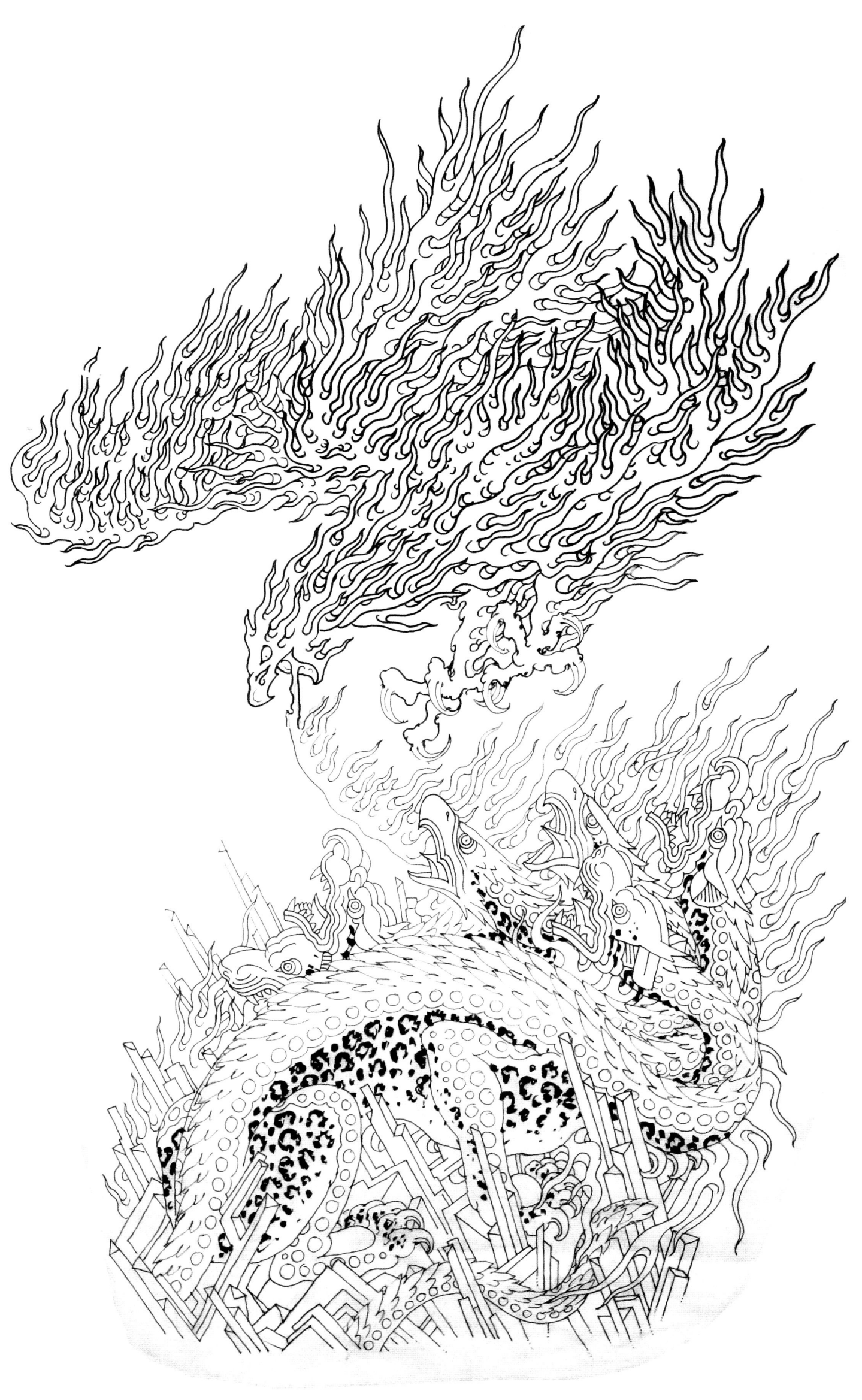

Firebird and Hydra
29 x 18

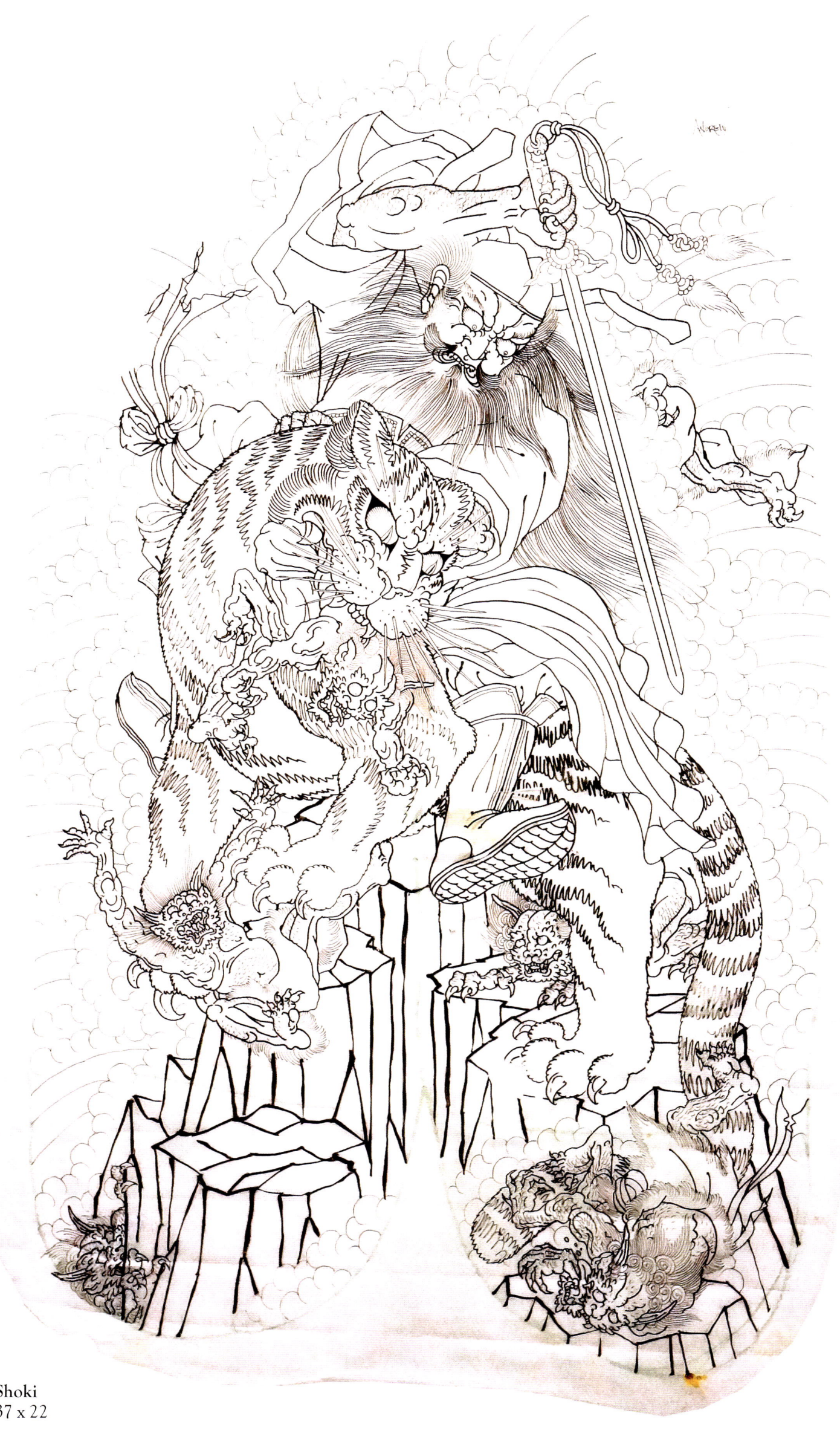

Shoki
37 x 22

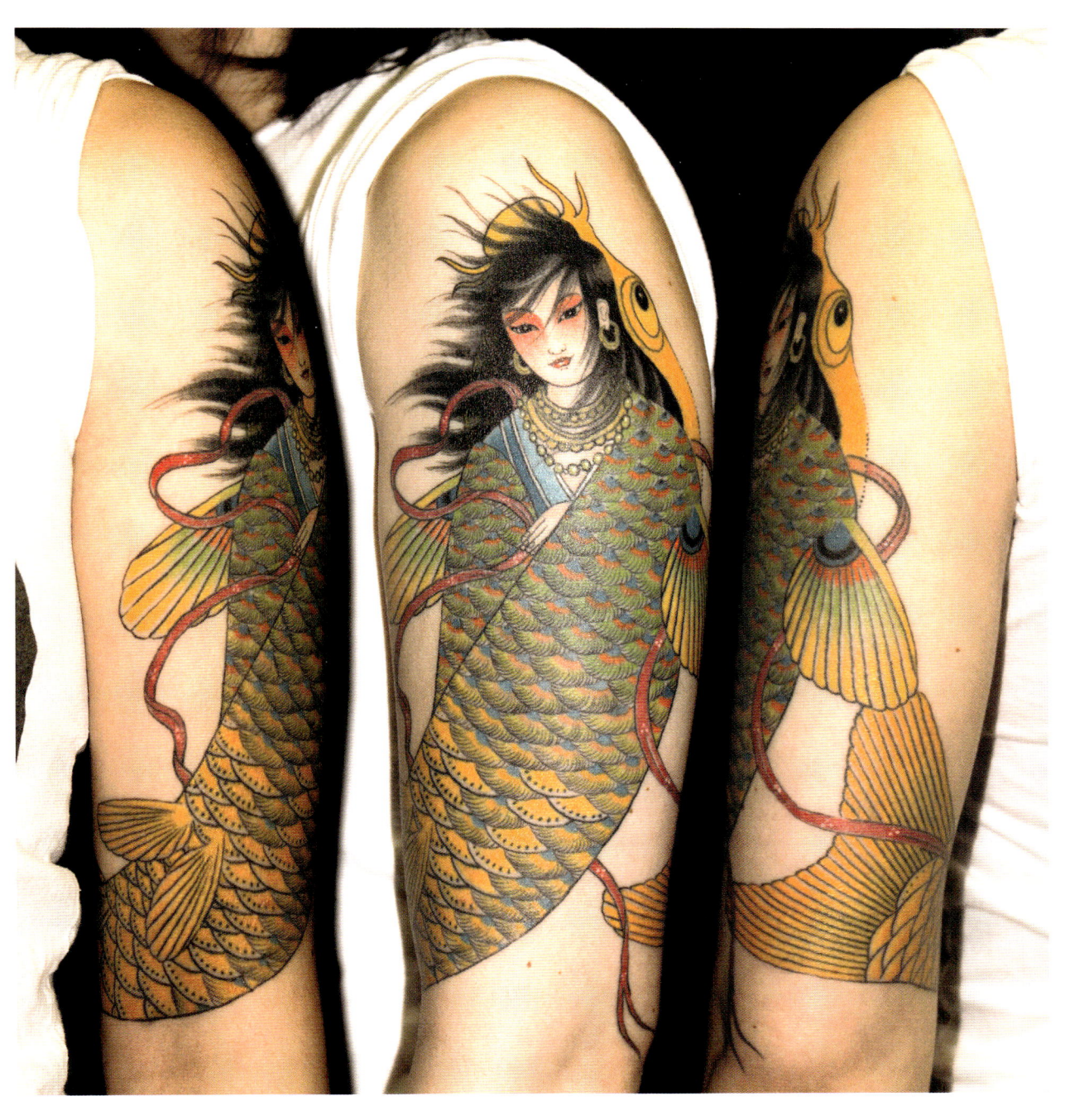

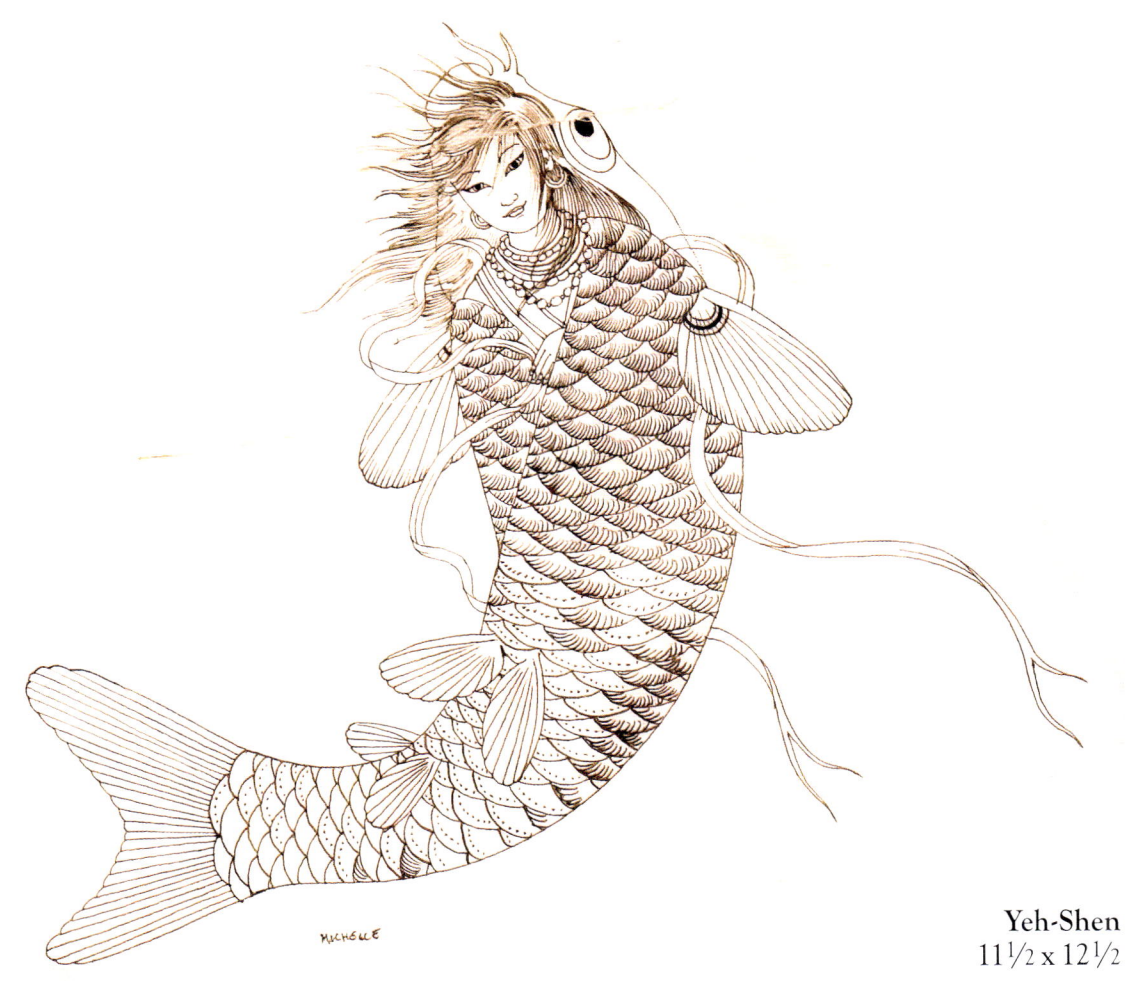

Yeh-Shen
$11\frac{1}{2} \times 12\frac{1}{2}$

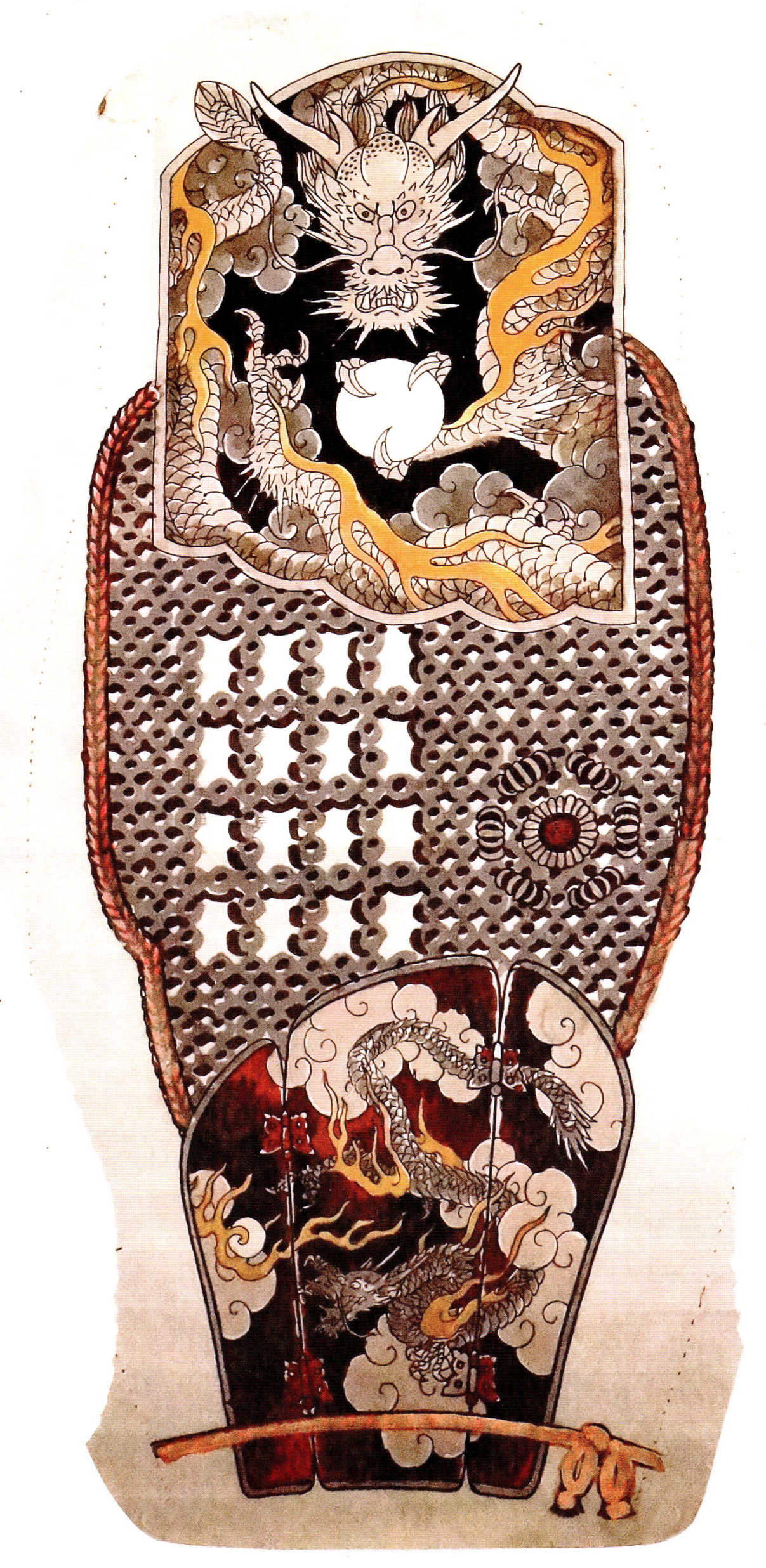

Armor
13 x 5½

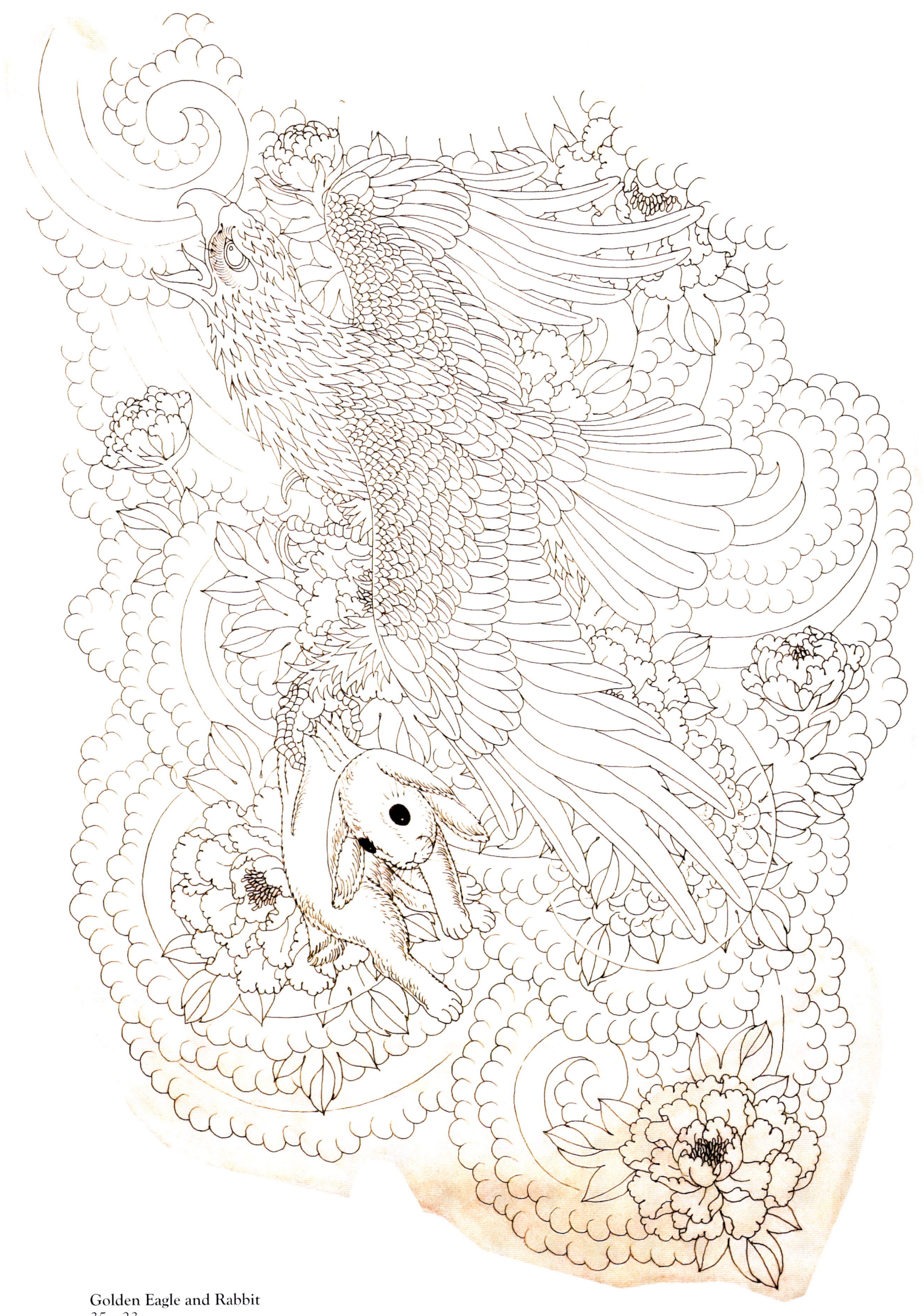

Golden Eagle and Rabbit
35 x 23

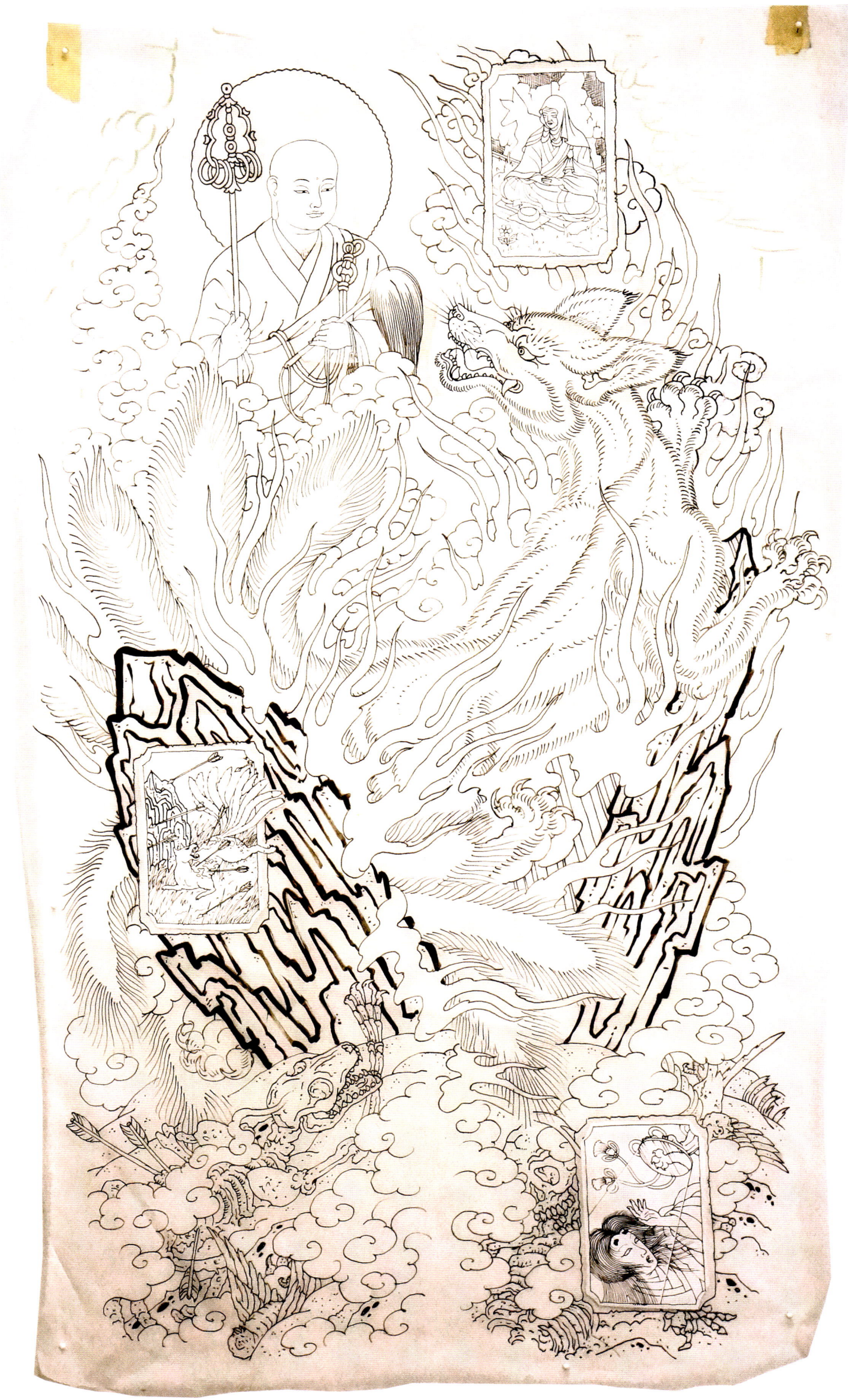

The 9-tailed Fox and the Killing Stone
39 x 23

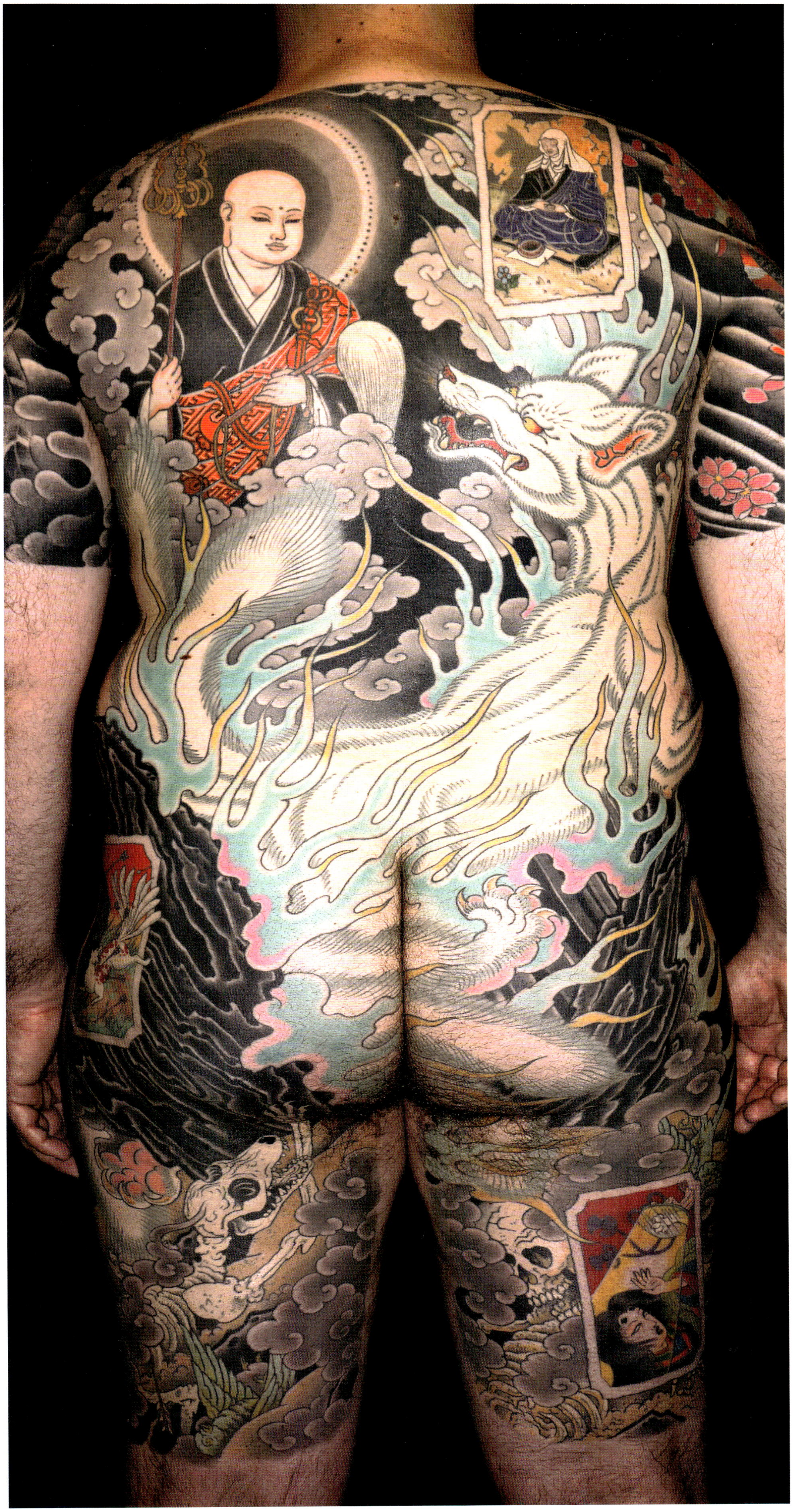

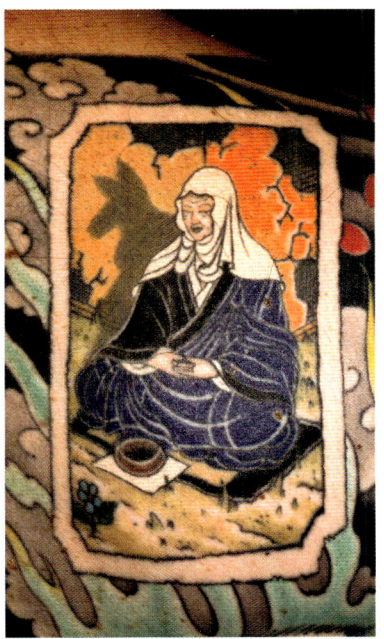

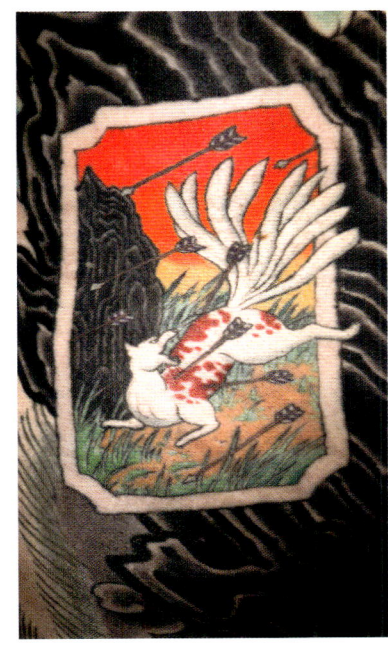

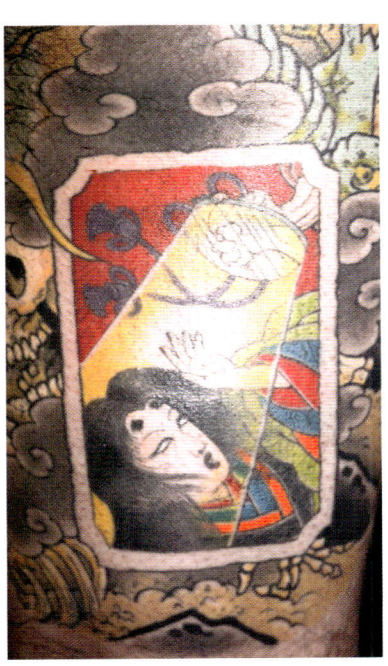

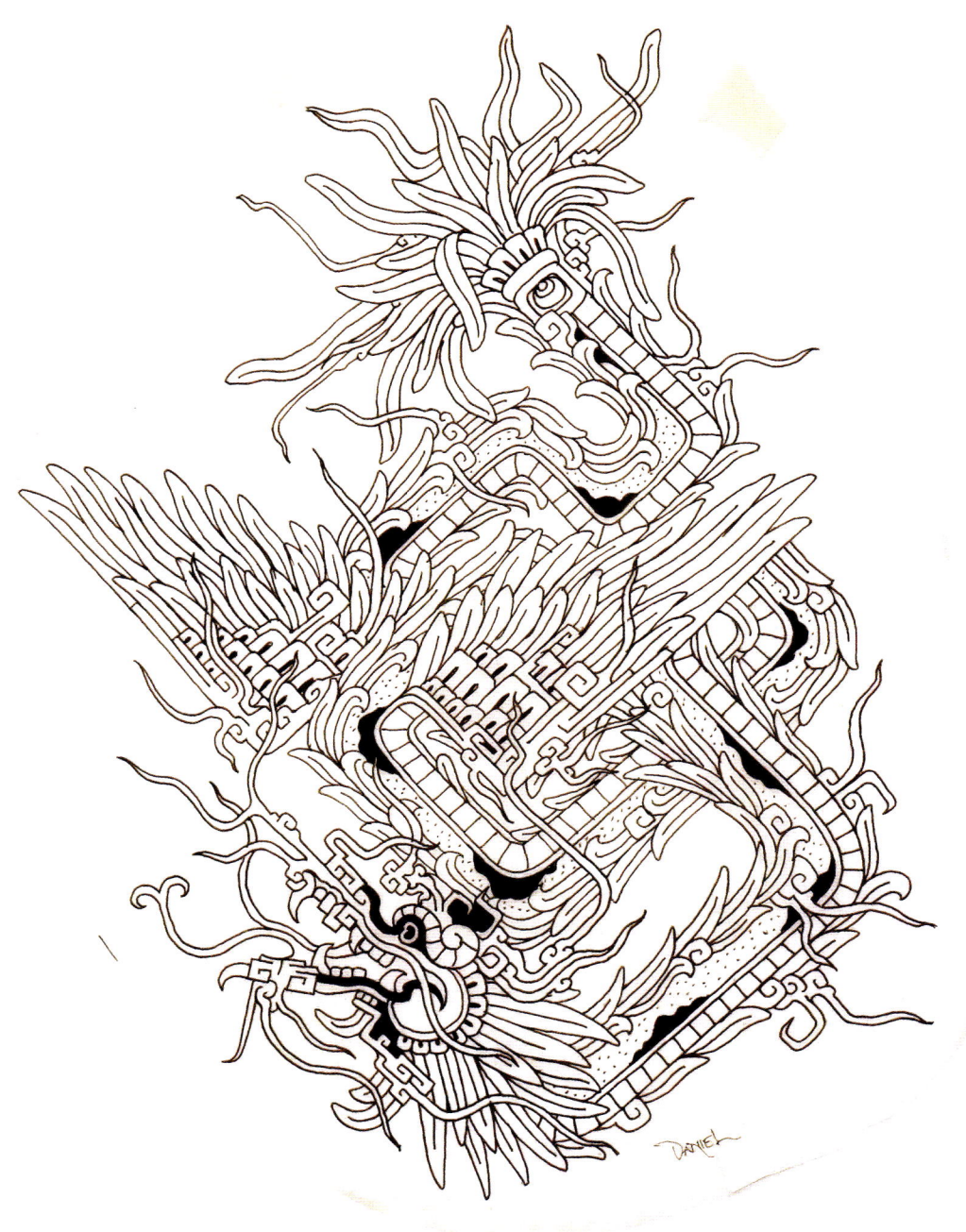

left:
Feathered Serpent
15 x 11½

bottom:
Quetzalcoatl
8 x 8½

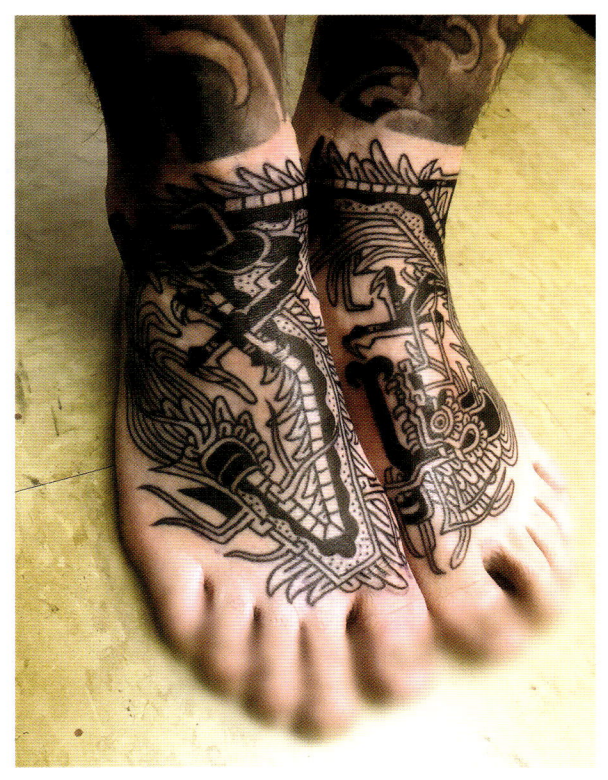

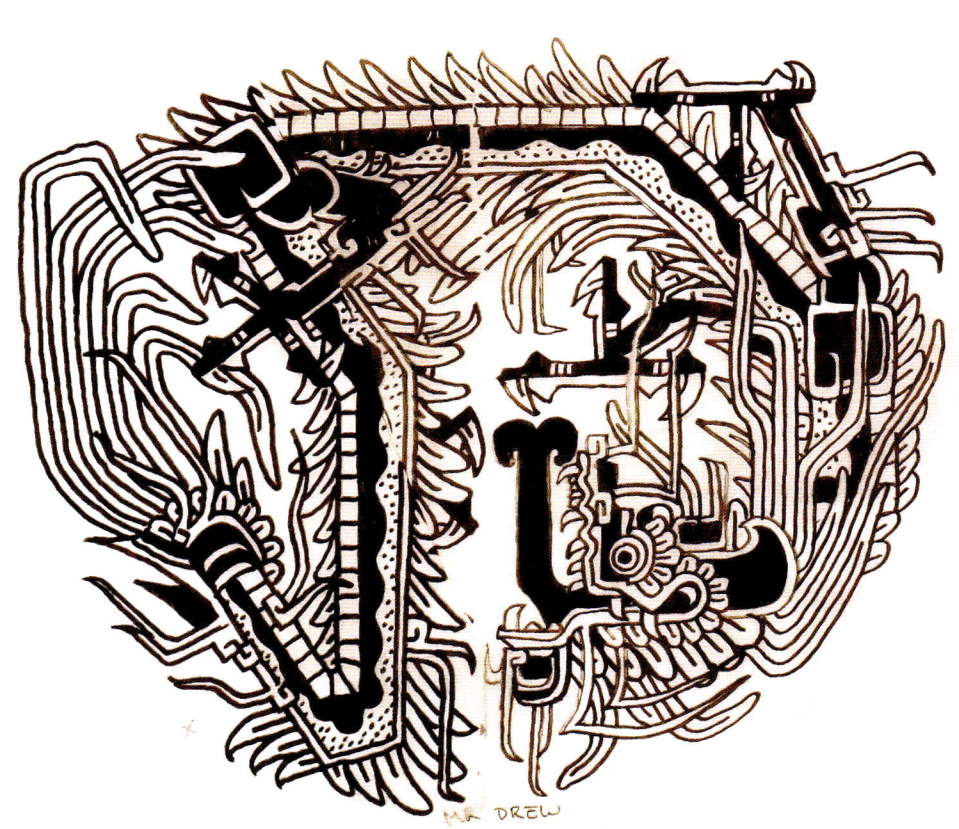

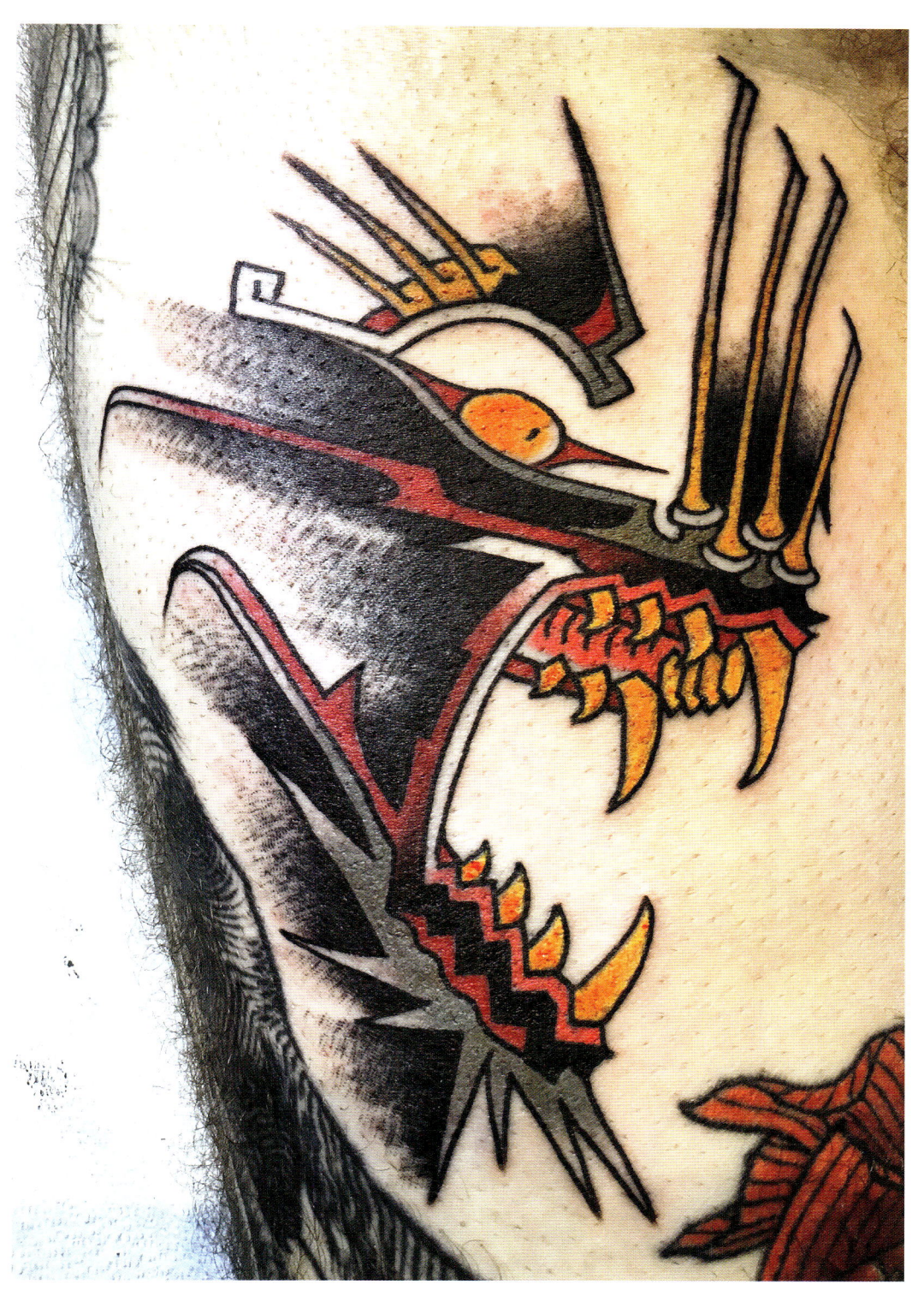

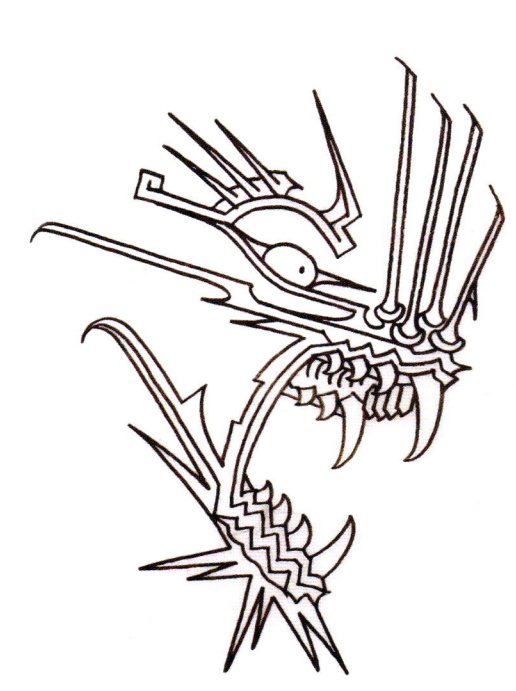

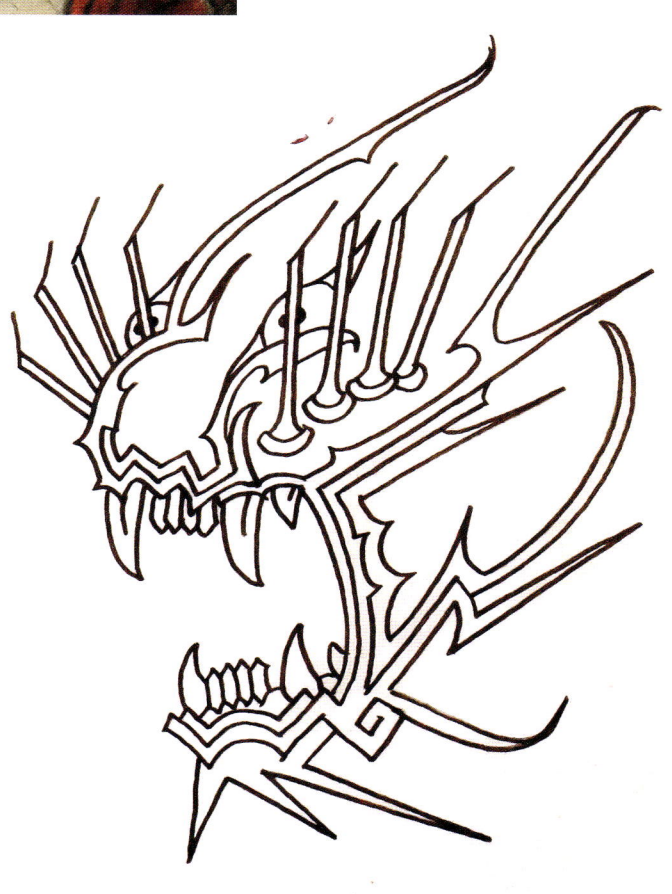

left:
Rawr
7½ x 5½

bottom:
Rawr 2
7½ x 5½

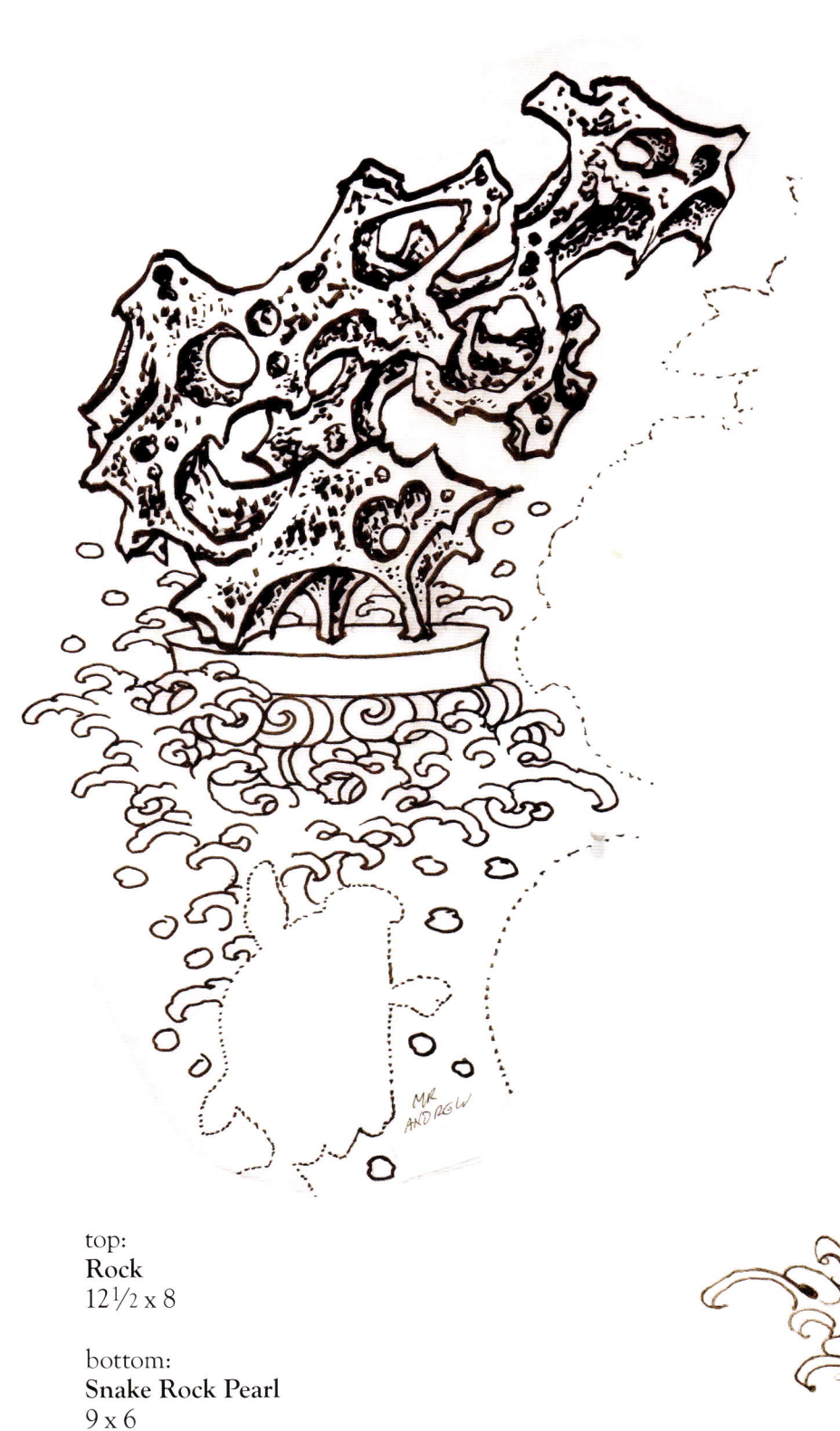

top:
Rock
12½ x 8

bottom:
Snake Rock Pearl
9 x 6

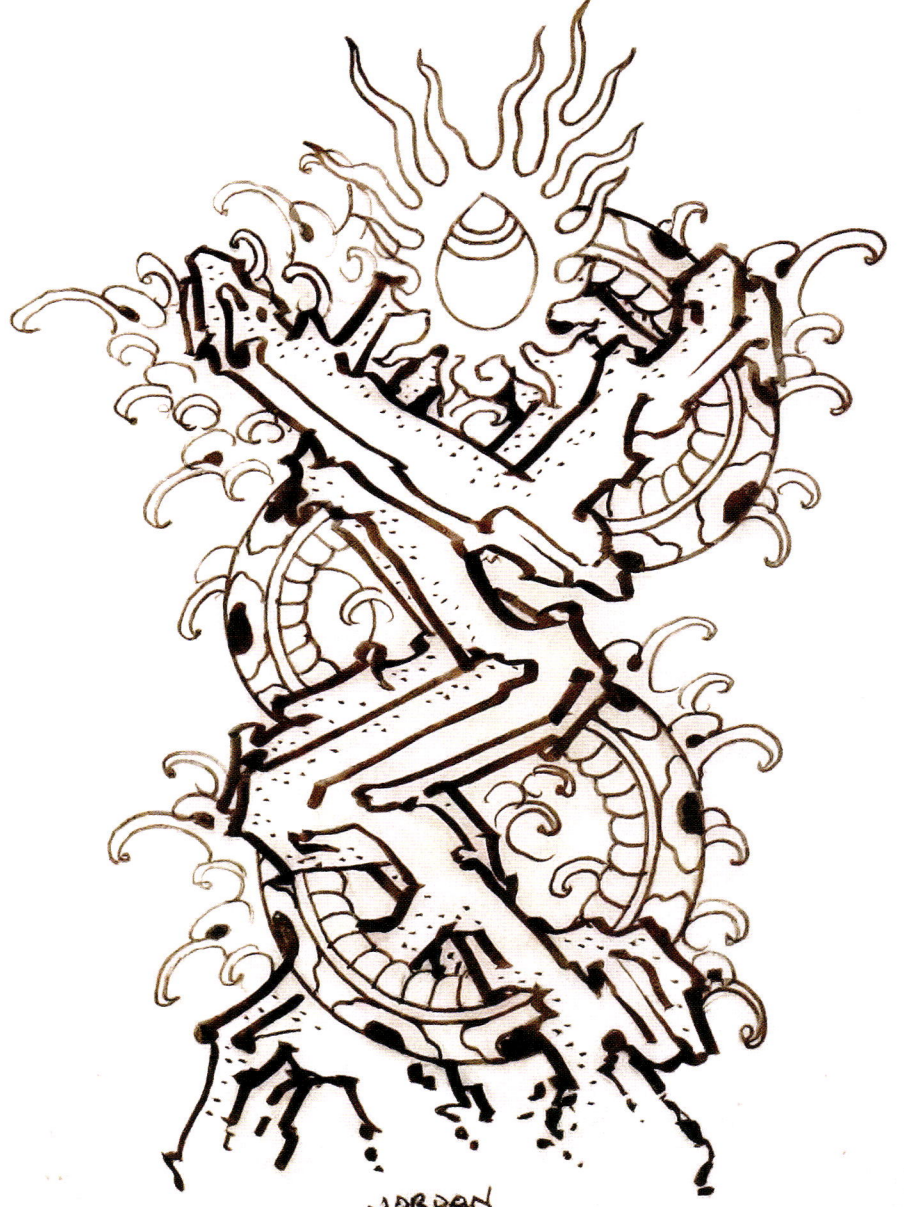

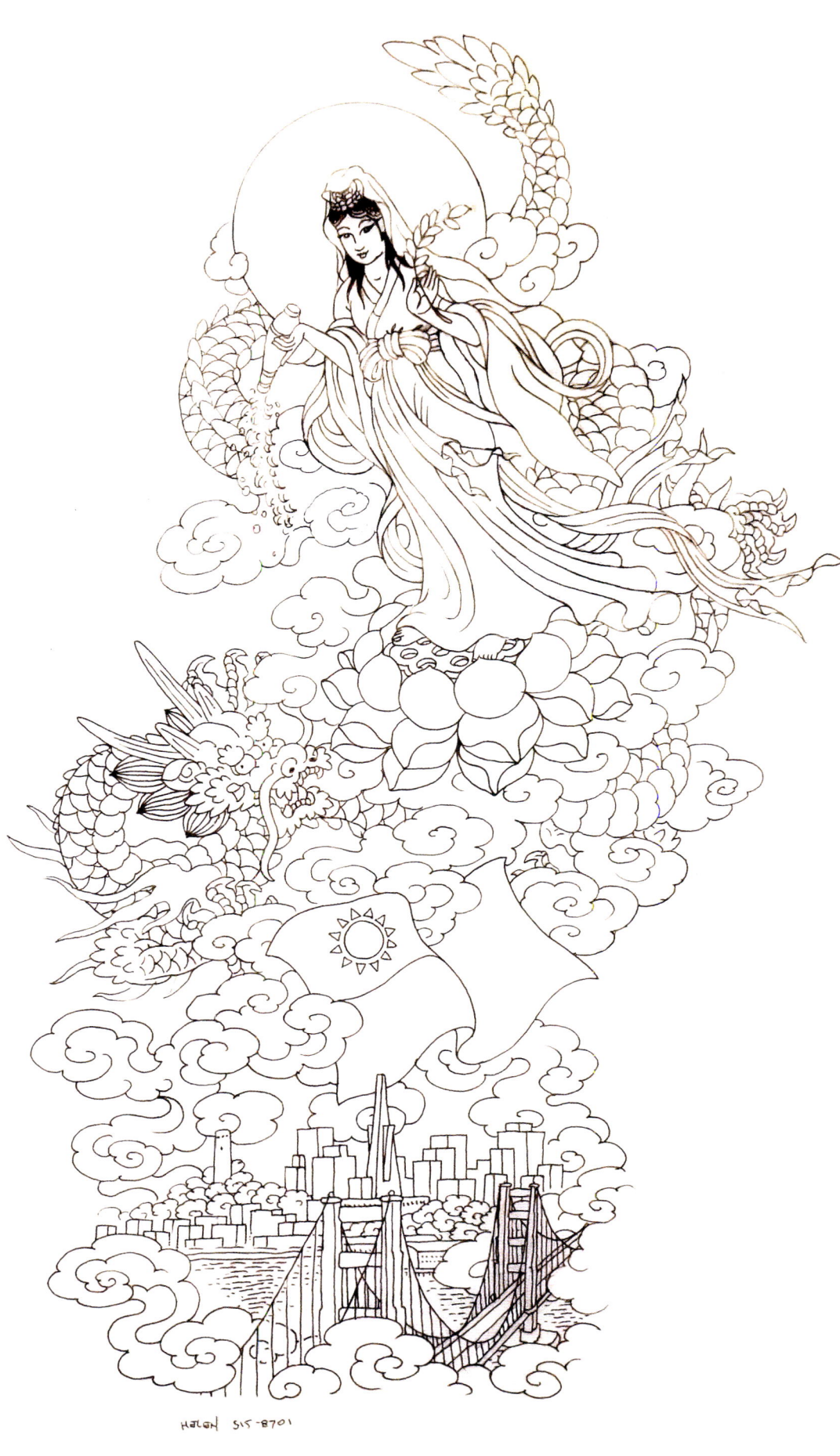

Taiwan SF
22 x 12

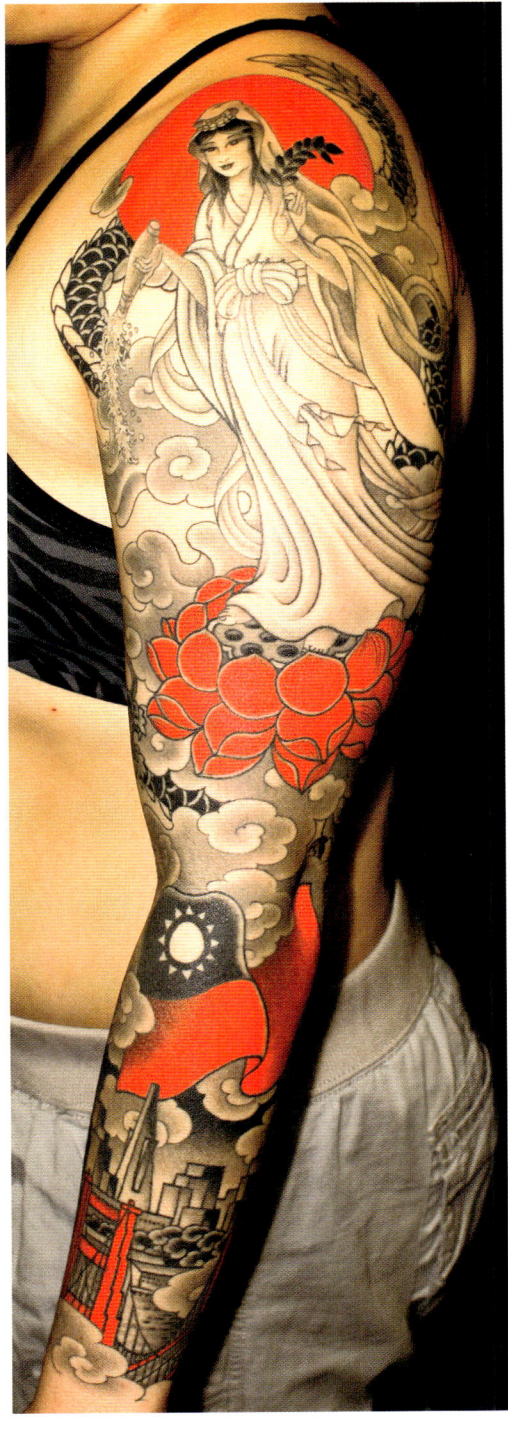

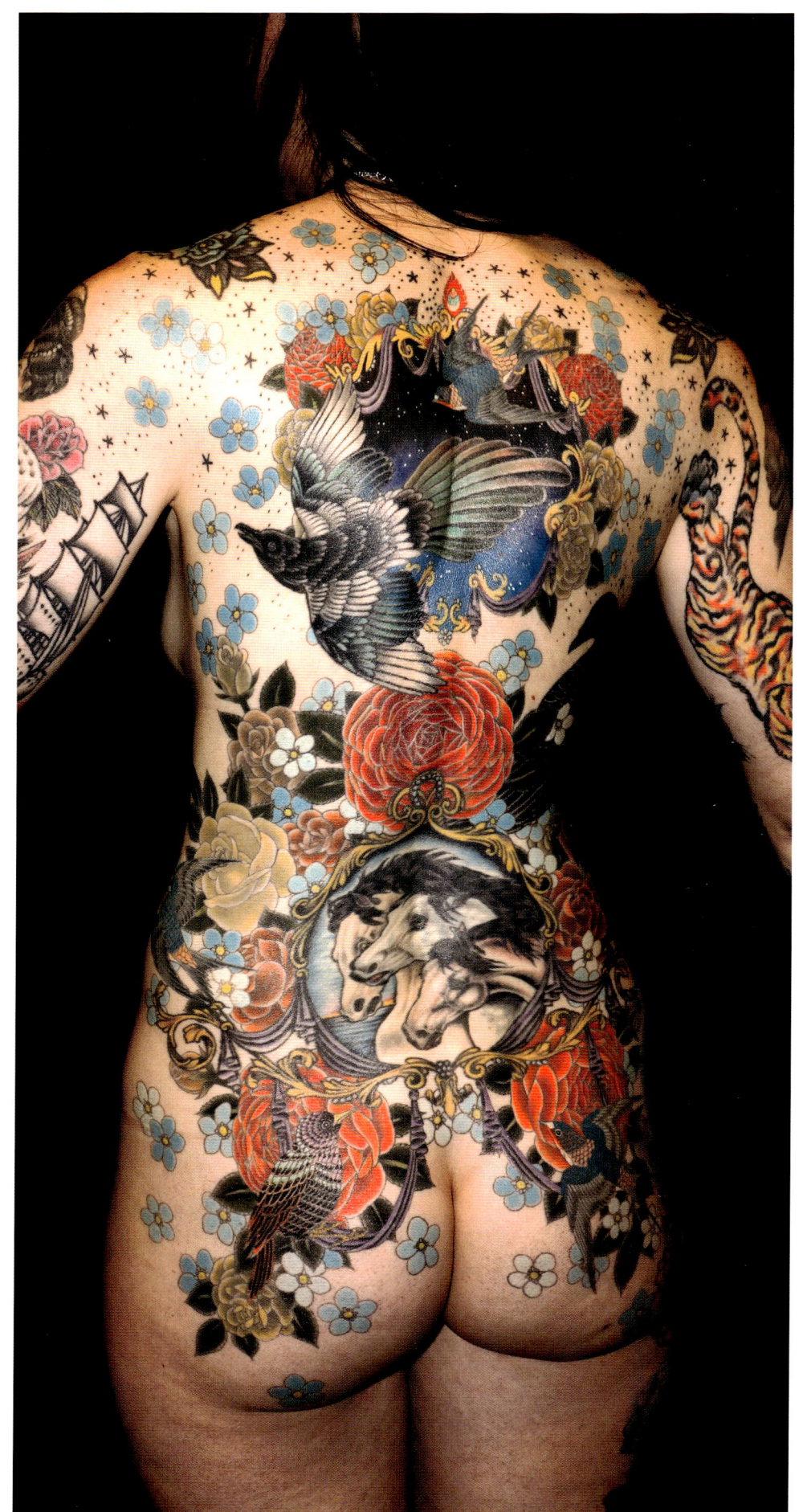

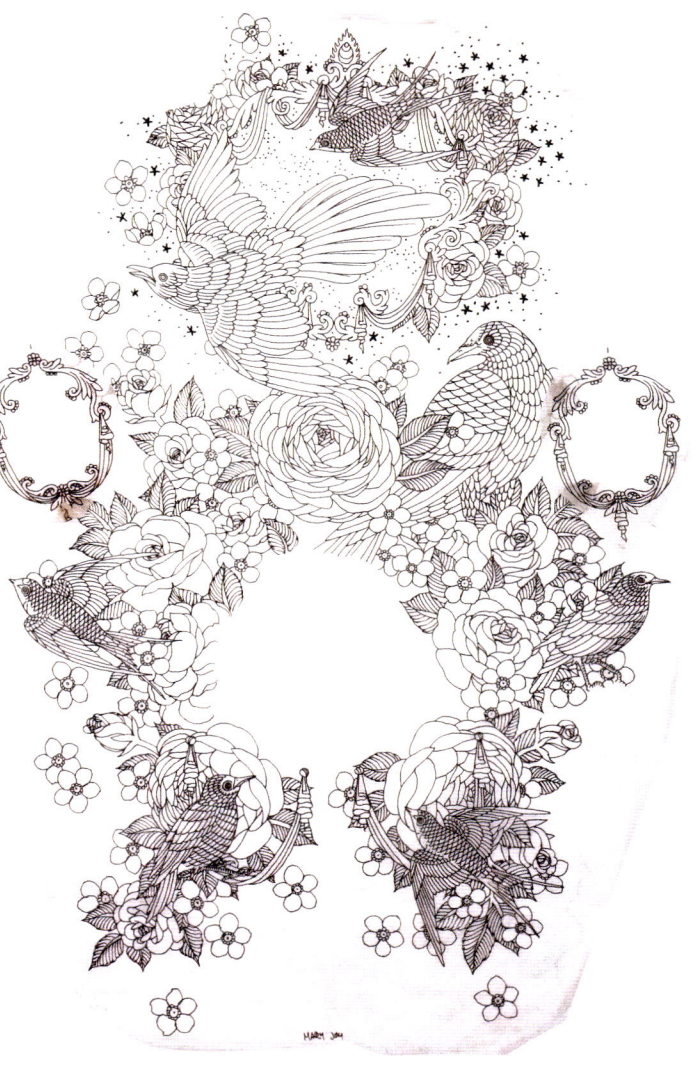

Mary Joy
26¹/₂ x 17

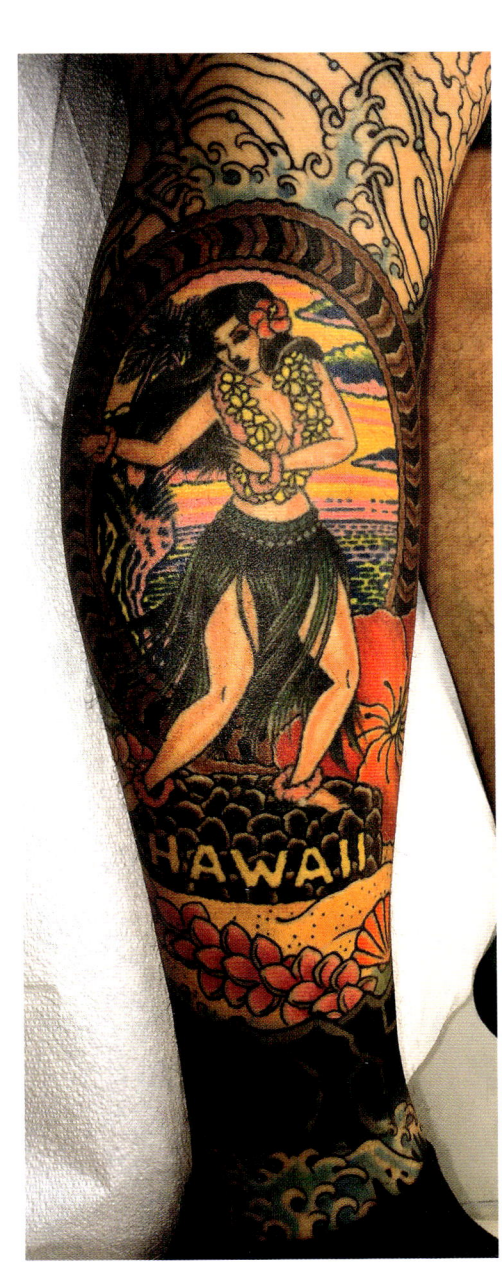

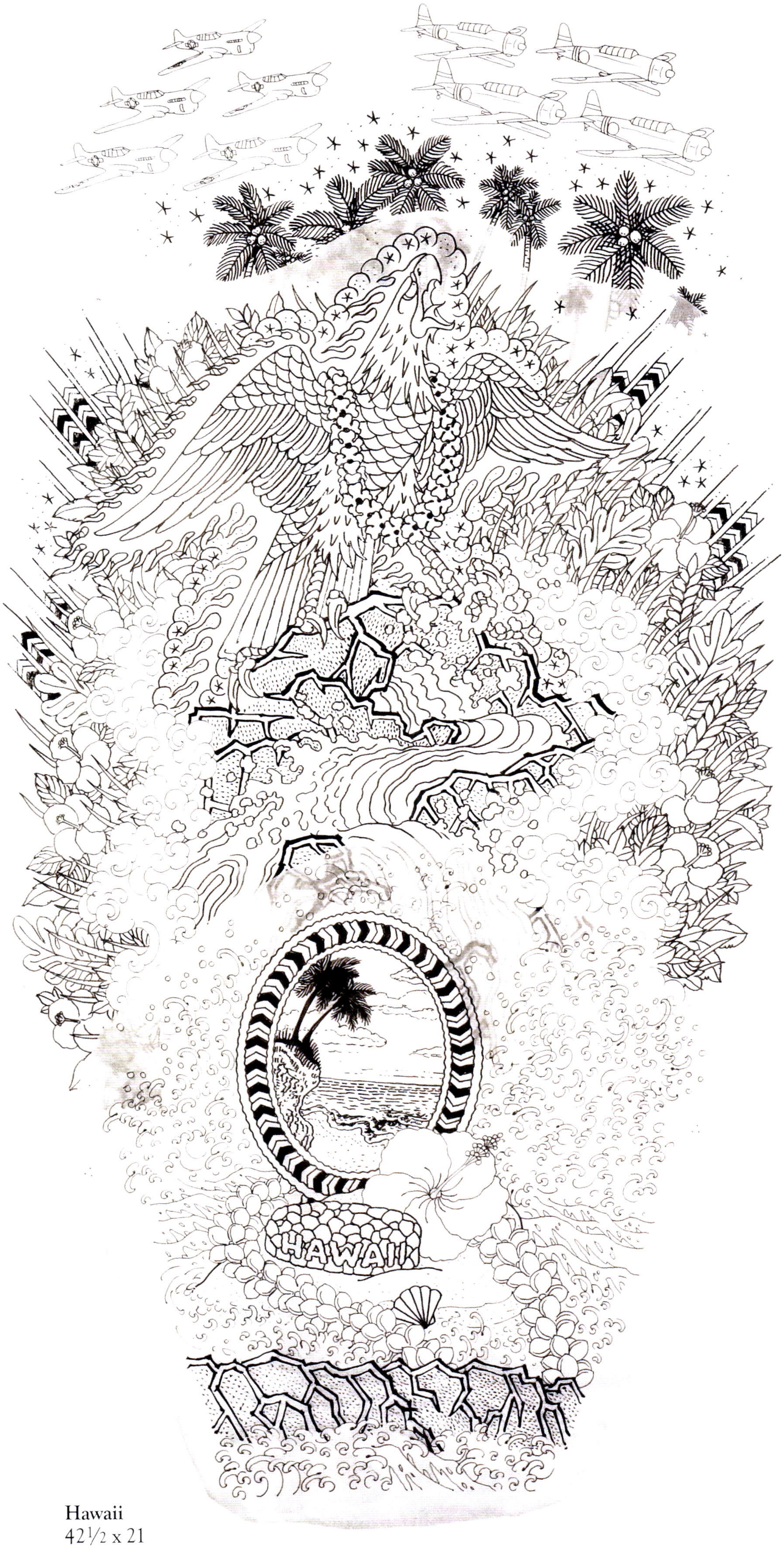

Hawaii
42½ x 21

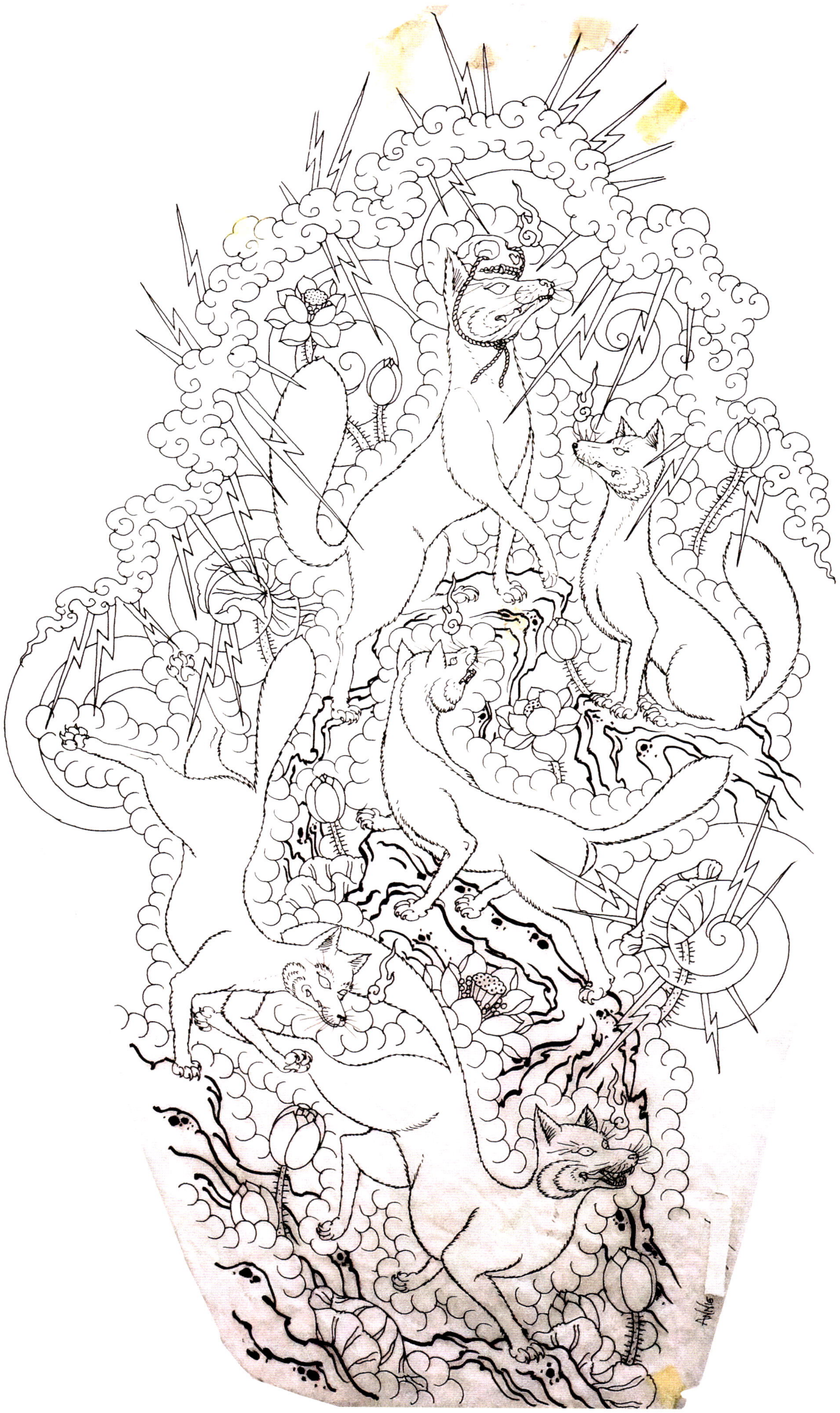

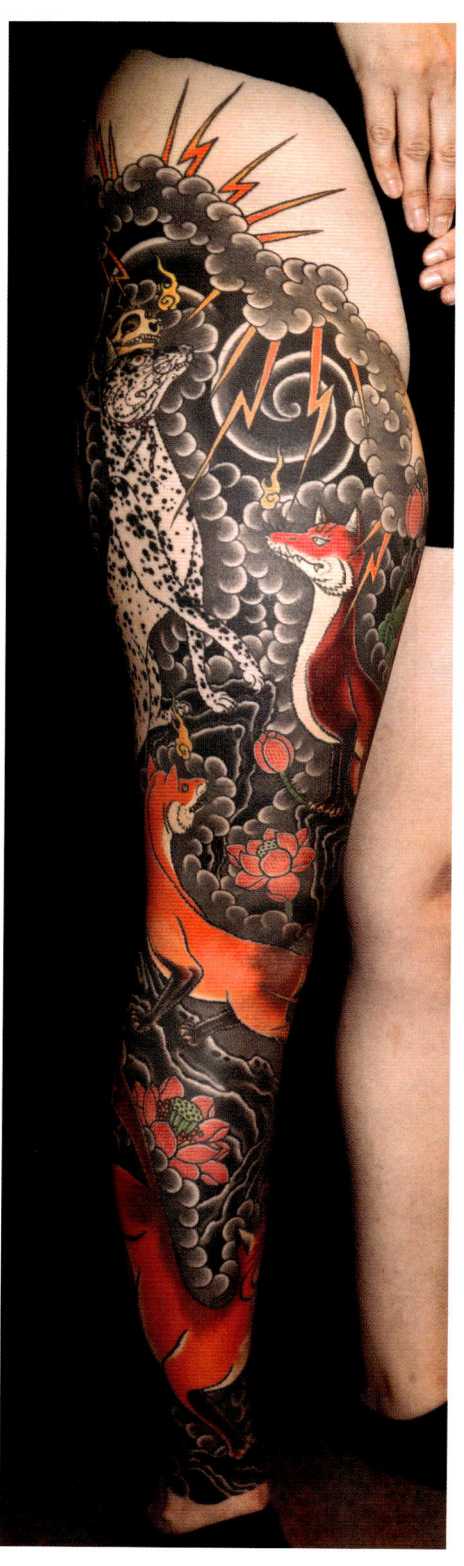

Kitsune
38 x 22

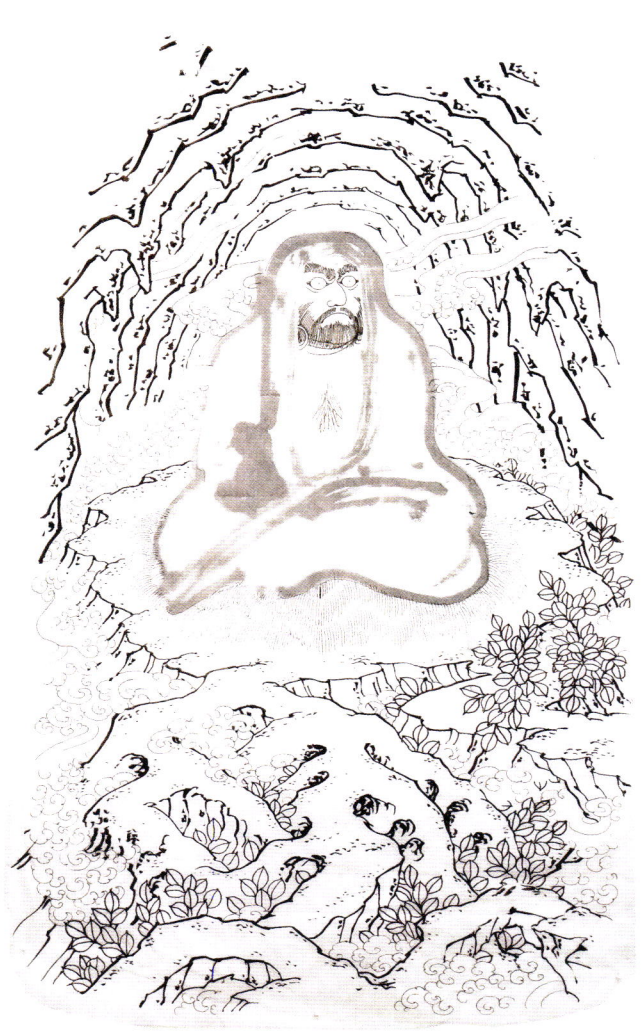

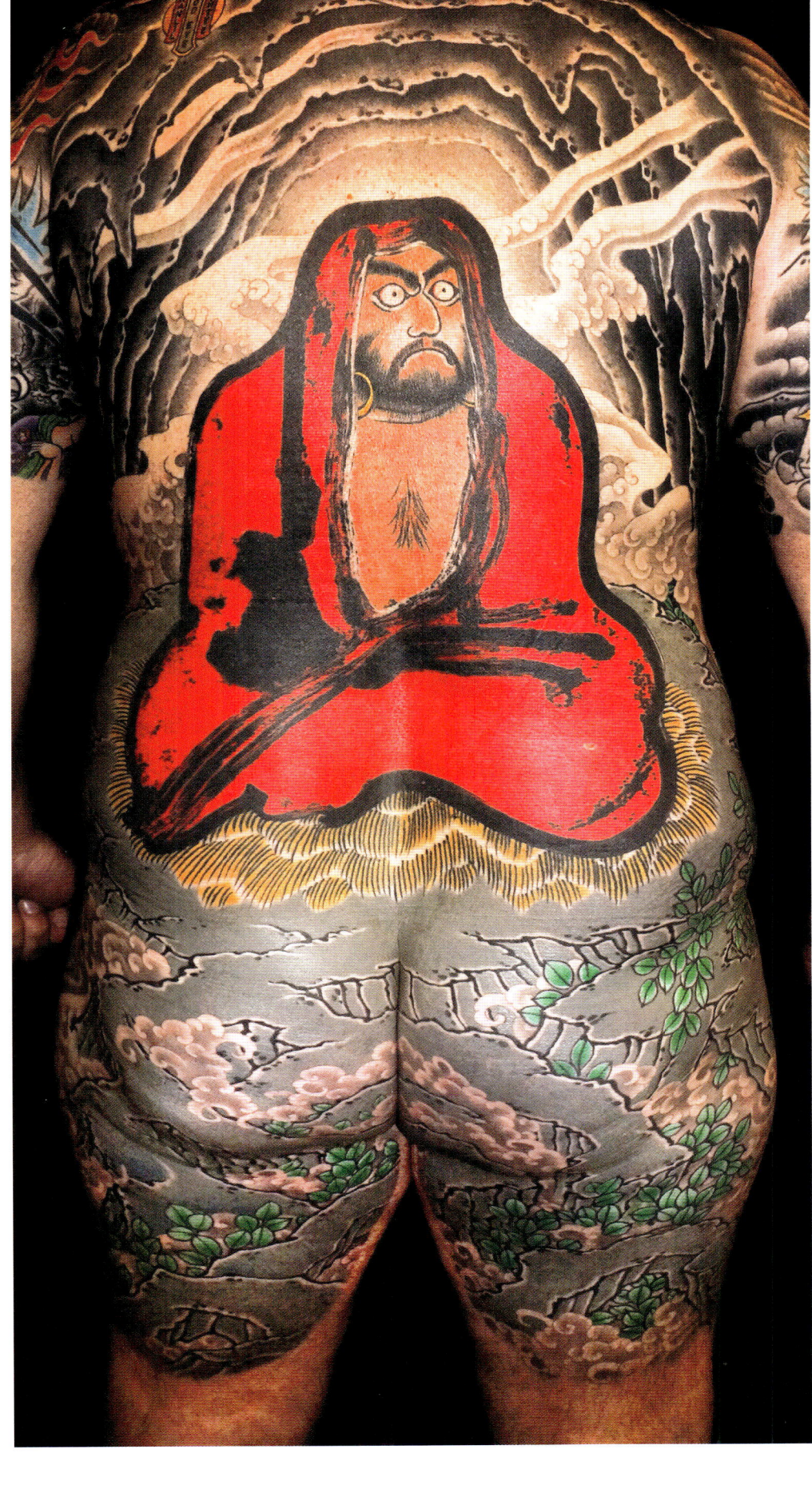

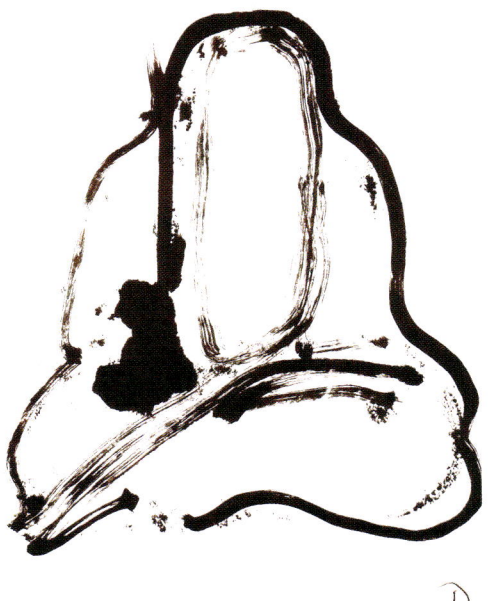

top left:
Daruma
35 x 22

bottom left:
Daruma One Stroke
14 x 12

43

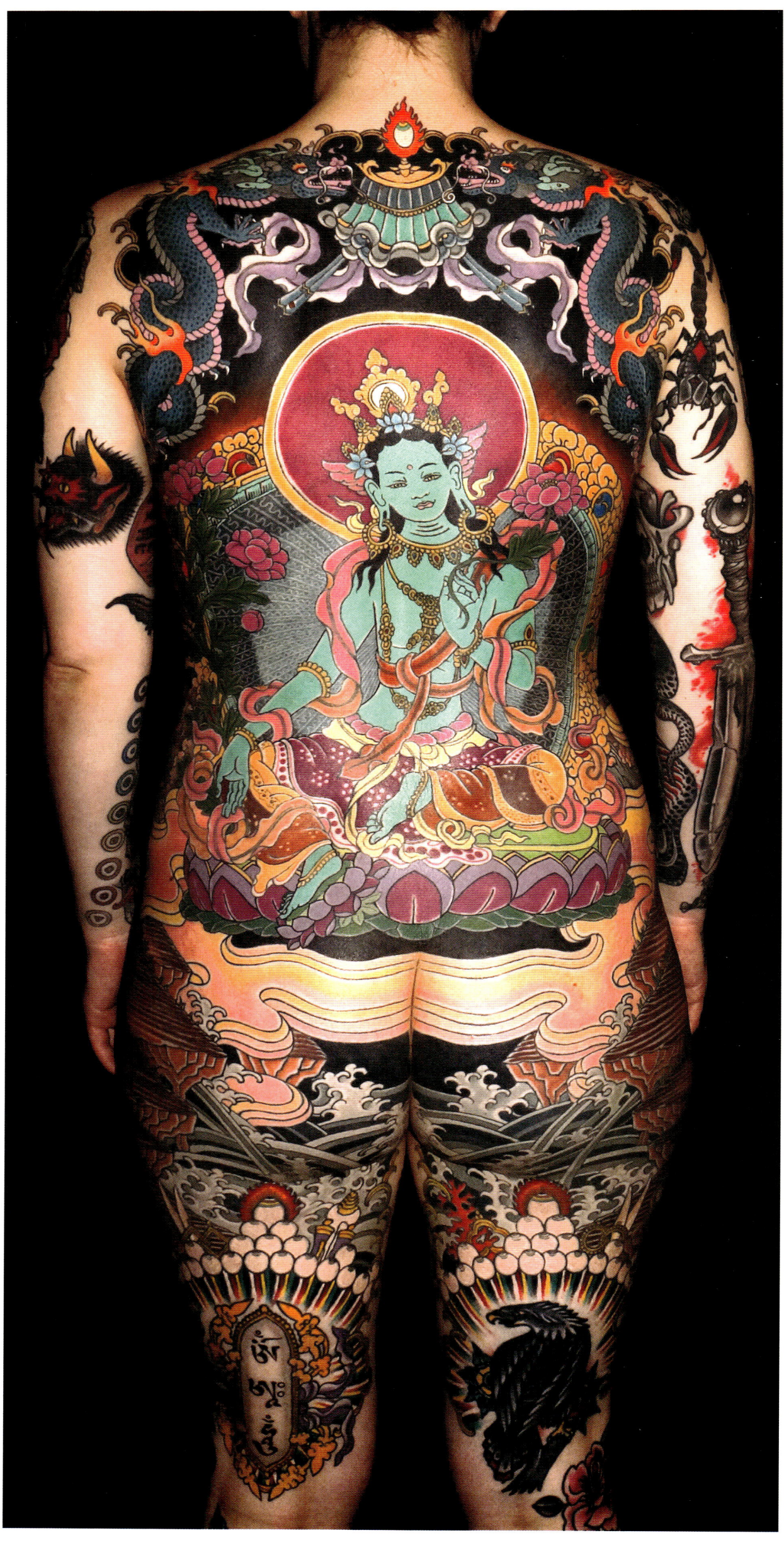

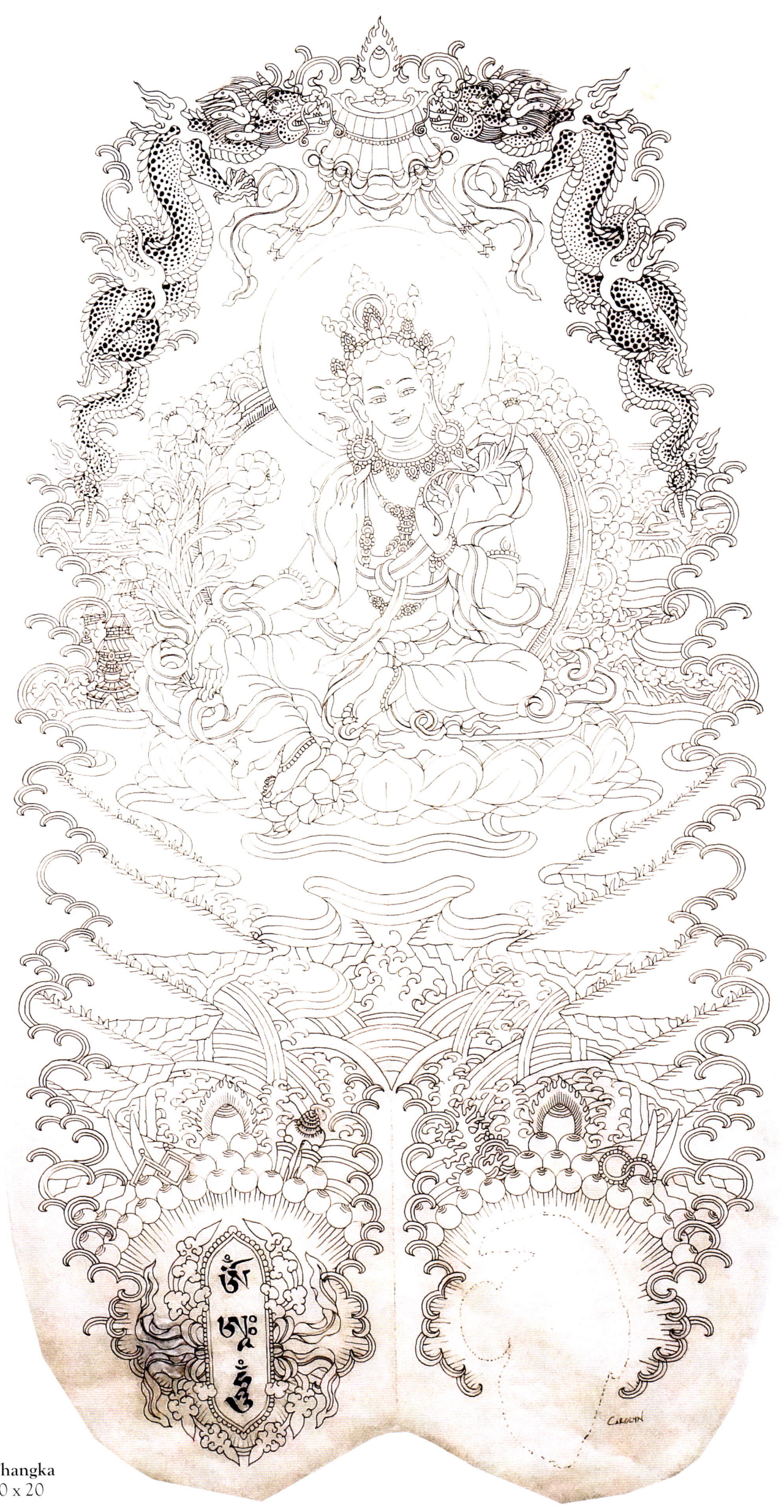

Thangka
40 x 20

45

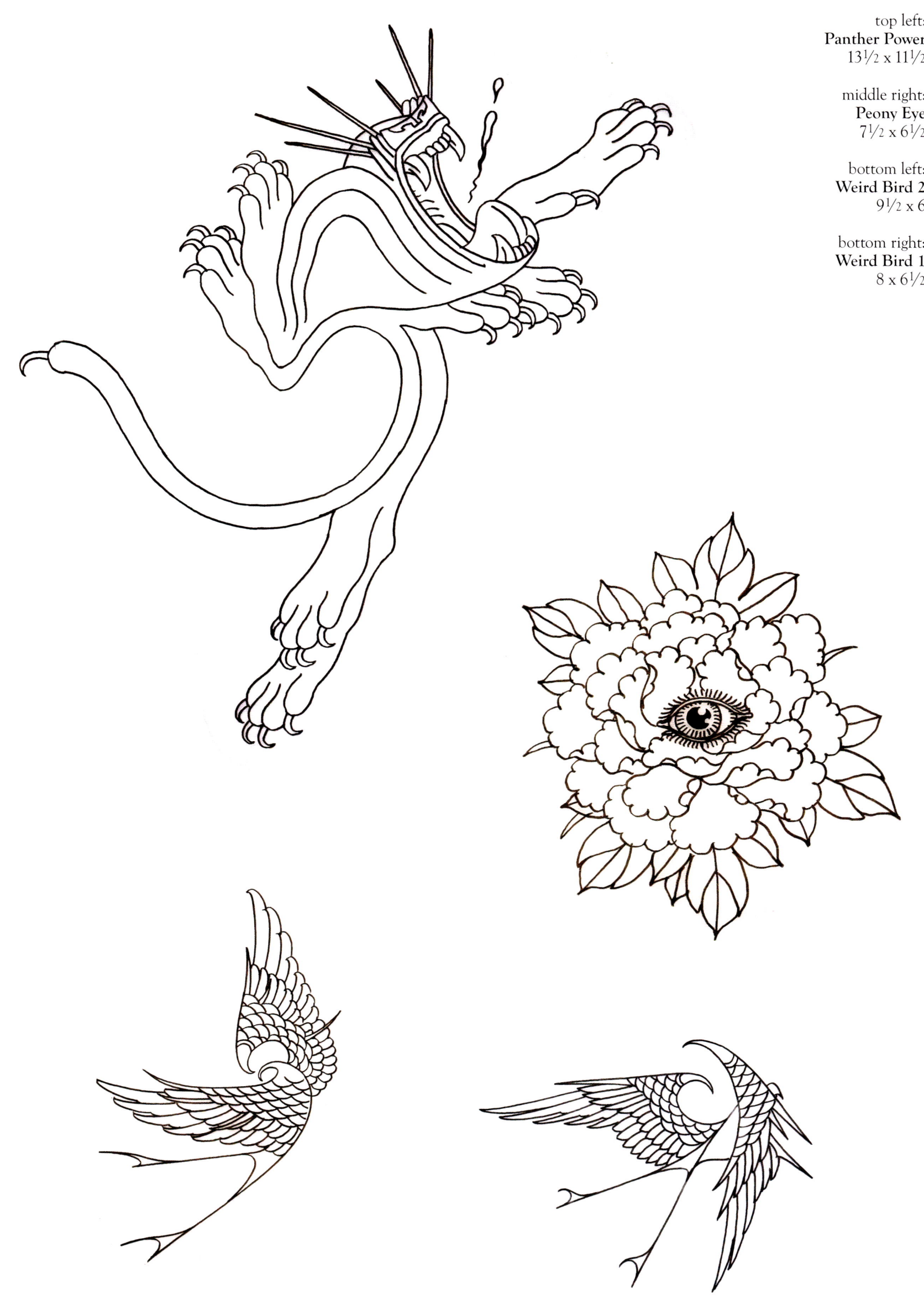

top left:
Panther Power
13½ x 11½

middle right:
Peony Eye
7½ x 6½

bottom left:
Weird Bird 2
9½ x 6

bottom right:
Weird Bird 1
8 x 6½

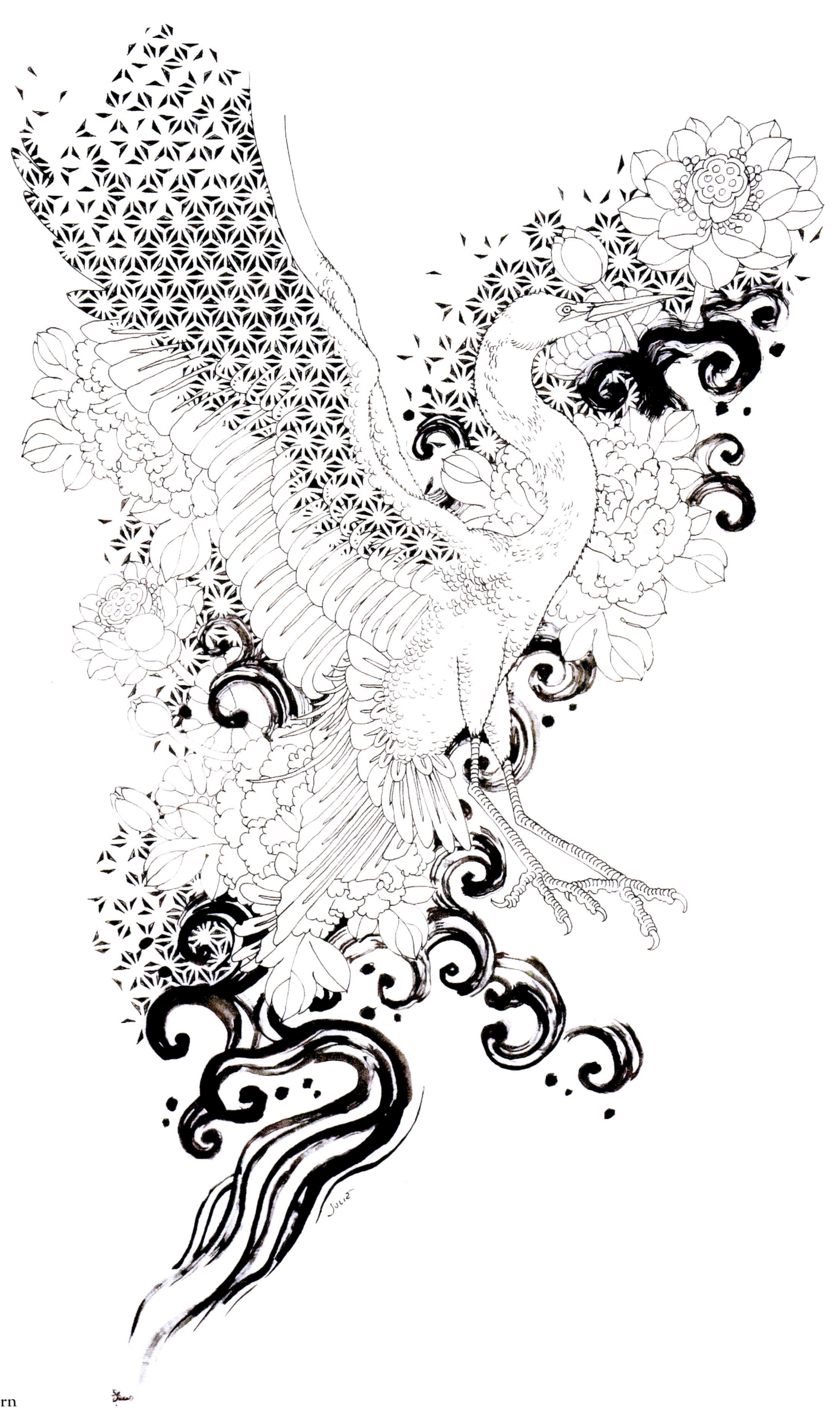

Heron Pattern
19 x 31

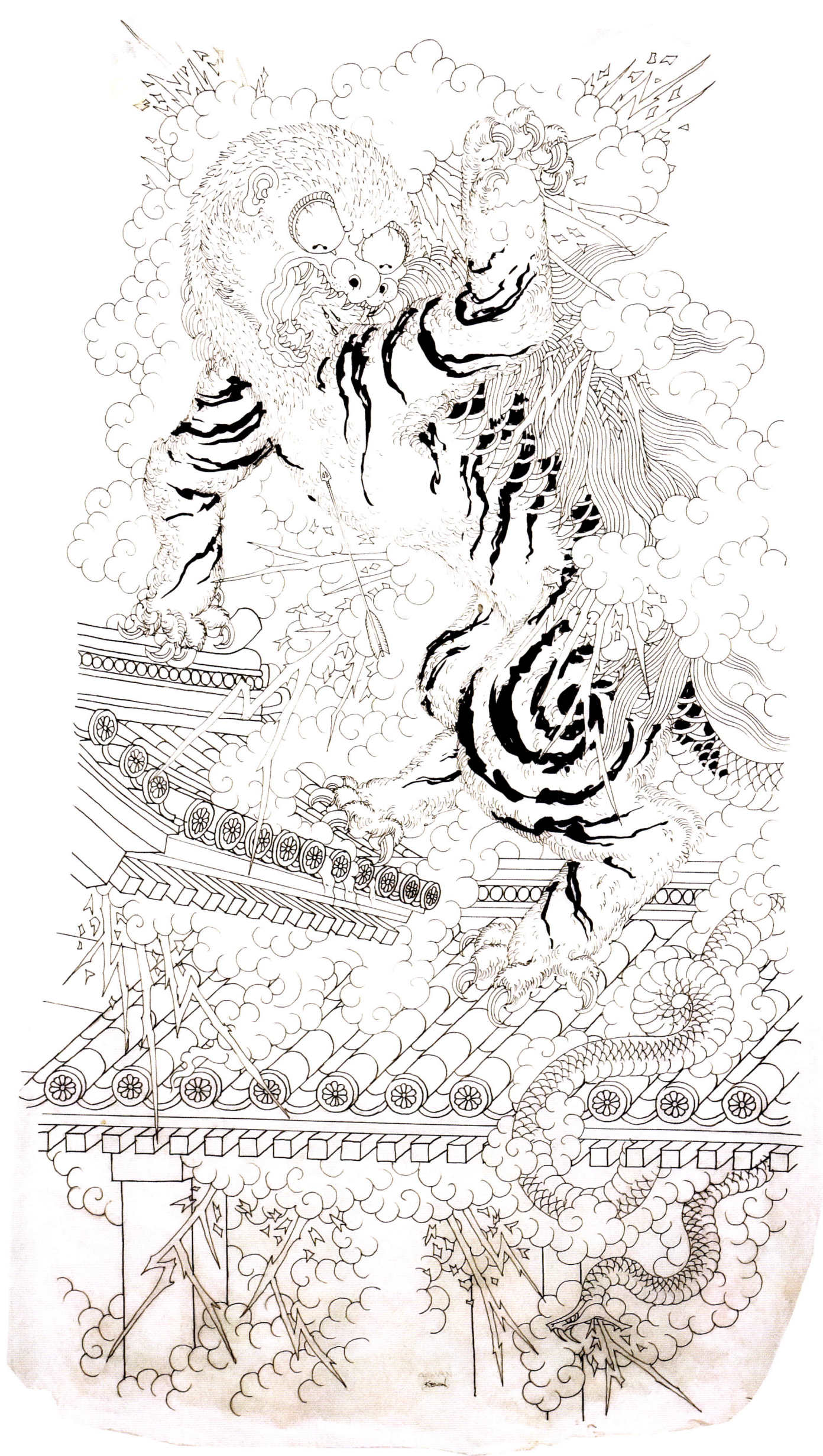

Nue
40 x 20

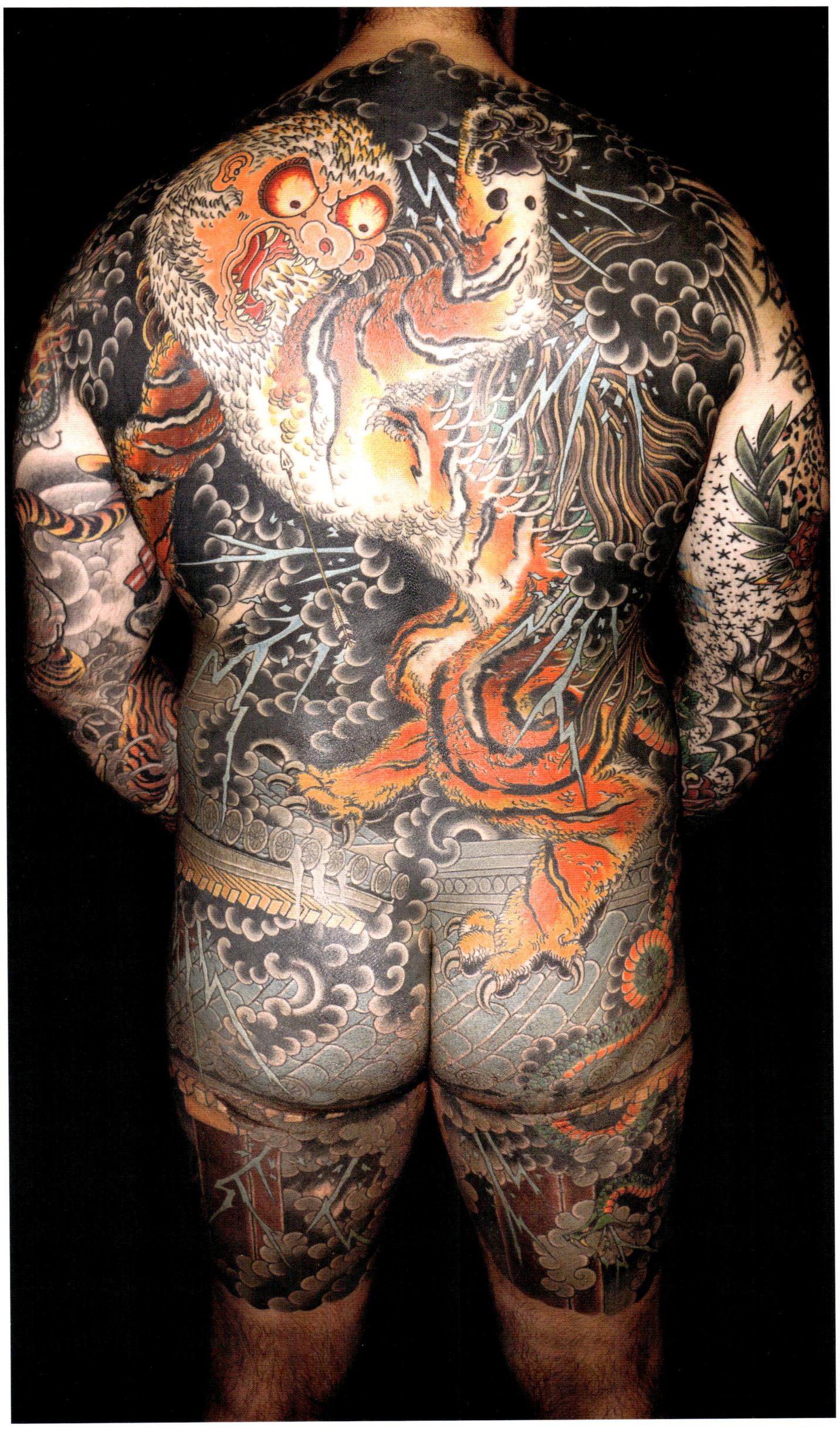

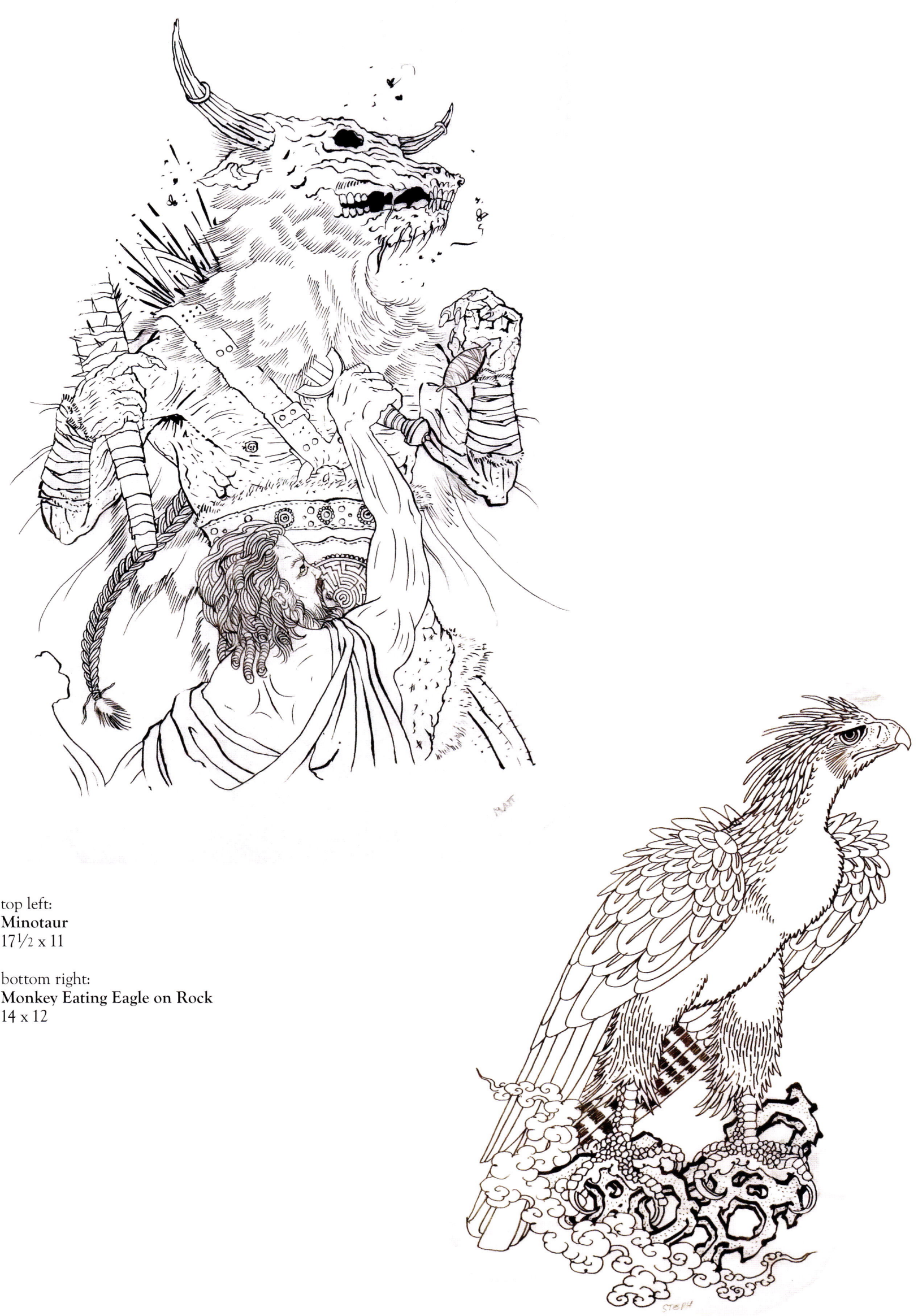

top left:
Minotaur
17½ x 11

bottom right:
Monkey Eating Eagle on Rock
14 x 12

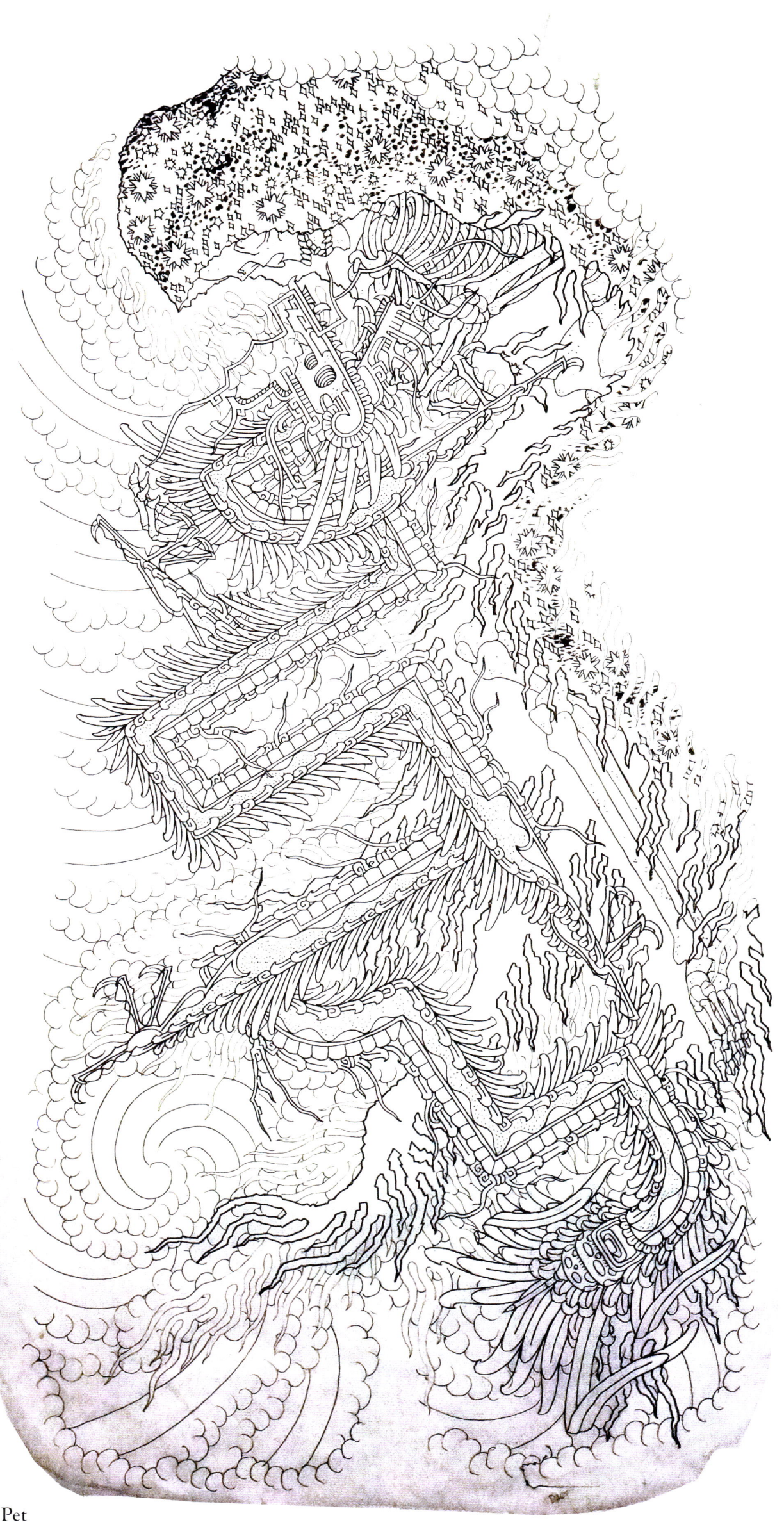

Heroin is Death's Pet
40 x 20

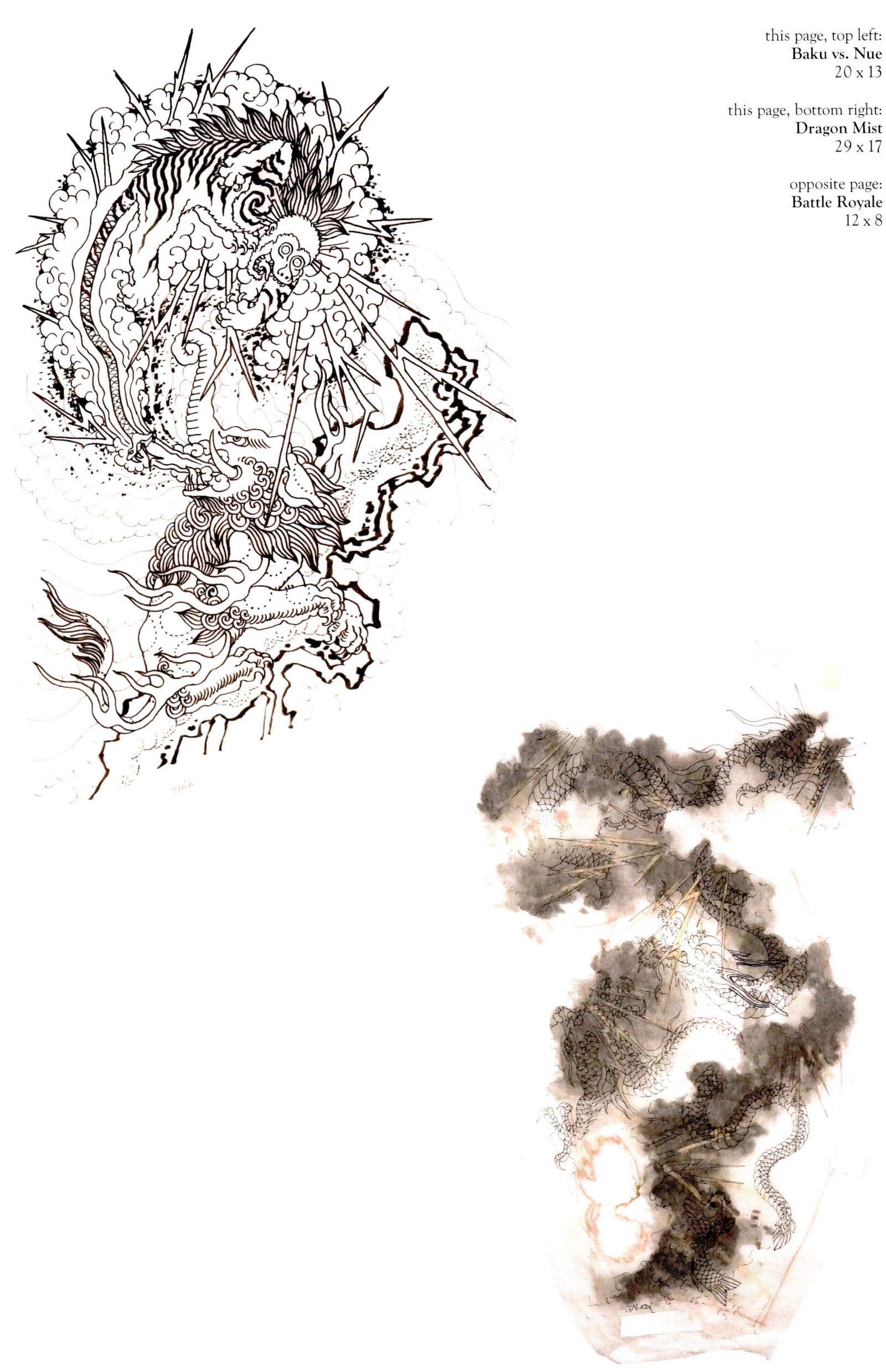

this page, top left:
Baku vs. Nue
20 x 13

this page, bottom right:
Dragon Mist
29 x 17

opposite page:
Battle Royale
12 x 8

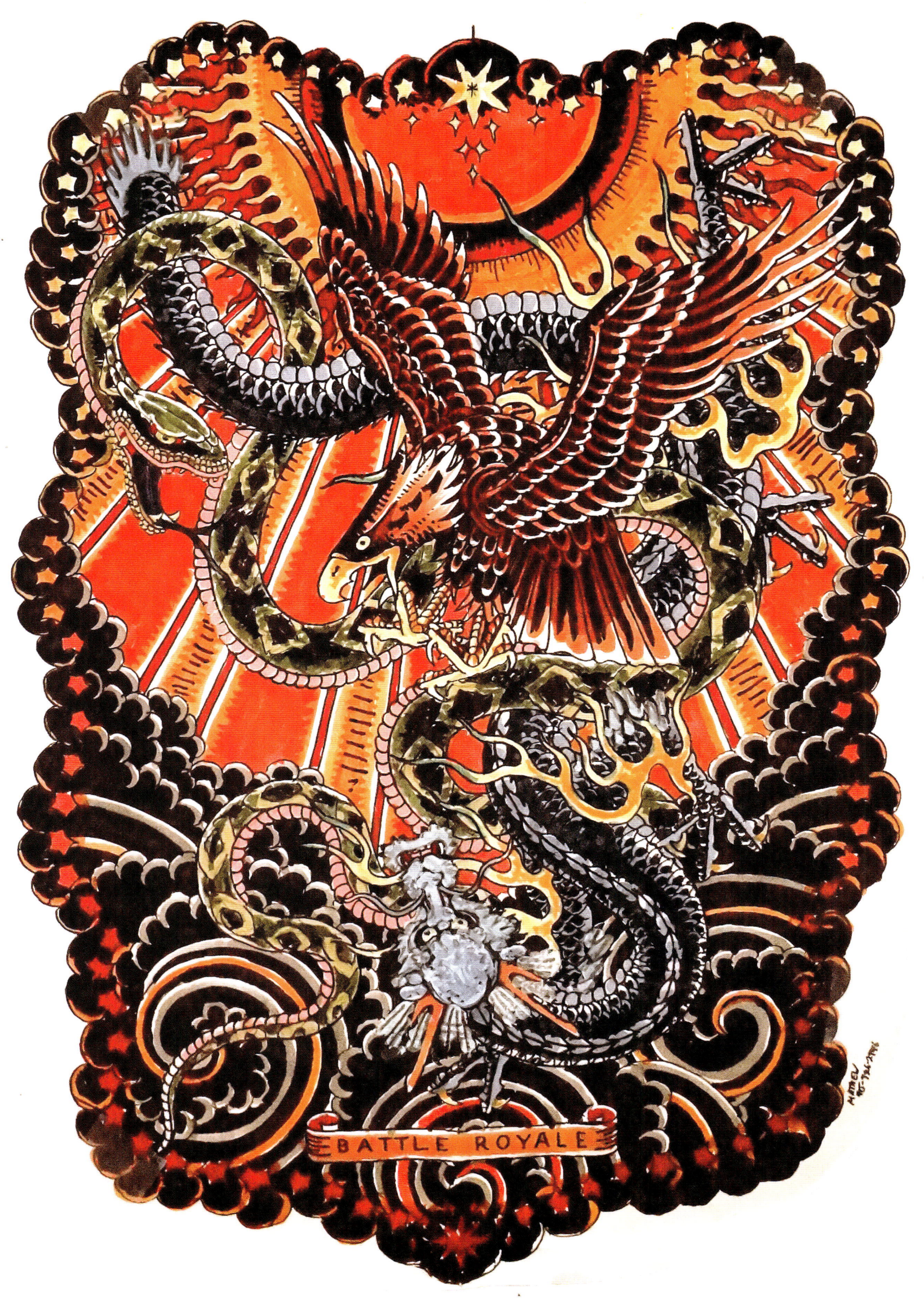

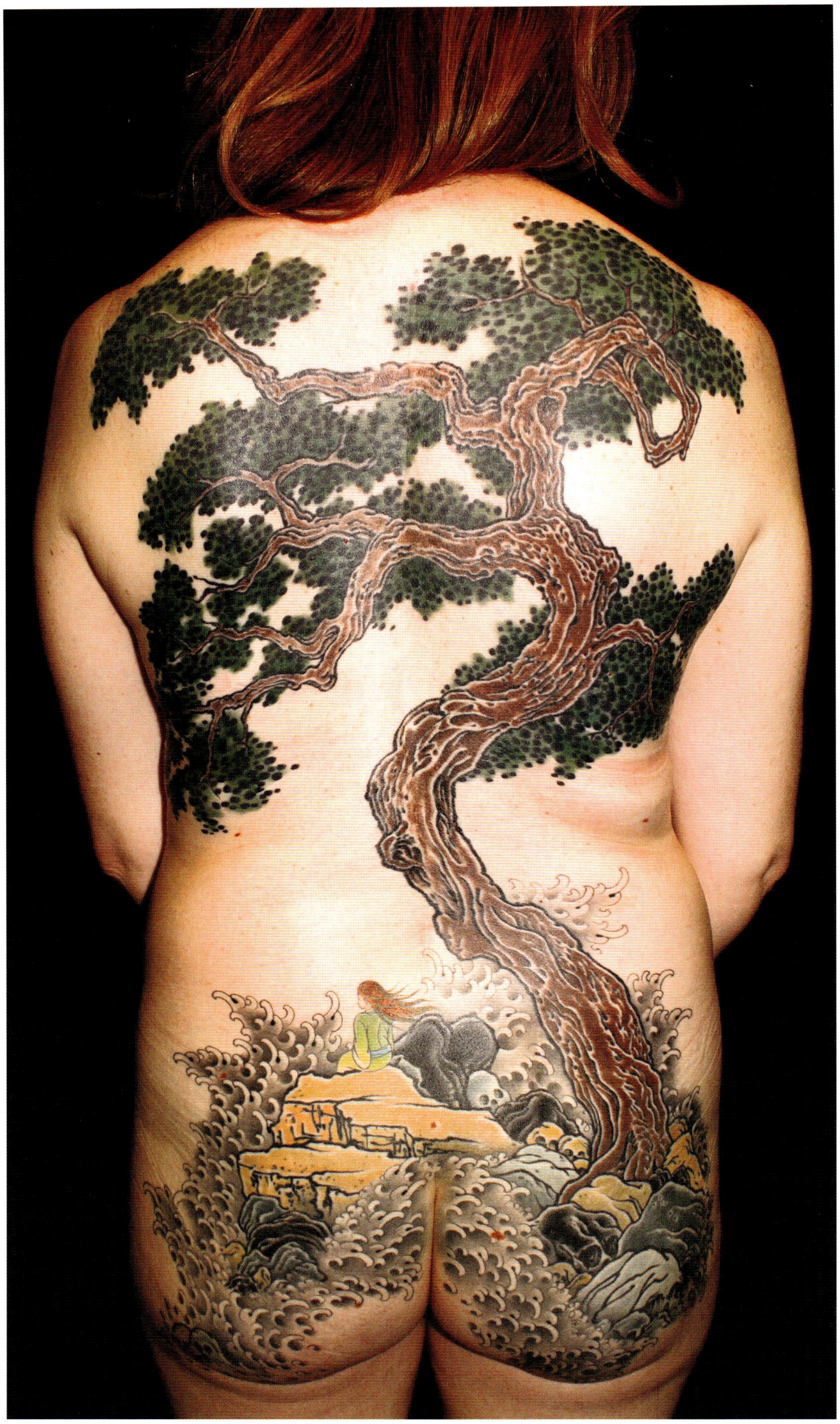

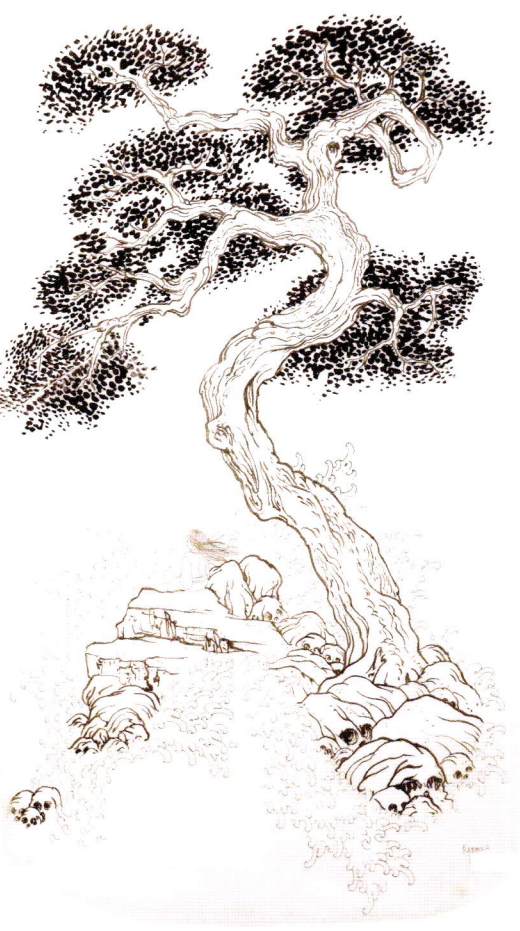

Ready
29 x 16

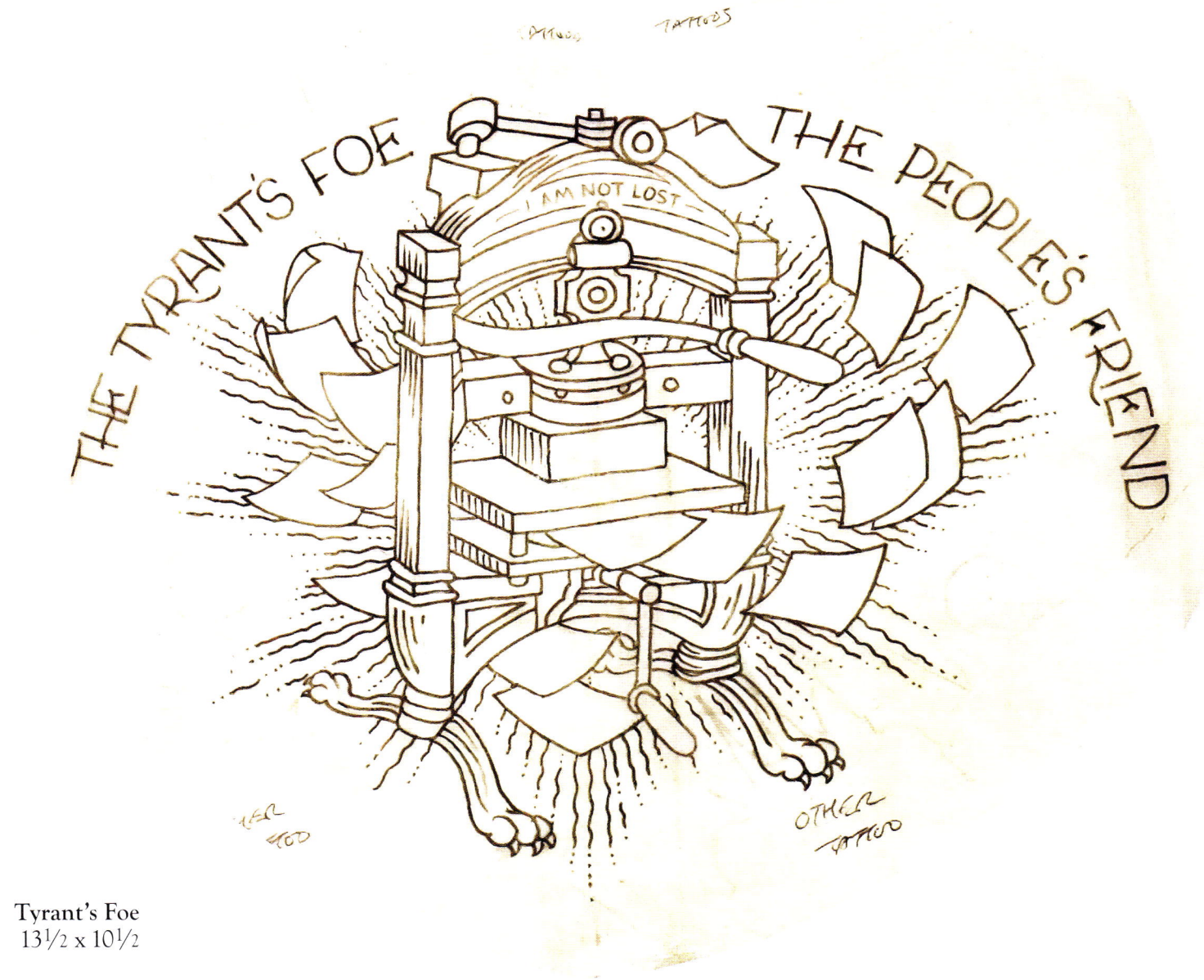

Tyrant's Foe
13½ x 10½

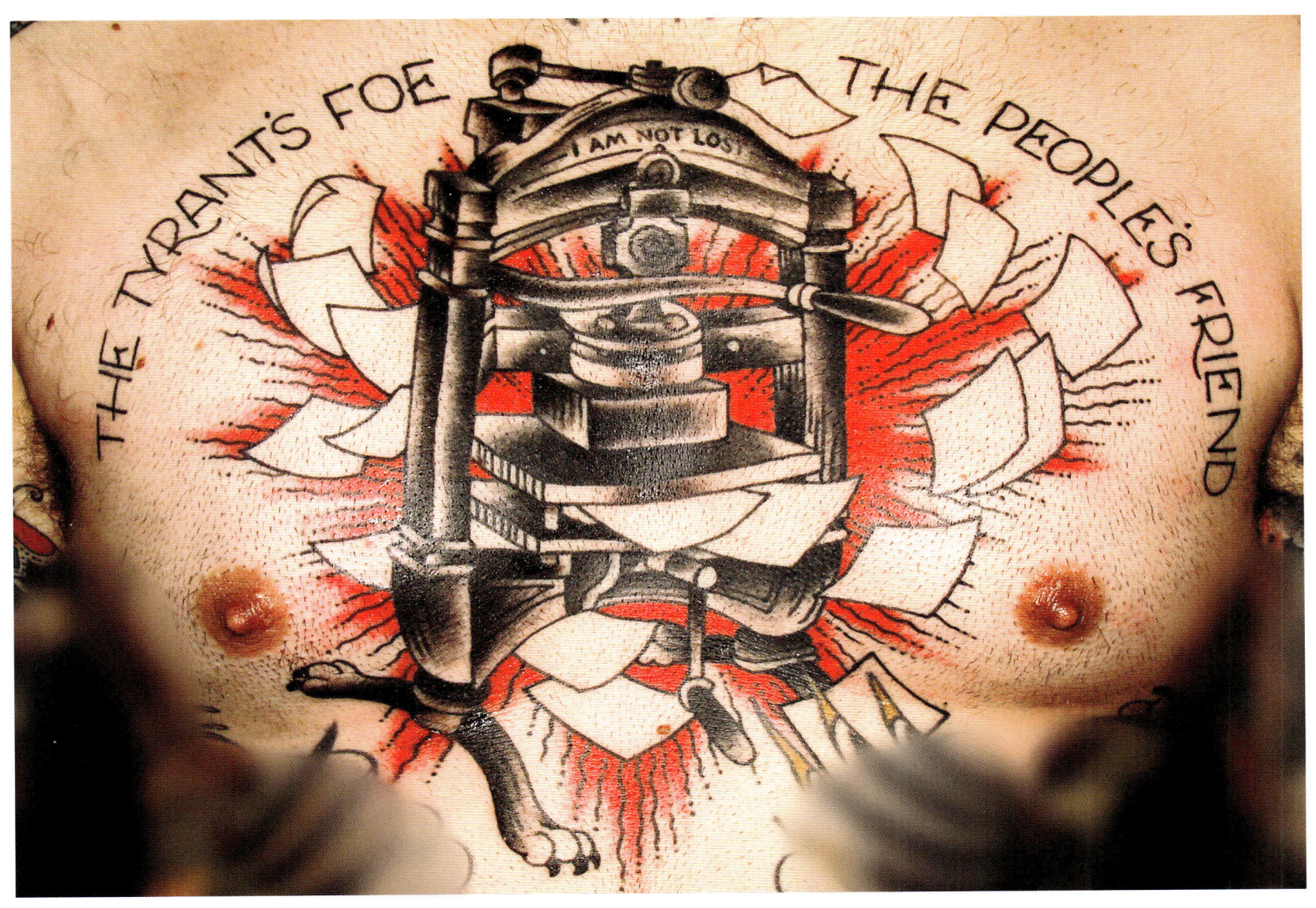

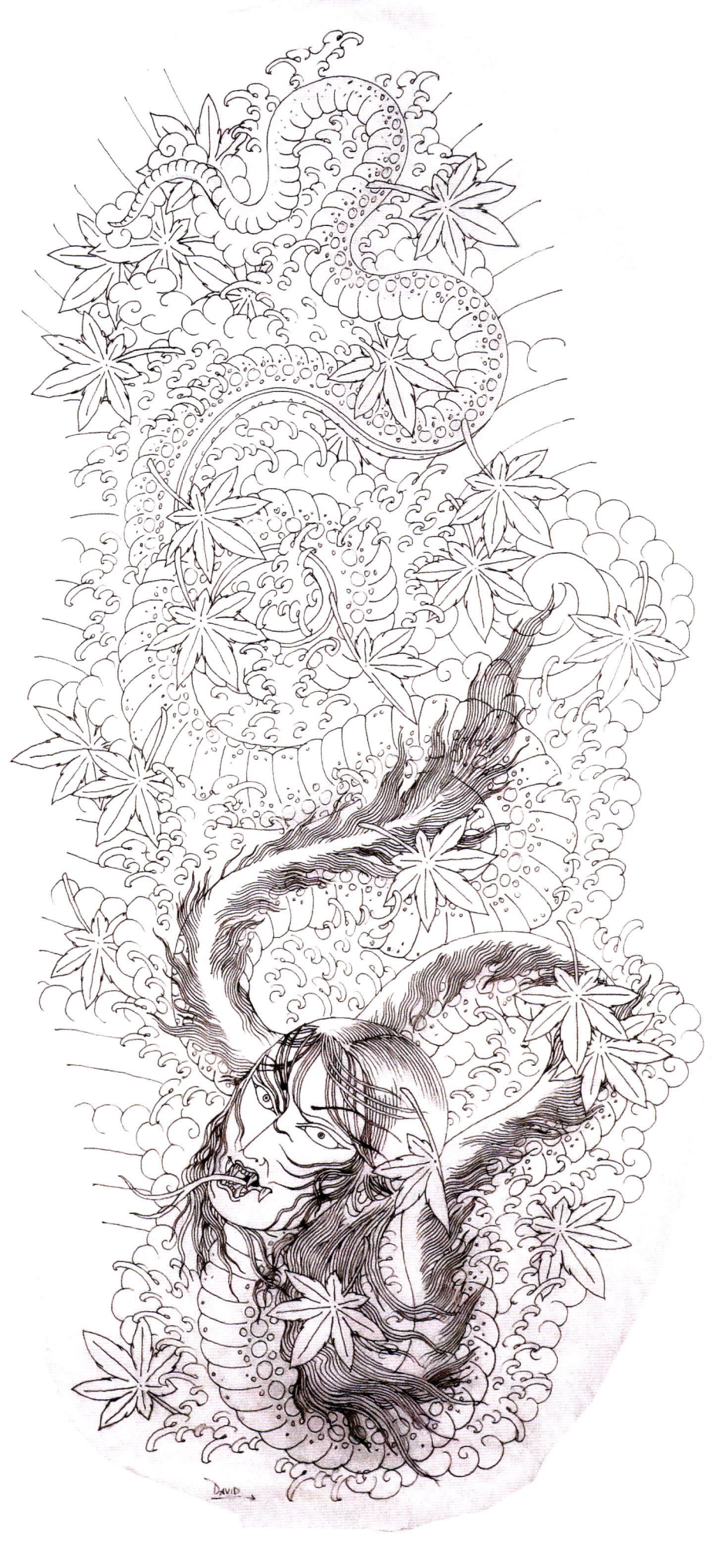

left:
Snake Lady
29 x 13

right:
Mega Oni
24 x 21

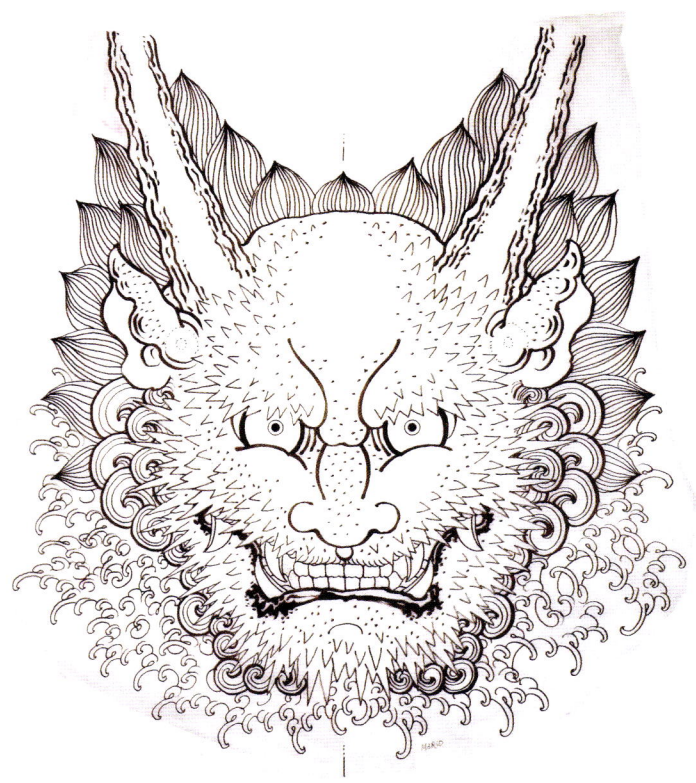

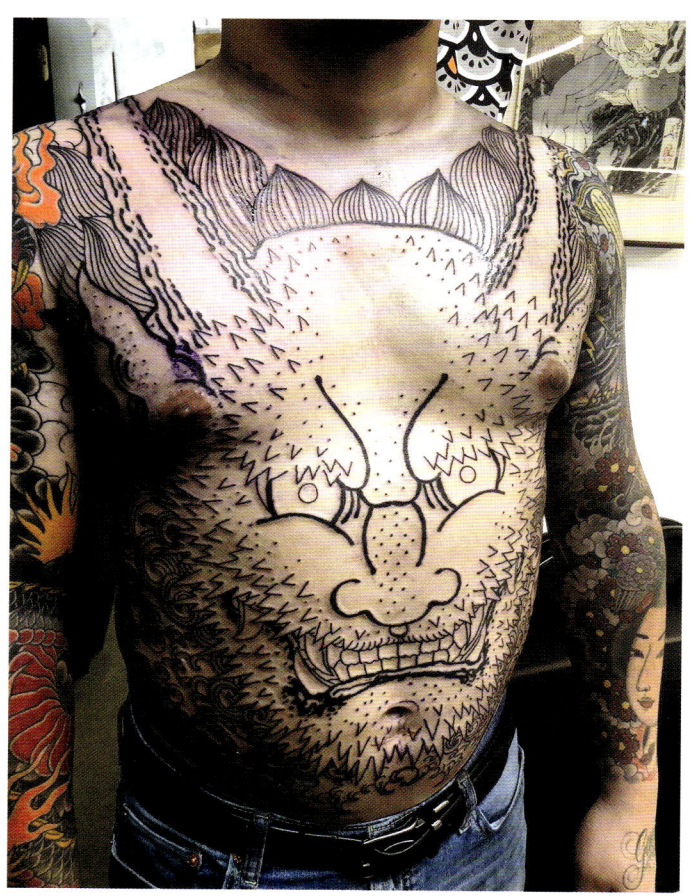

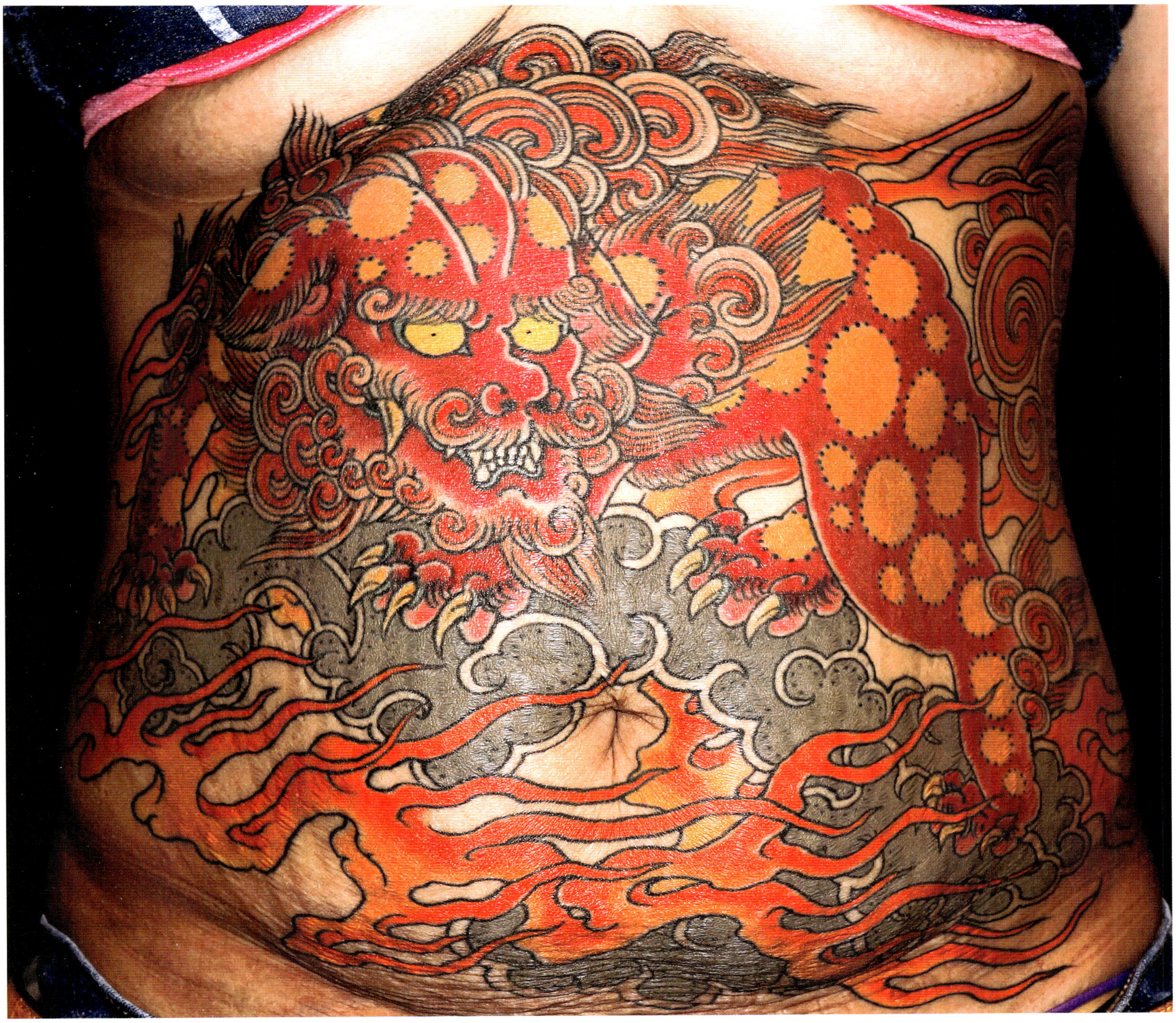

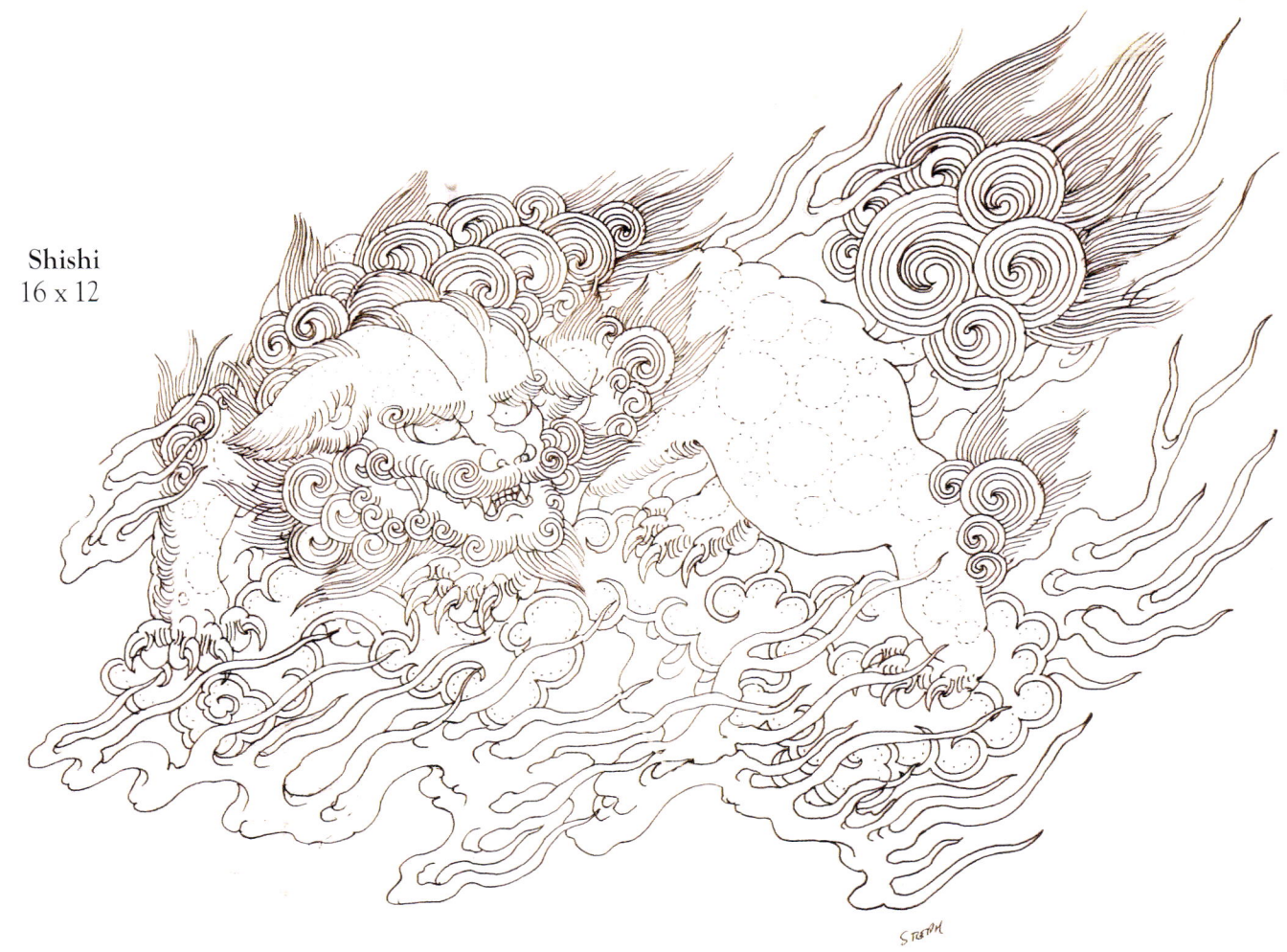

Shishi
16 x 12

57

Mongaku
35 x 21

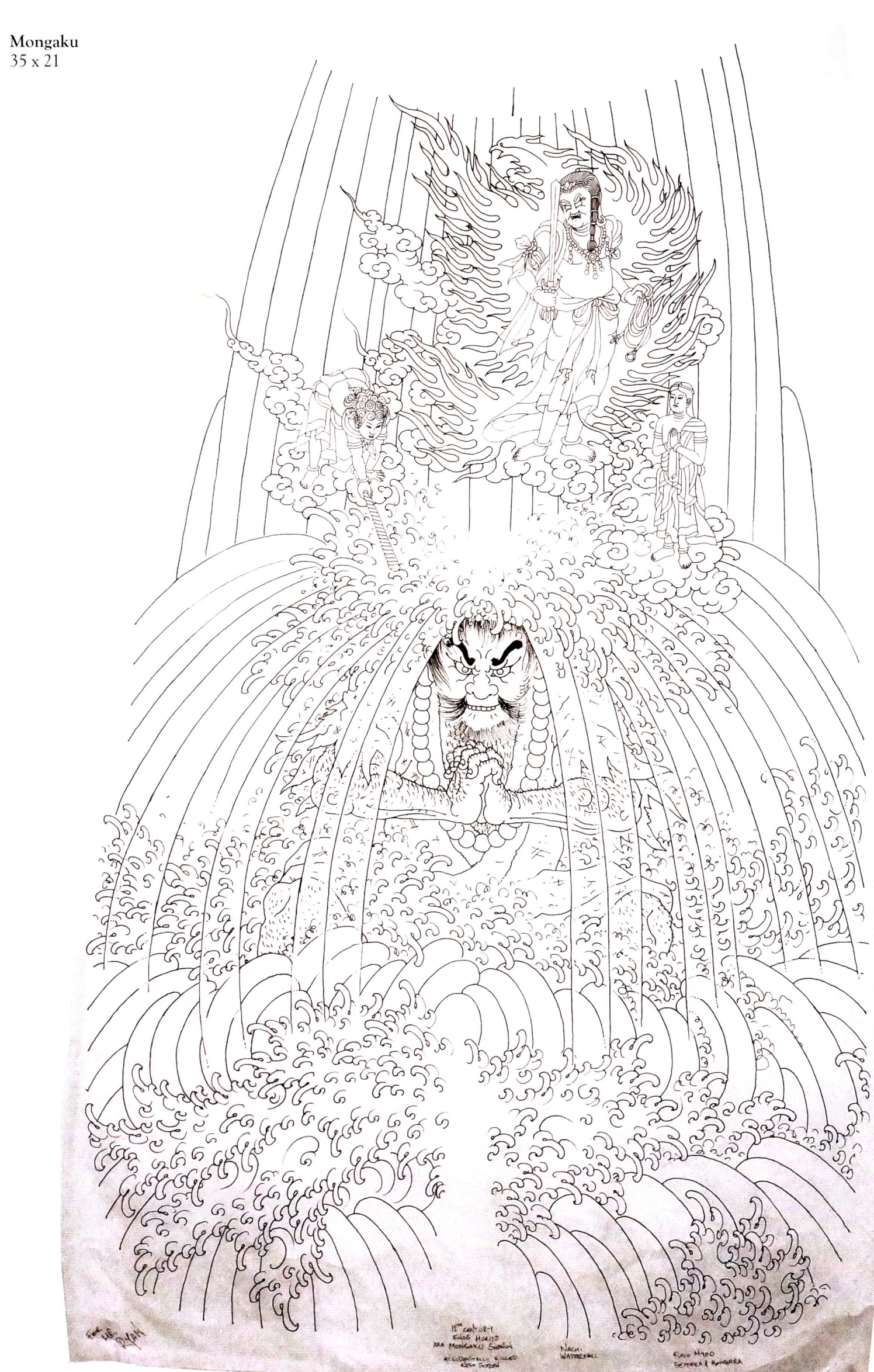

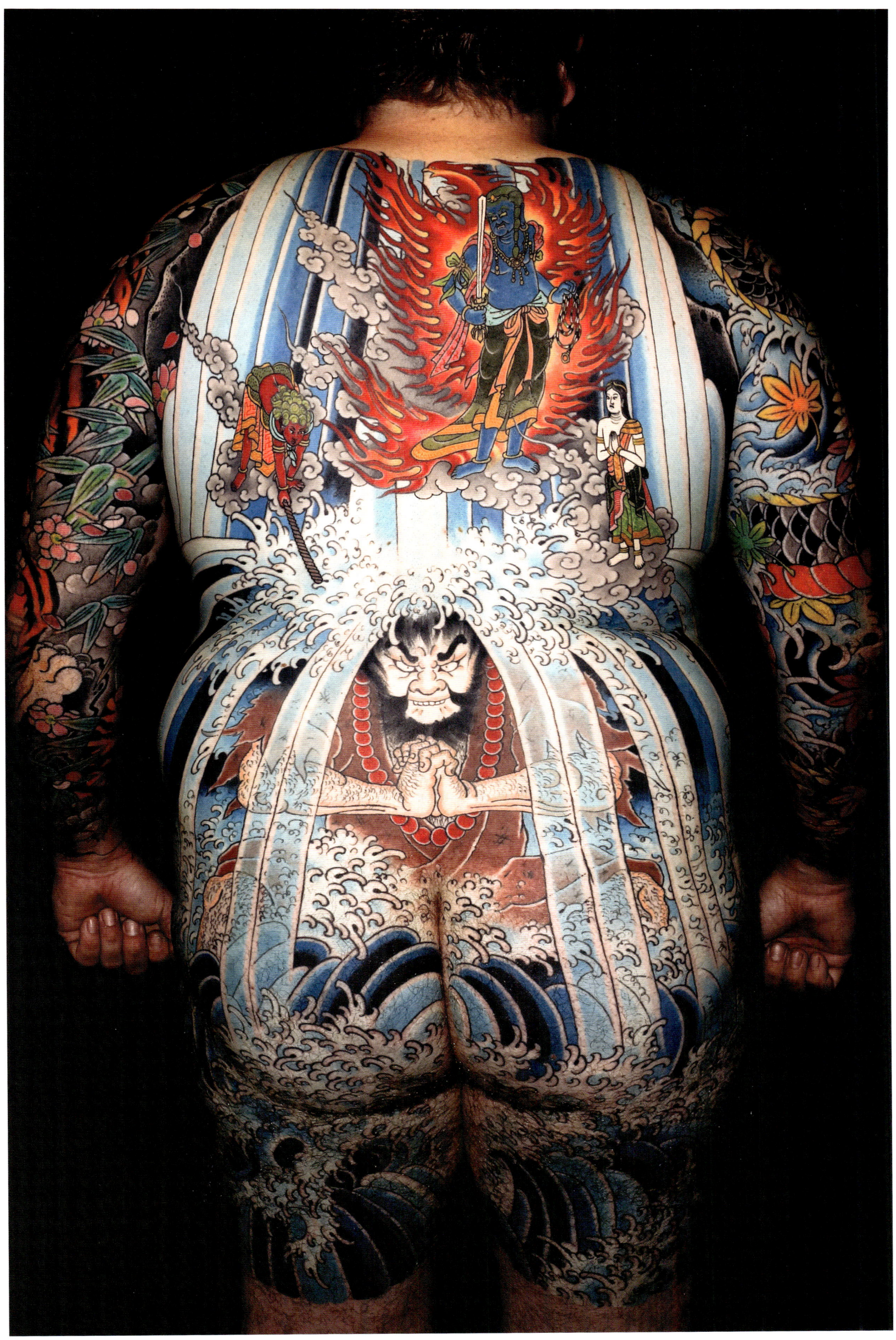

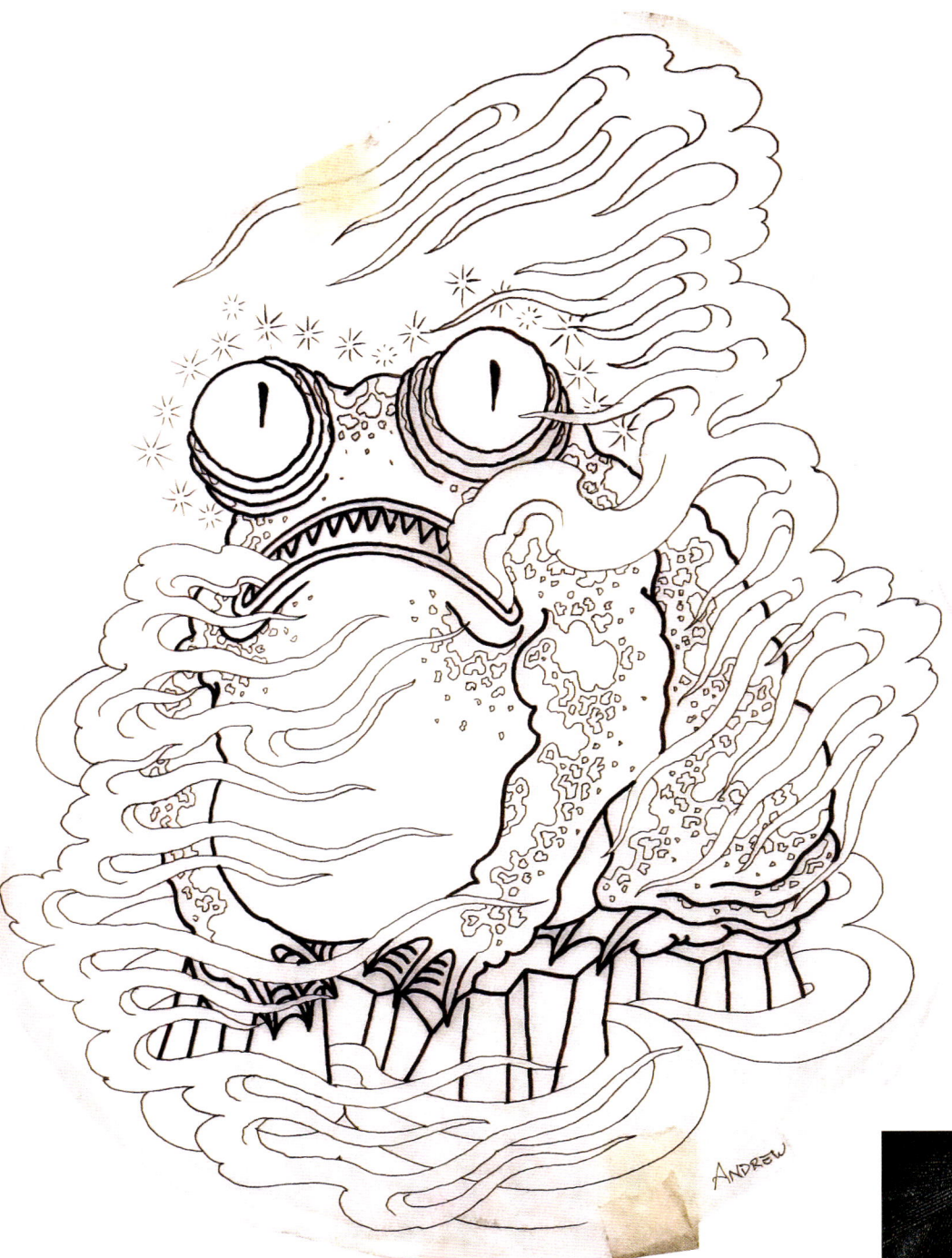

Hypno Toad
14½ x 10½

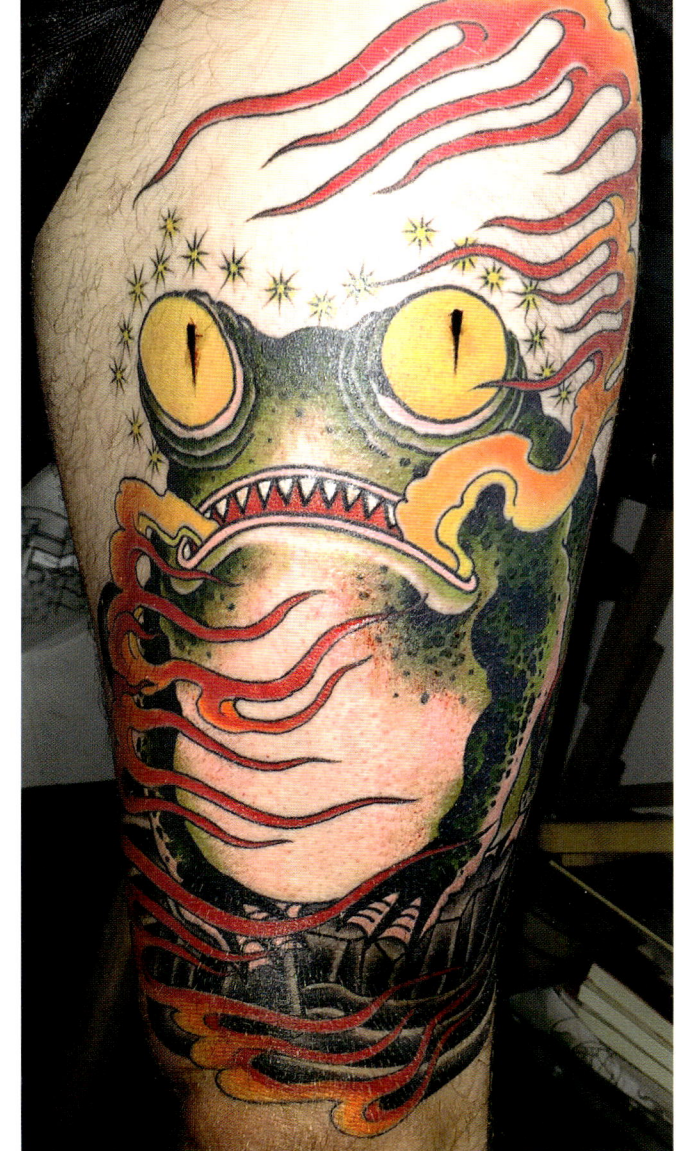

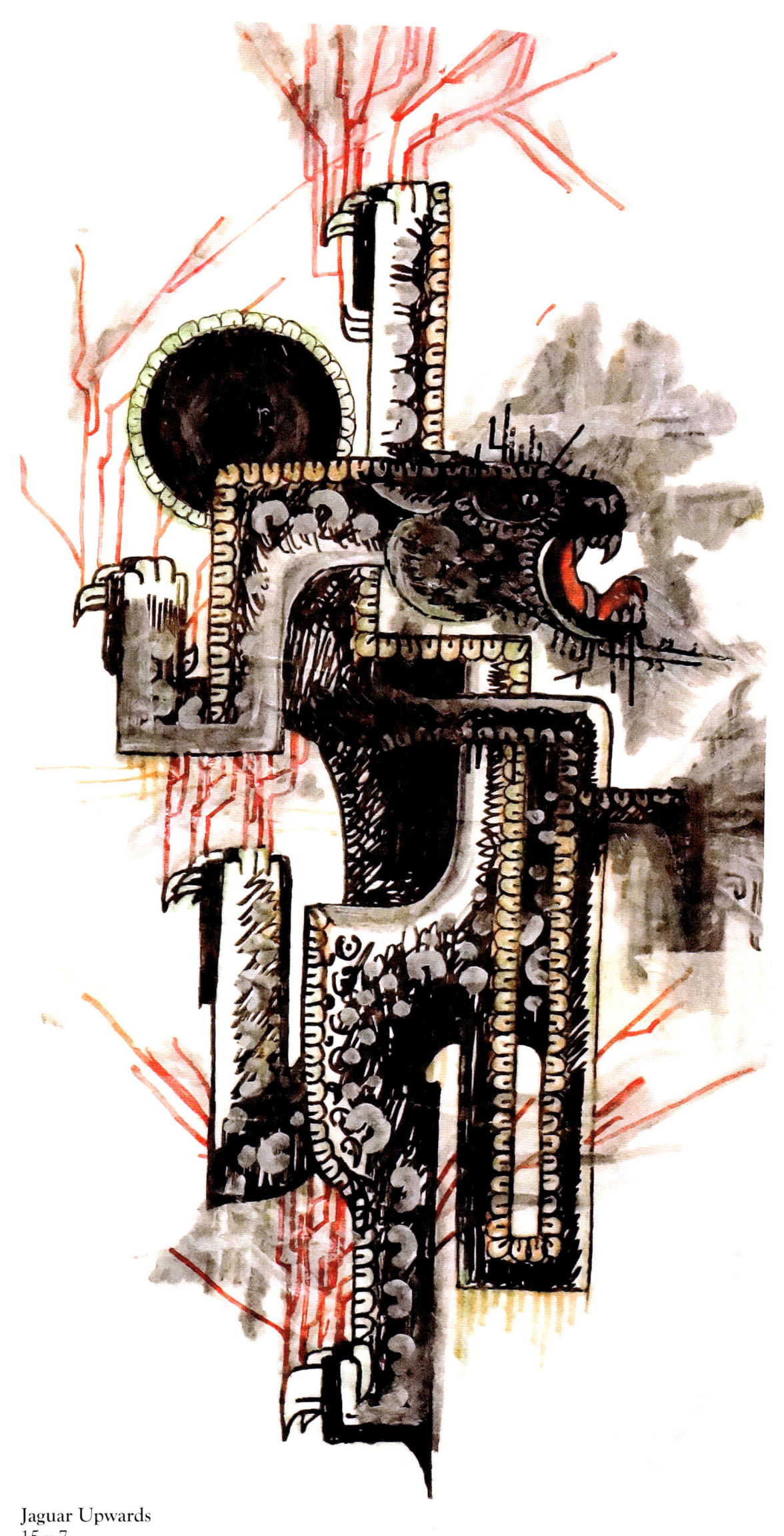

Jaguar Upwards
15 x 7

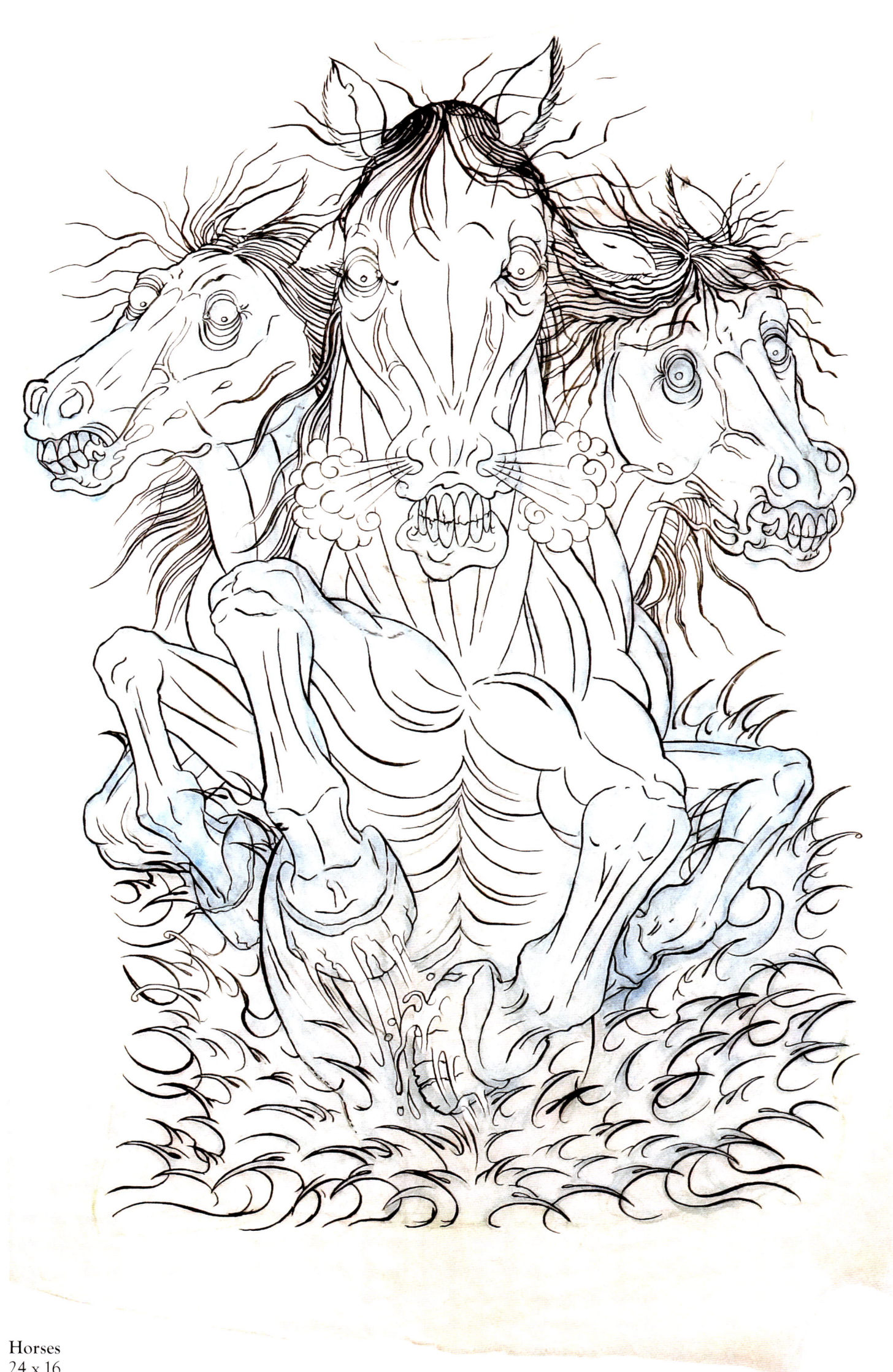

Horses
24 x 16

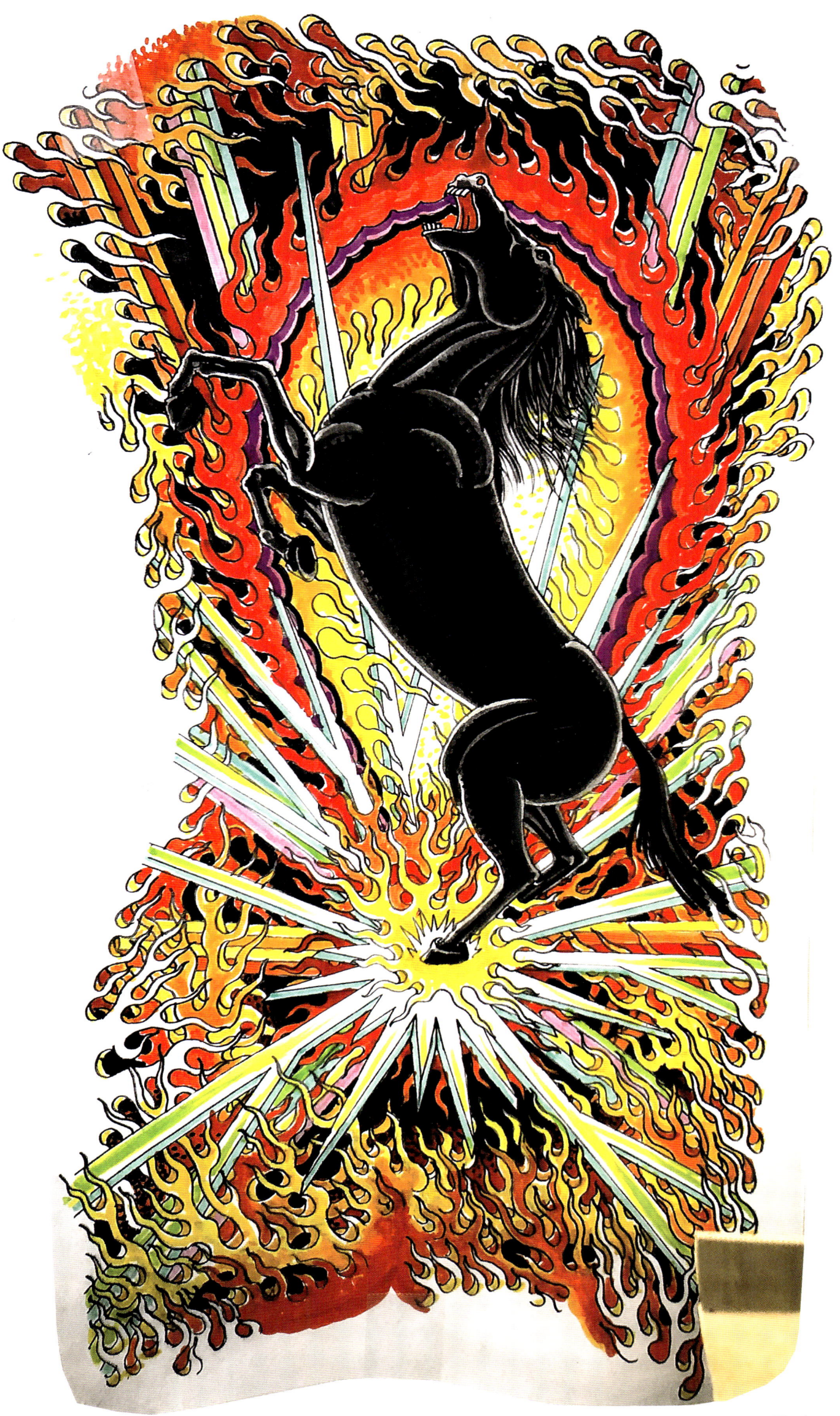

Firehorse
27 x 15

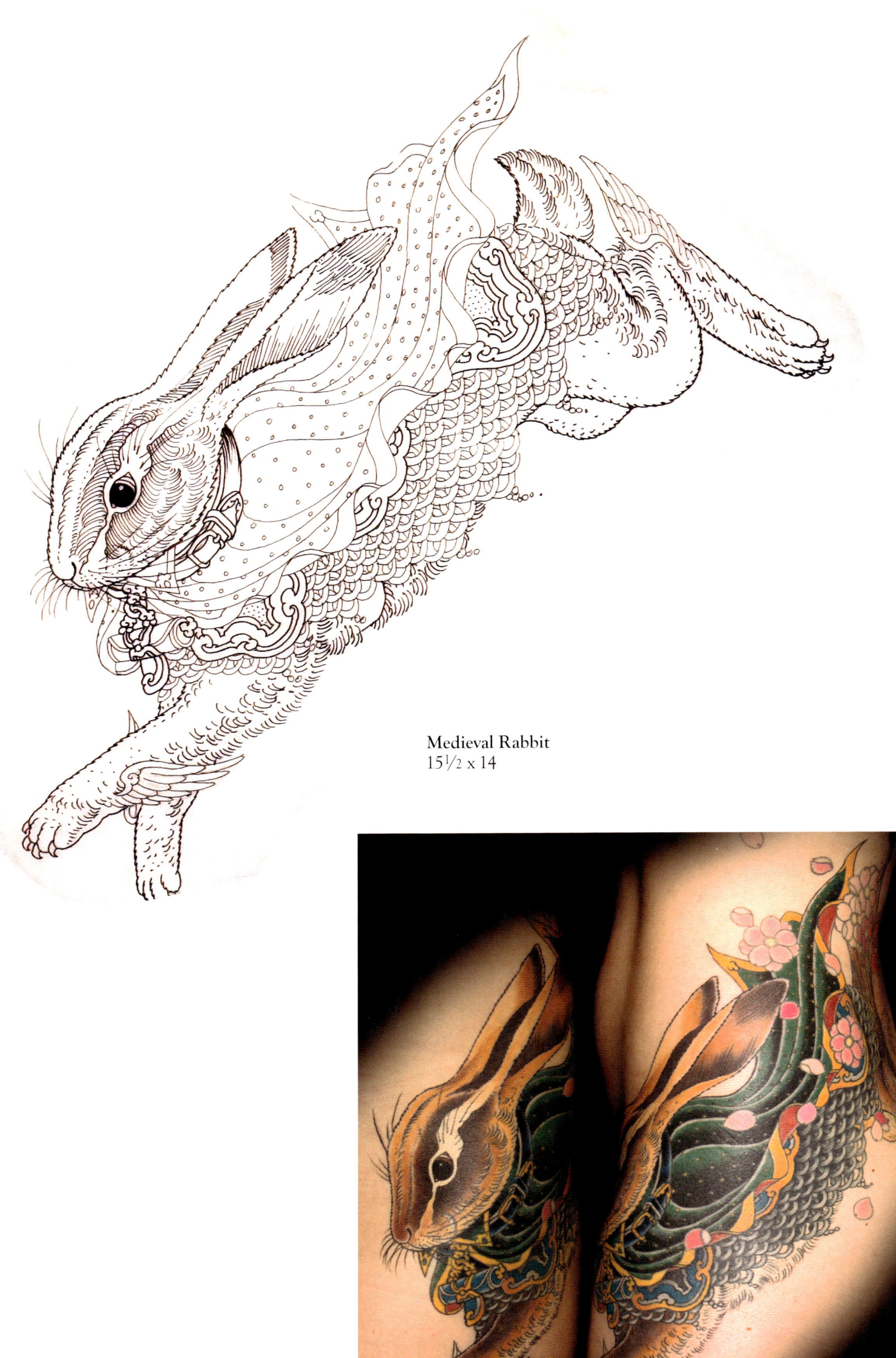

Medieval Rabbit
$15^{1}/_2$ x 14

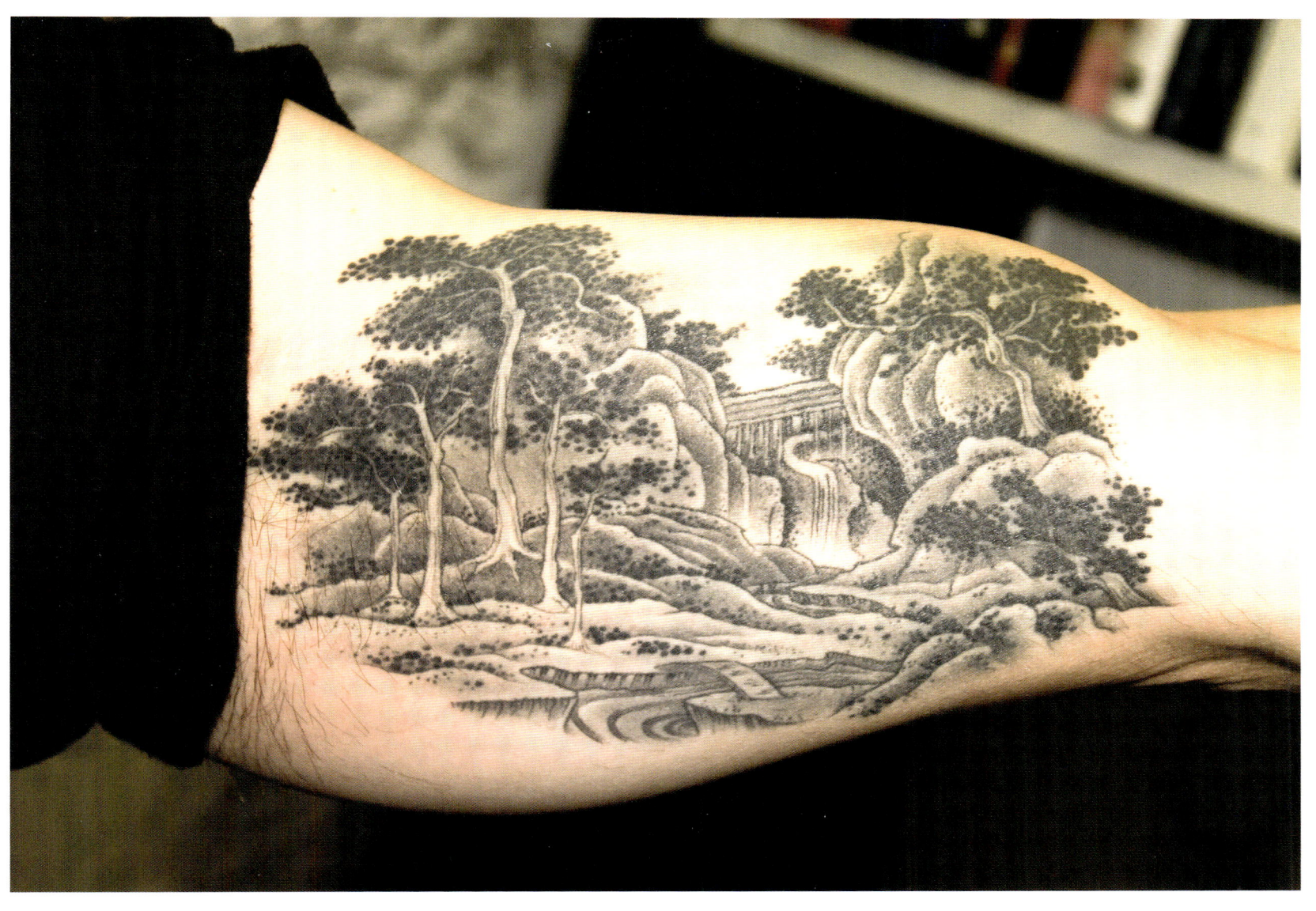

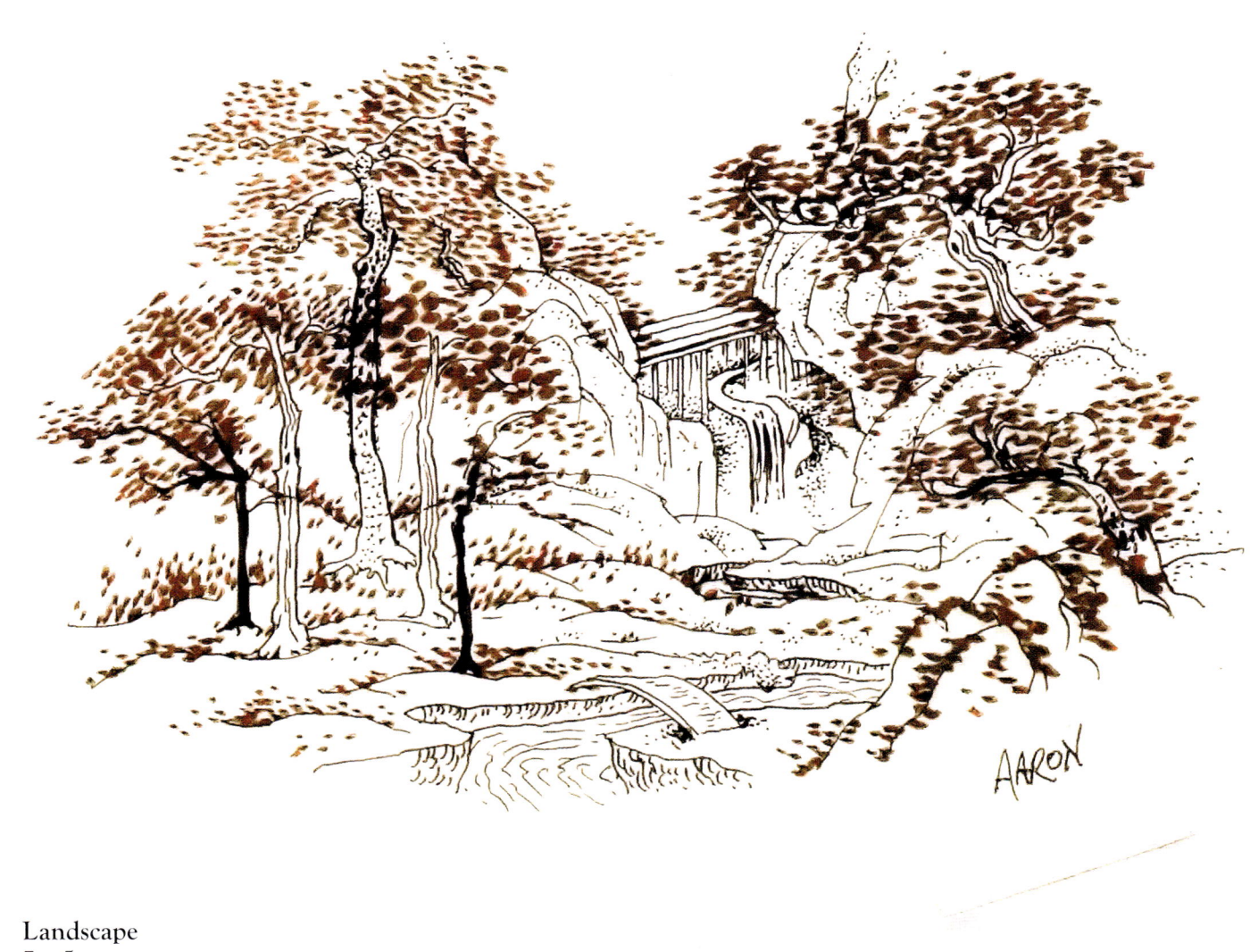

Landscape
7 x 5

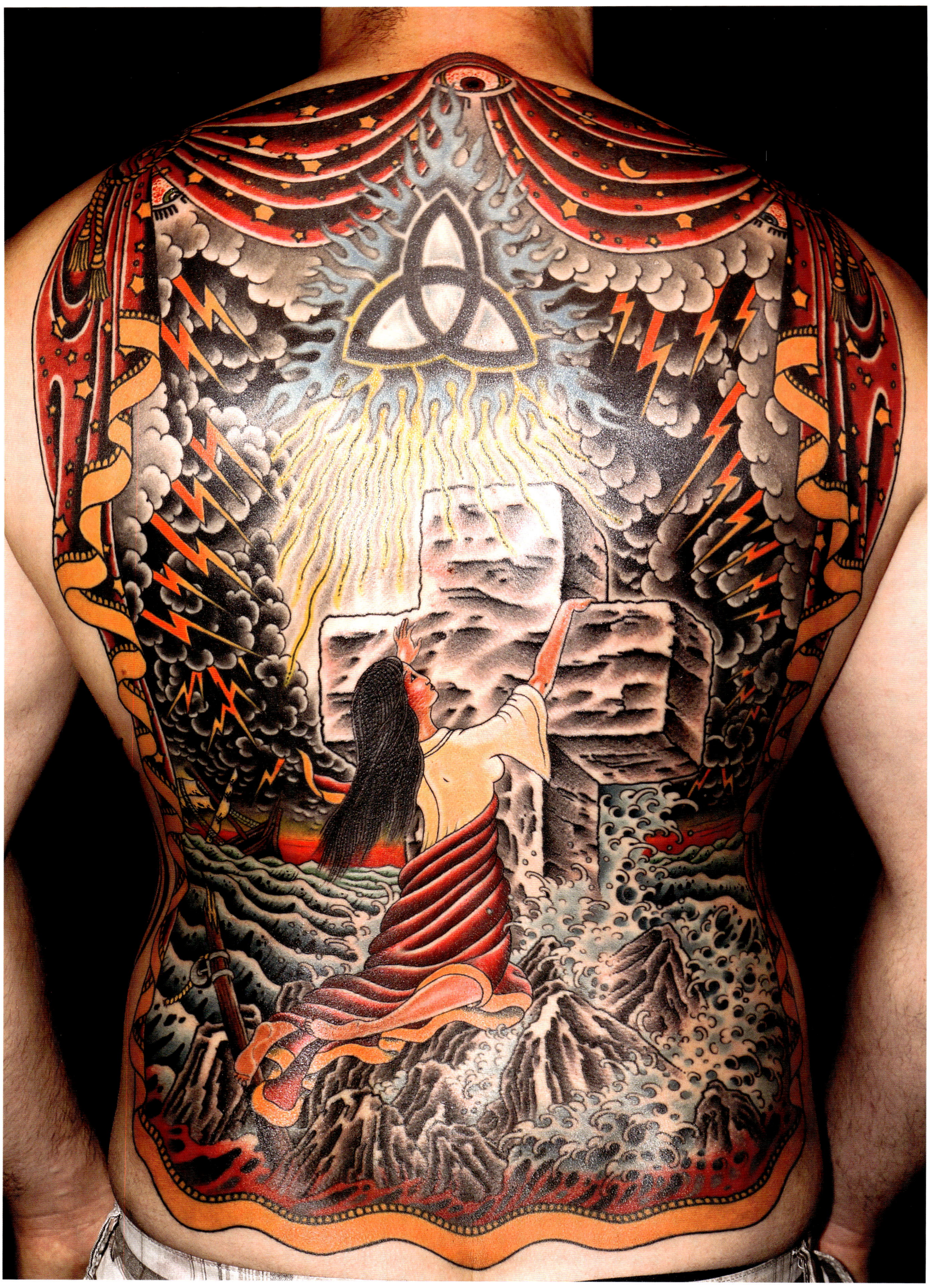

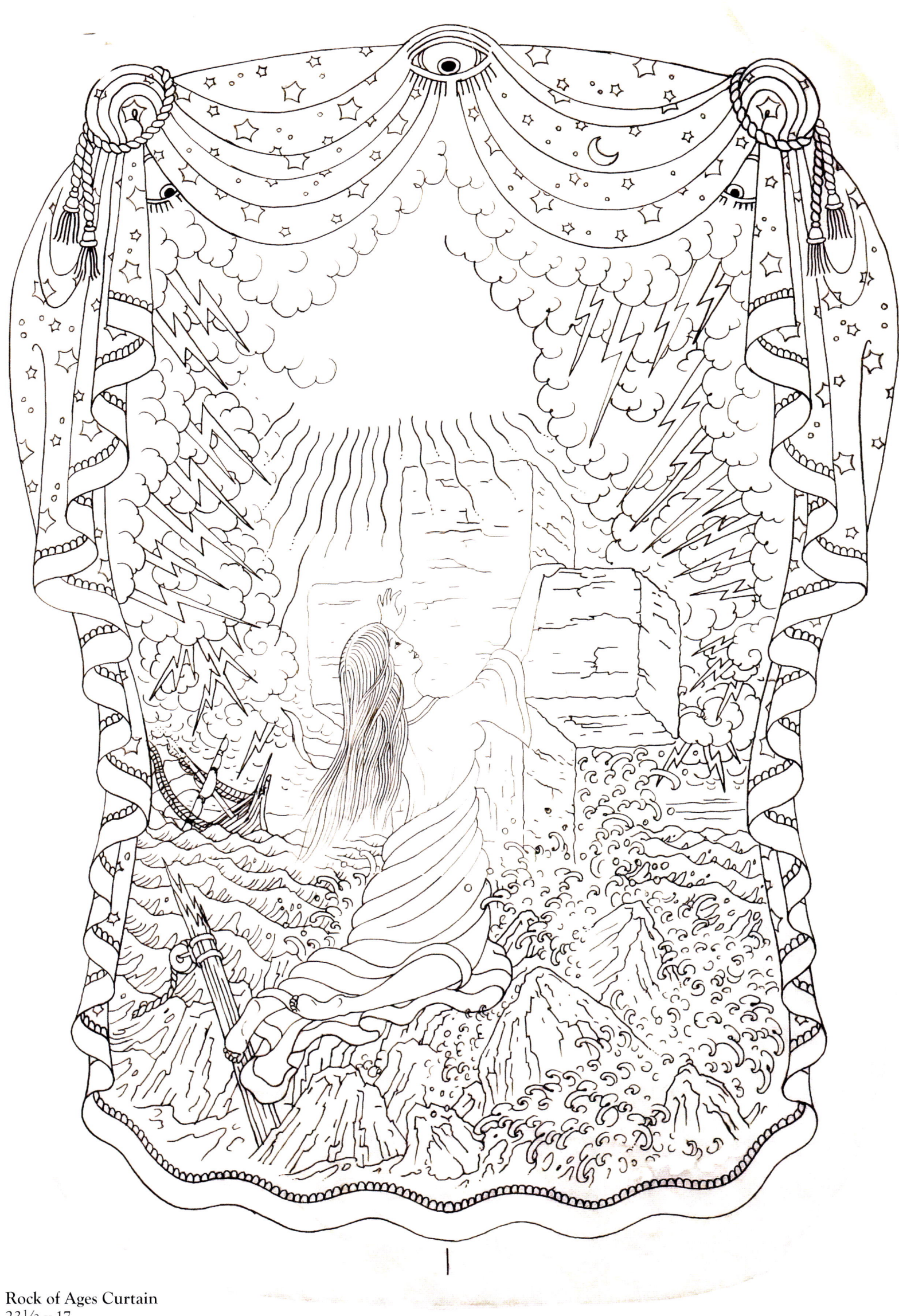

Rock of Ages Curtain
23½ x 17

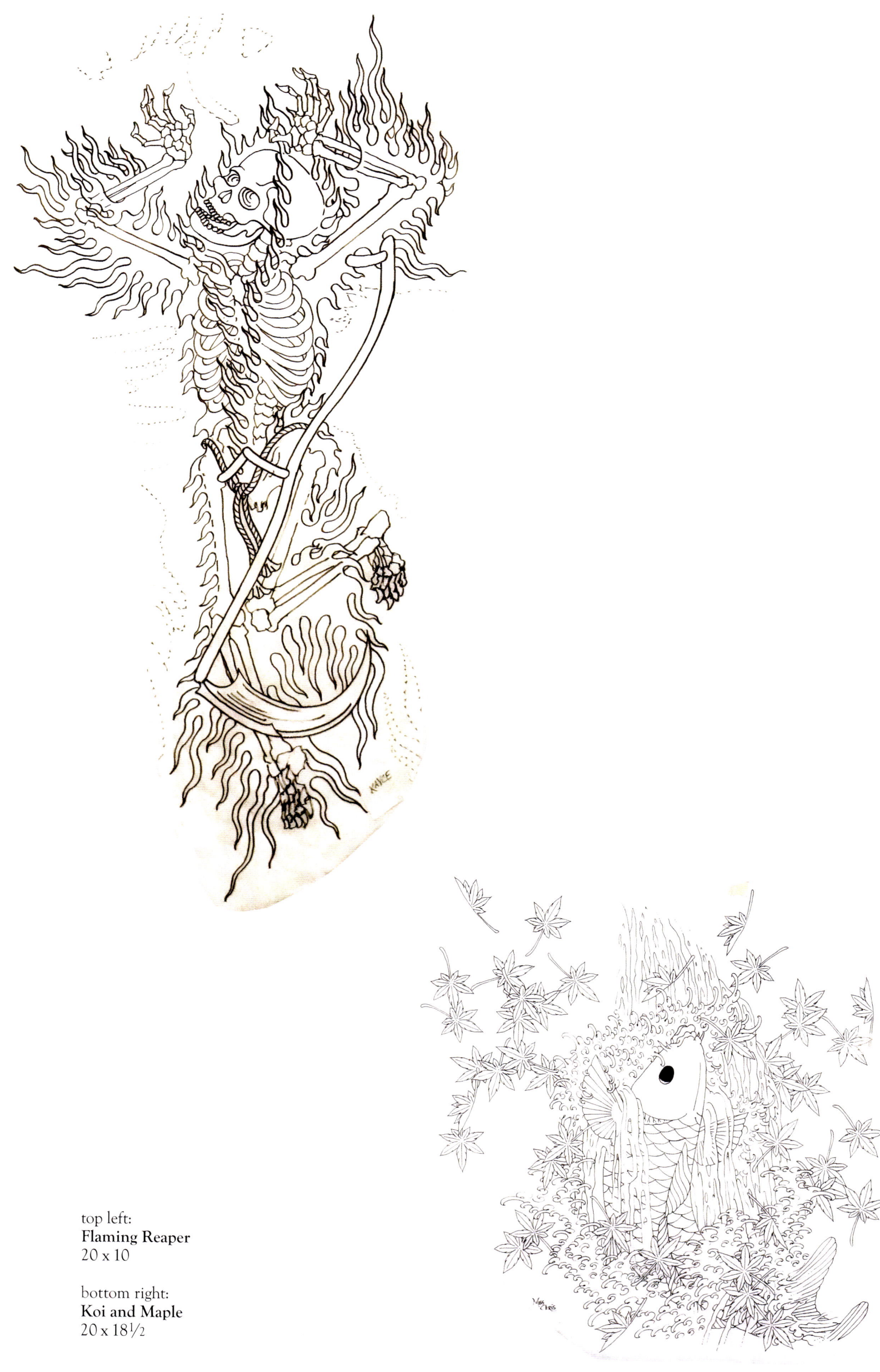

top left:
Flaming Reaper
20 x 10

bottom right:
Koi and Maple
20 x 18½

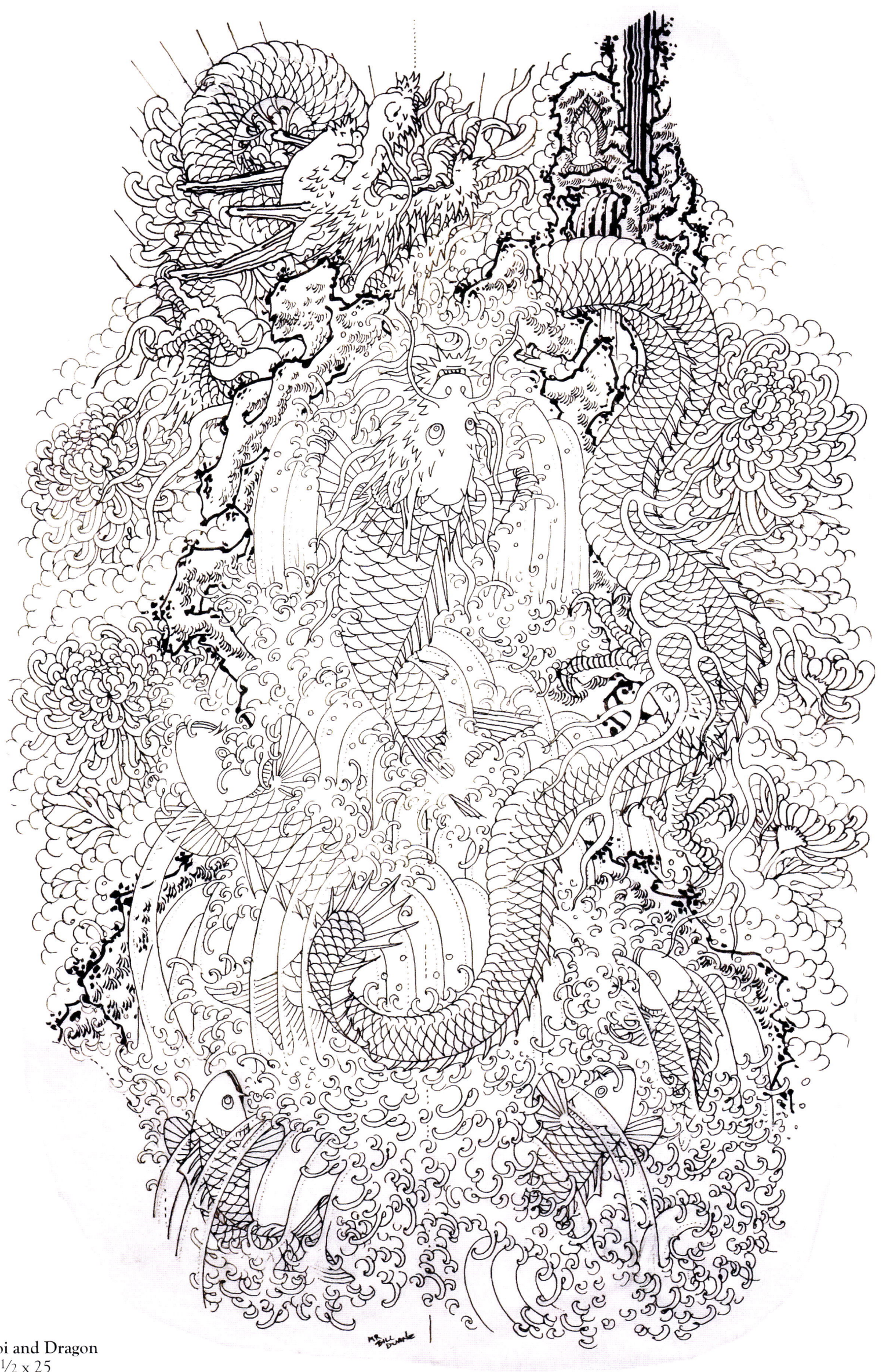

Koi and Dragon
39½ x 25

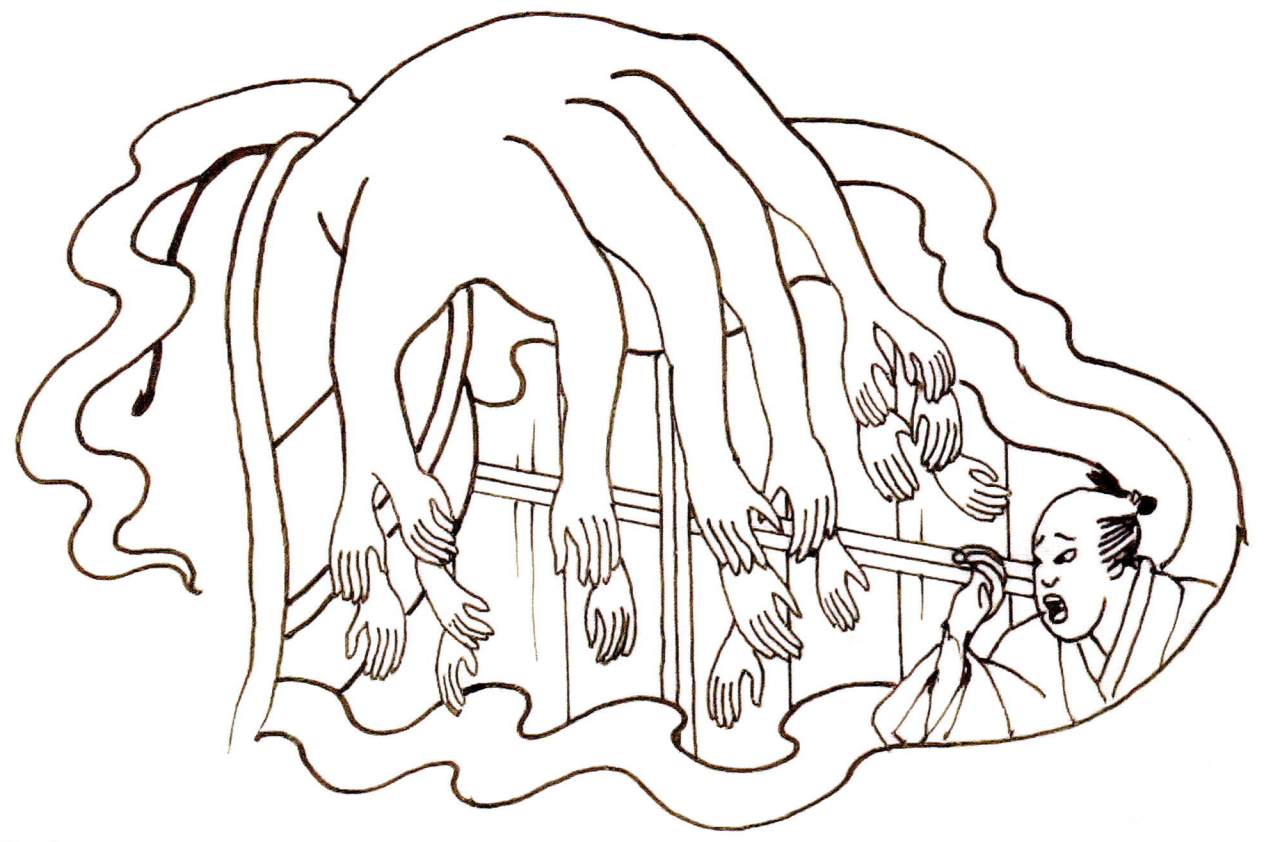

Creepy Hand
6 x 4

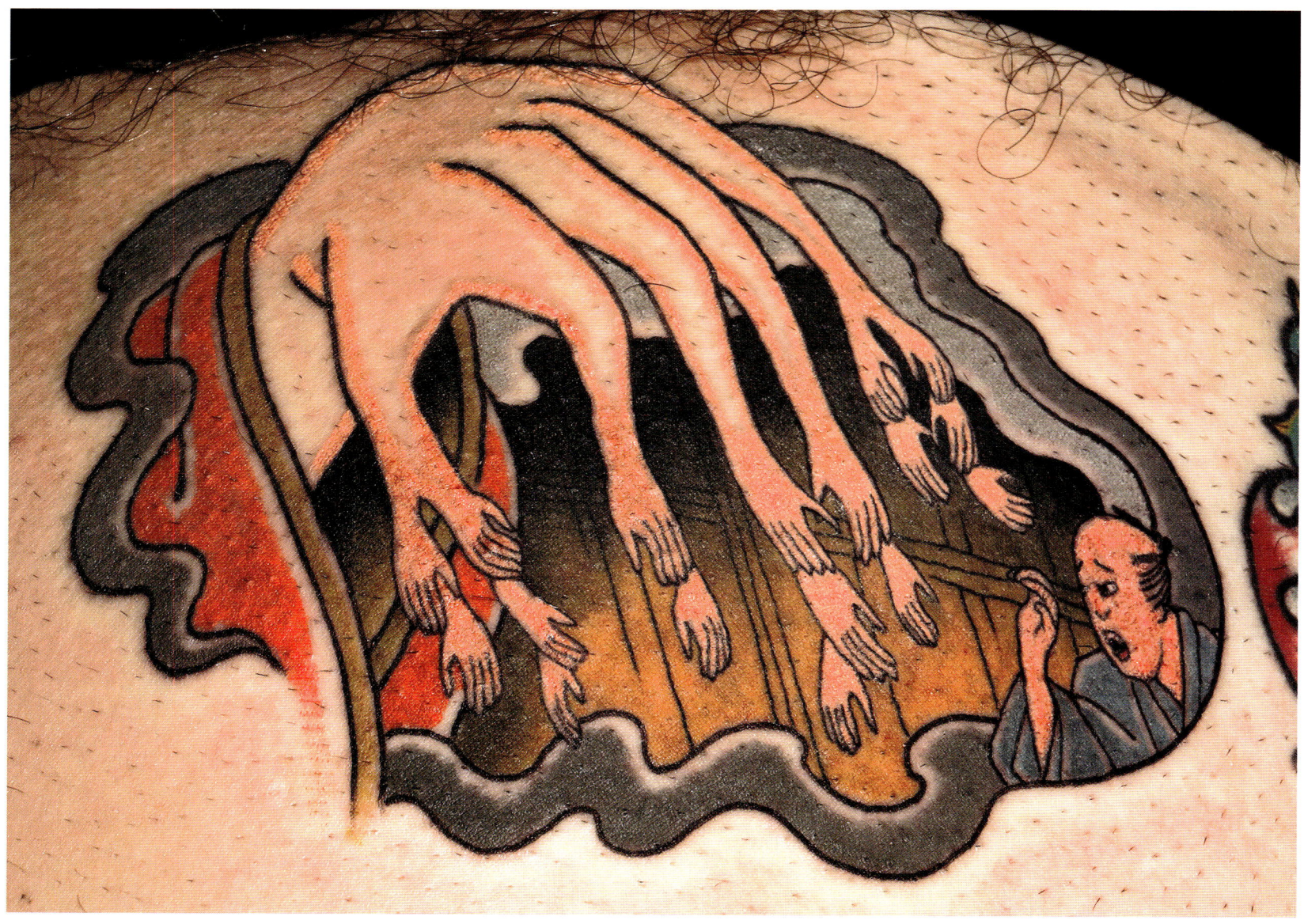

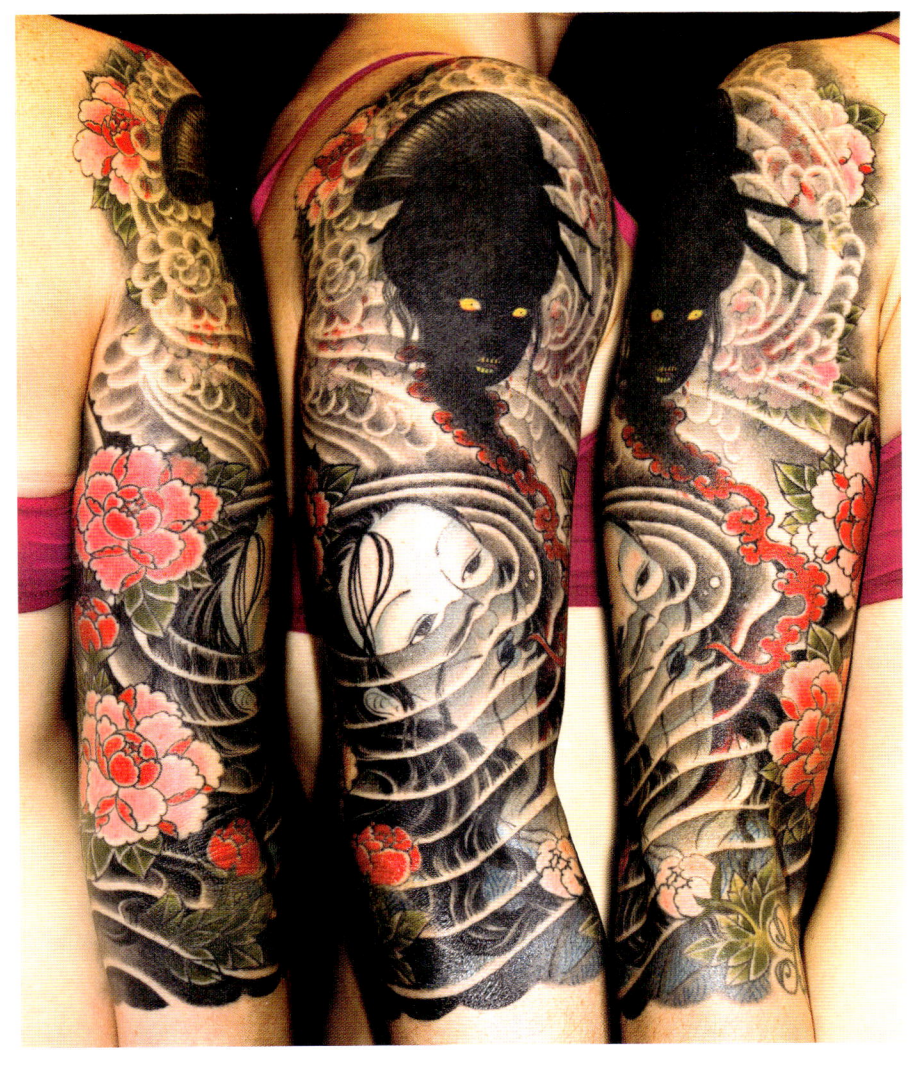

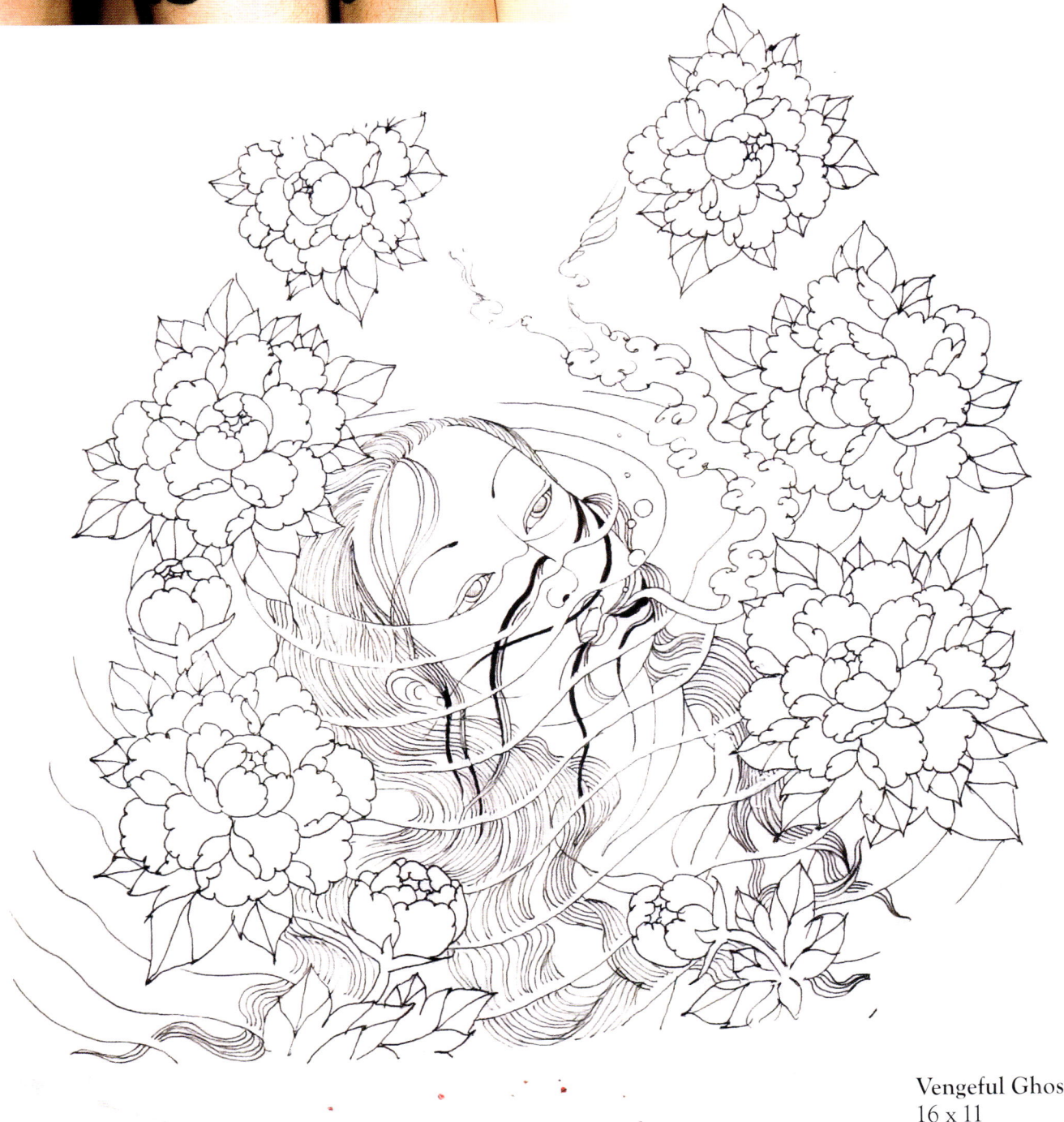

Vengeful Ghost
16 x 11

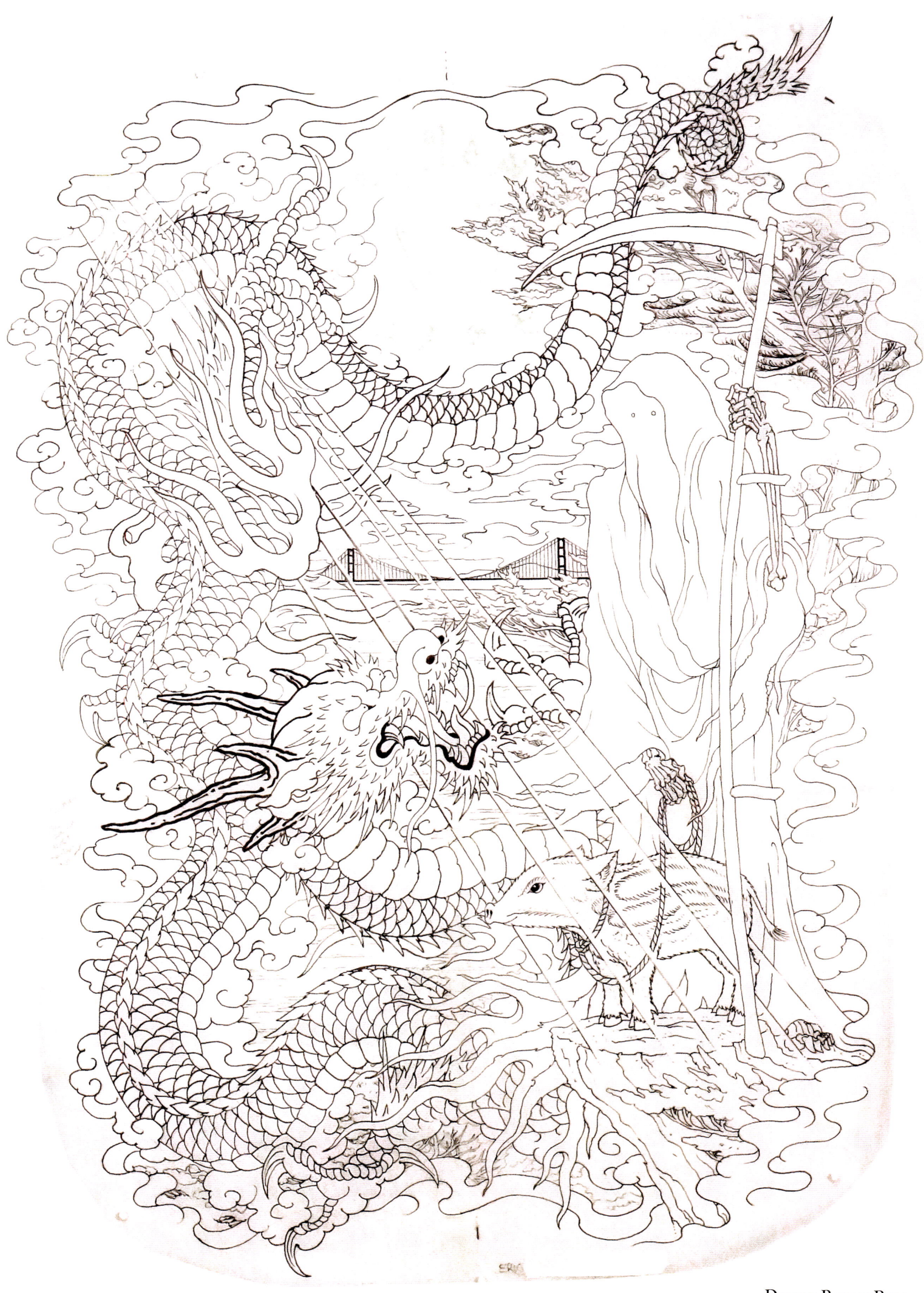

Dragon Reaper Boar
26 x 19

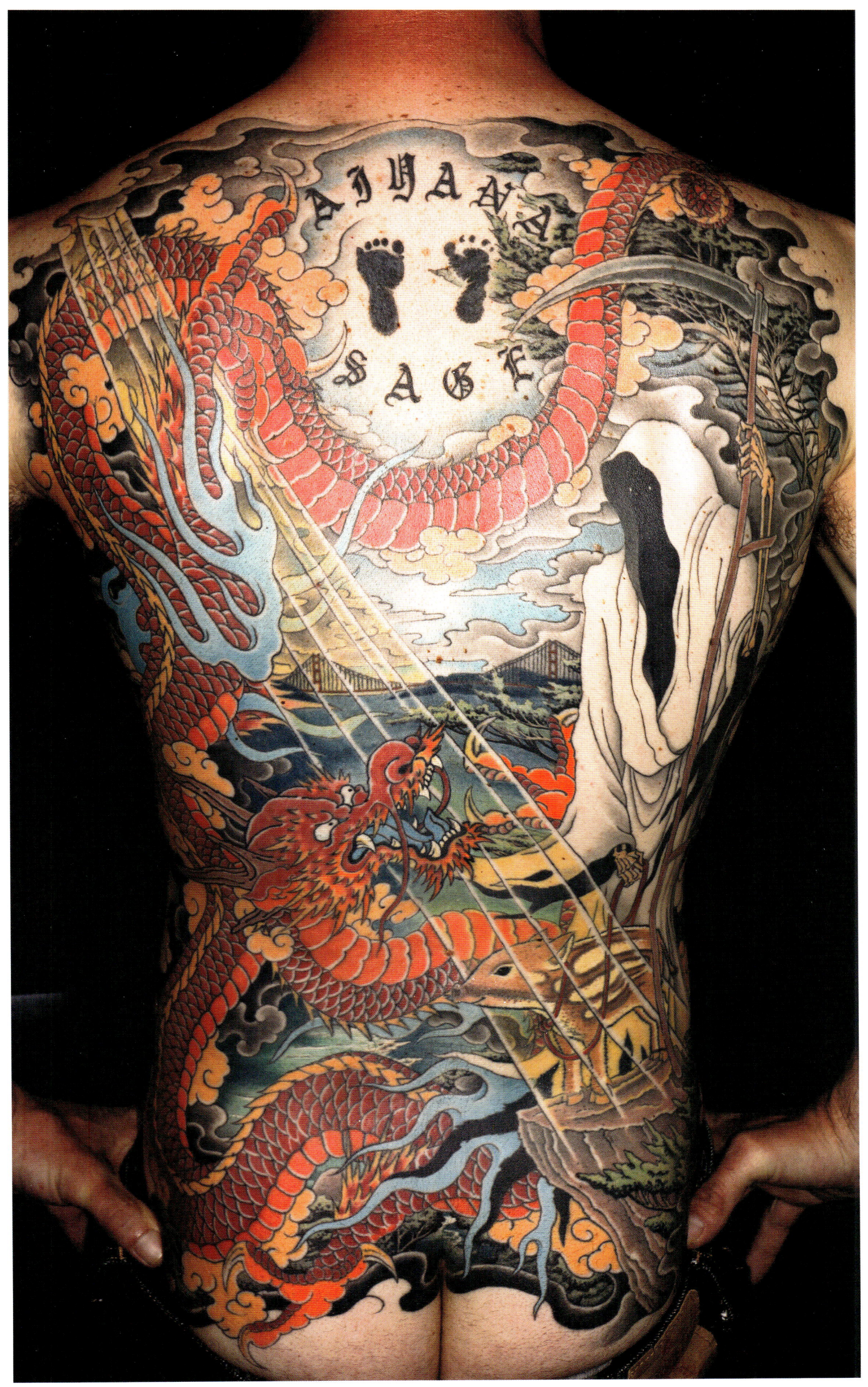

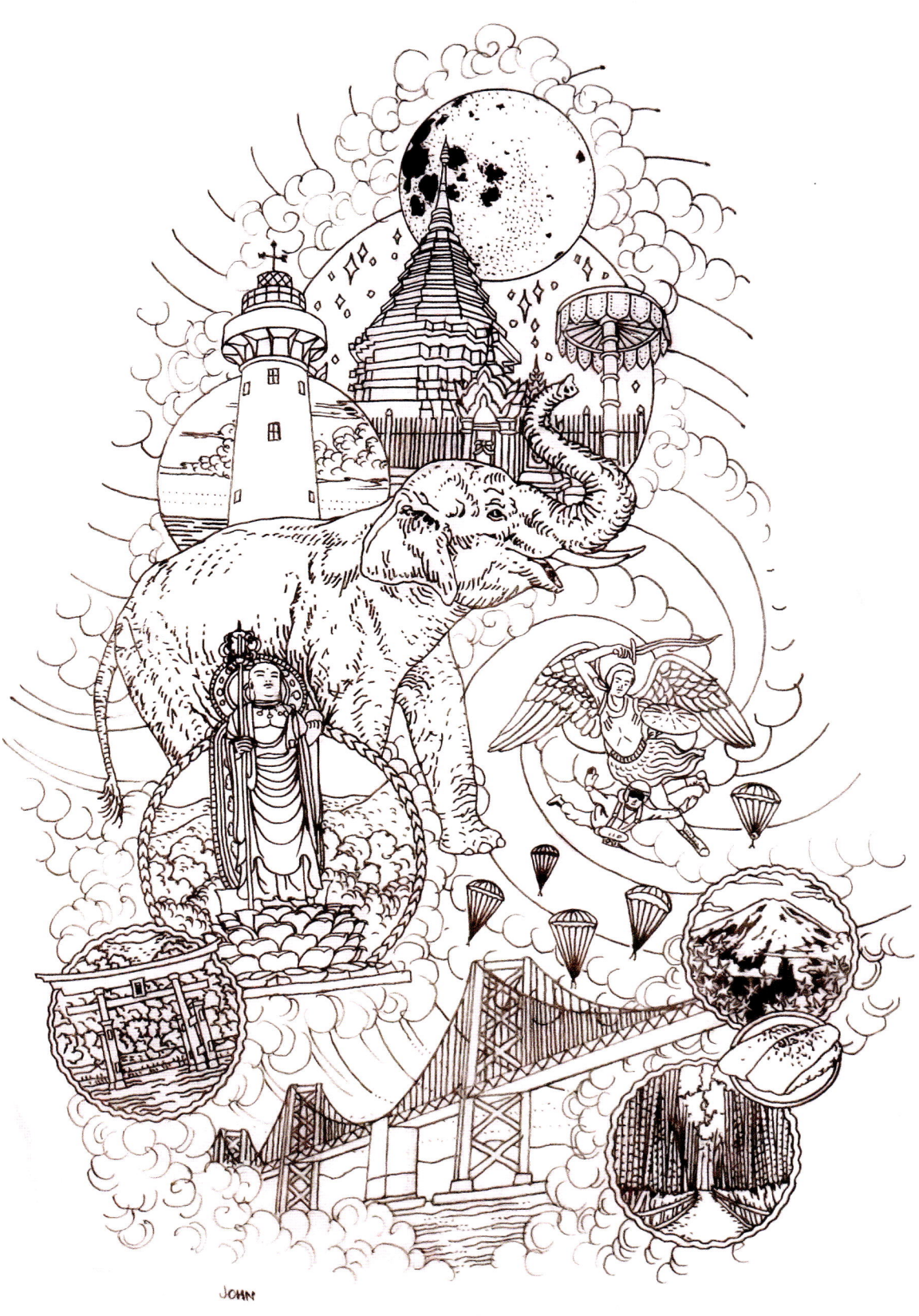

Travel
20 x 14

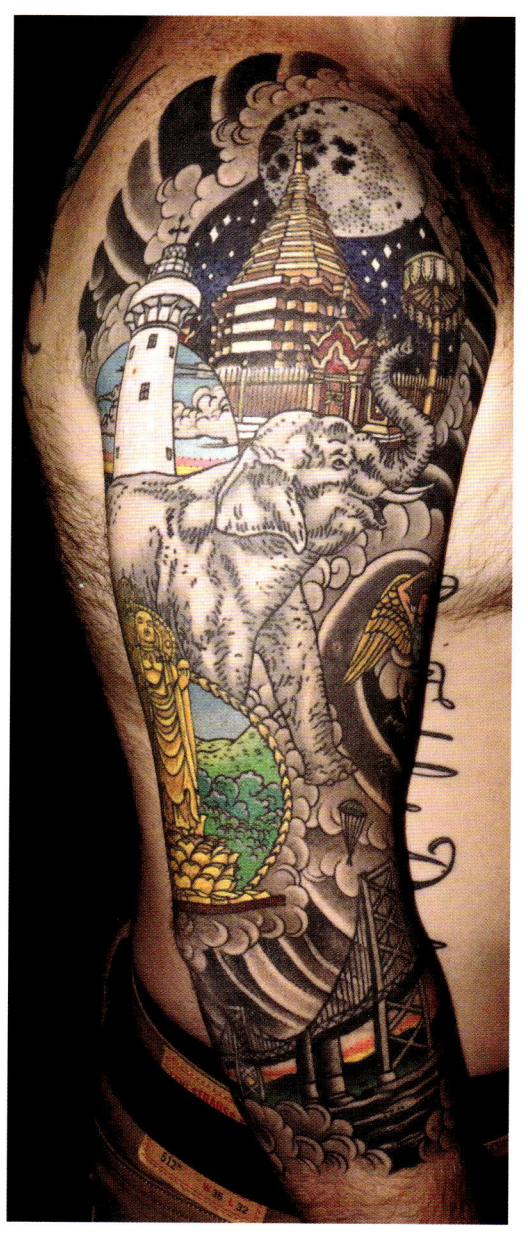

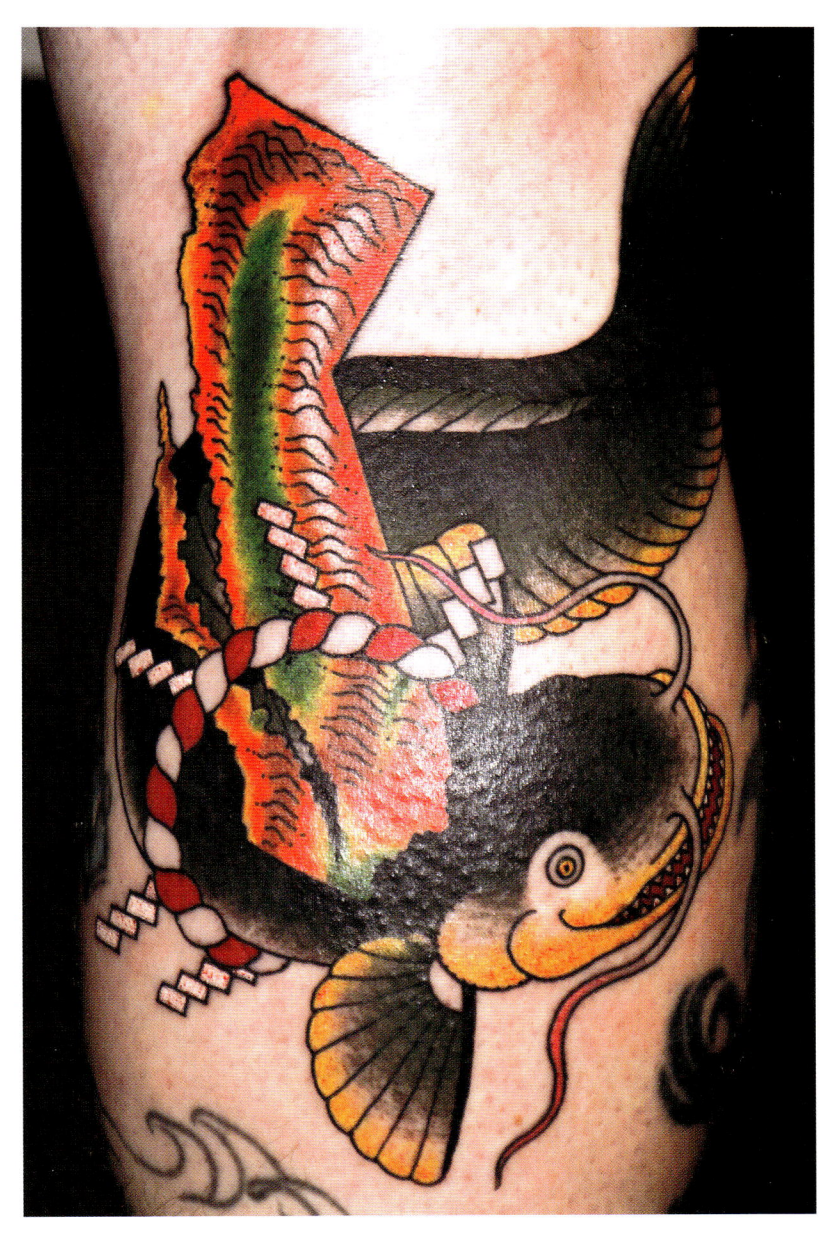

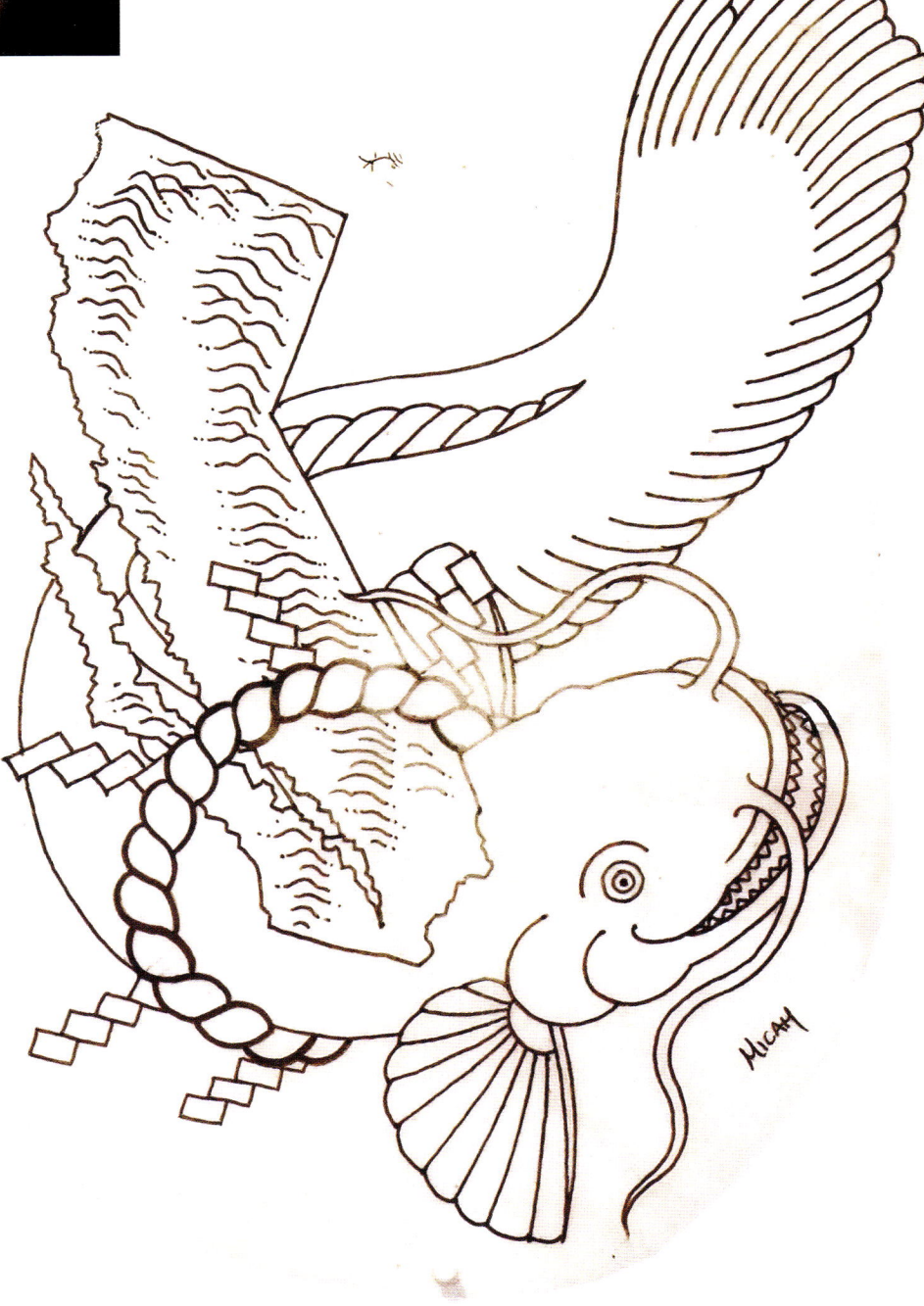

Earthquake Fish
10 x 8½

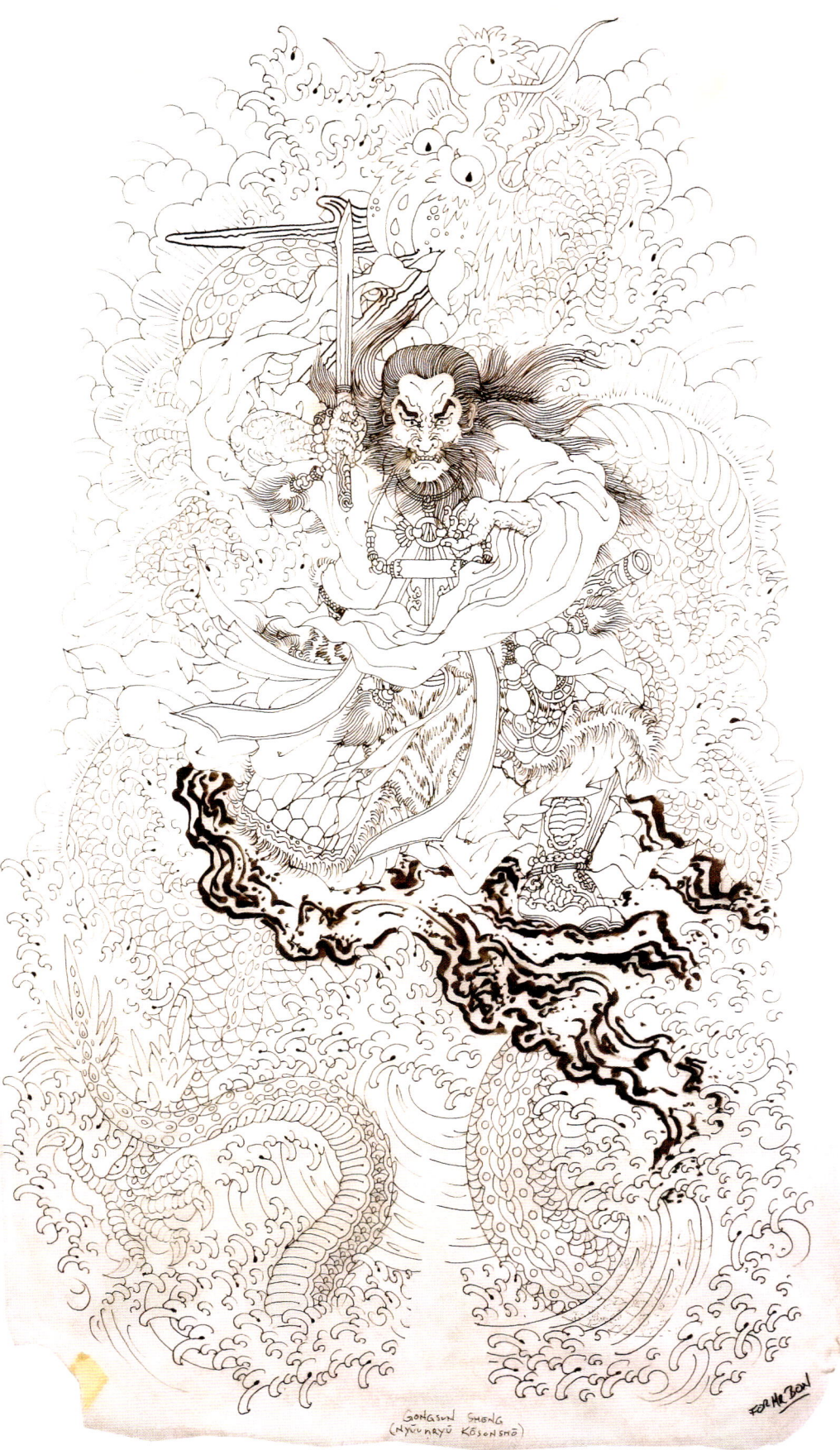

Suikoden Wizard
35 x 19

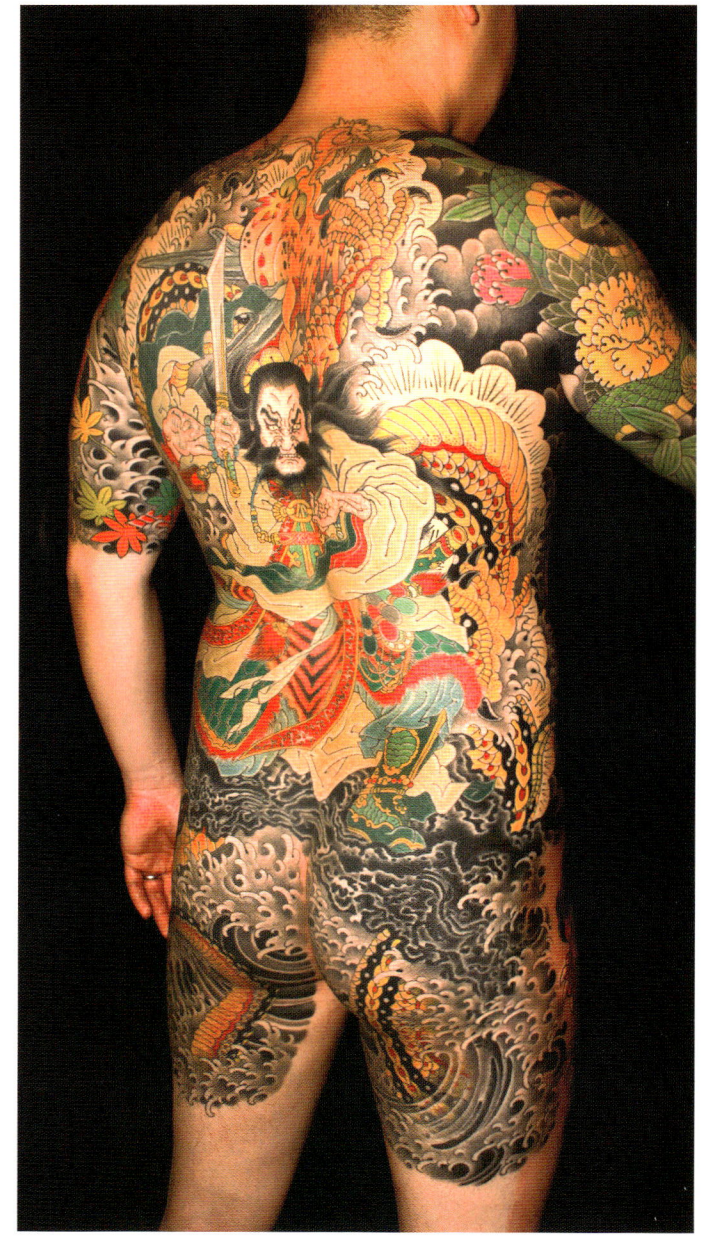

Quan Yin
34 x 16½

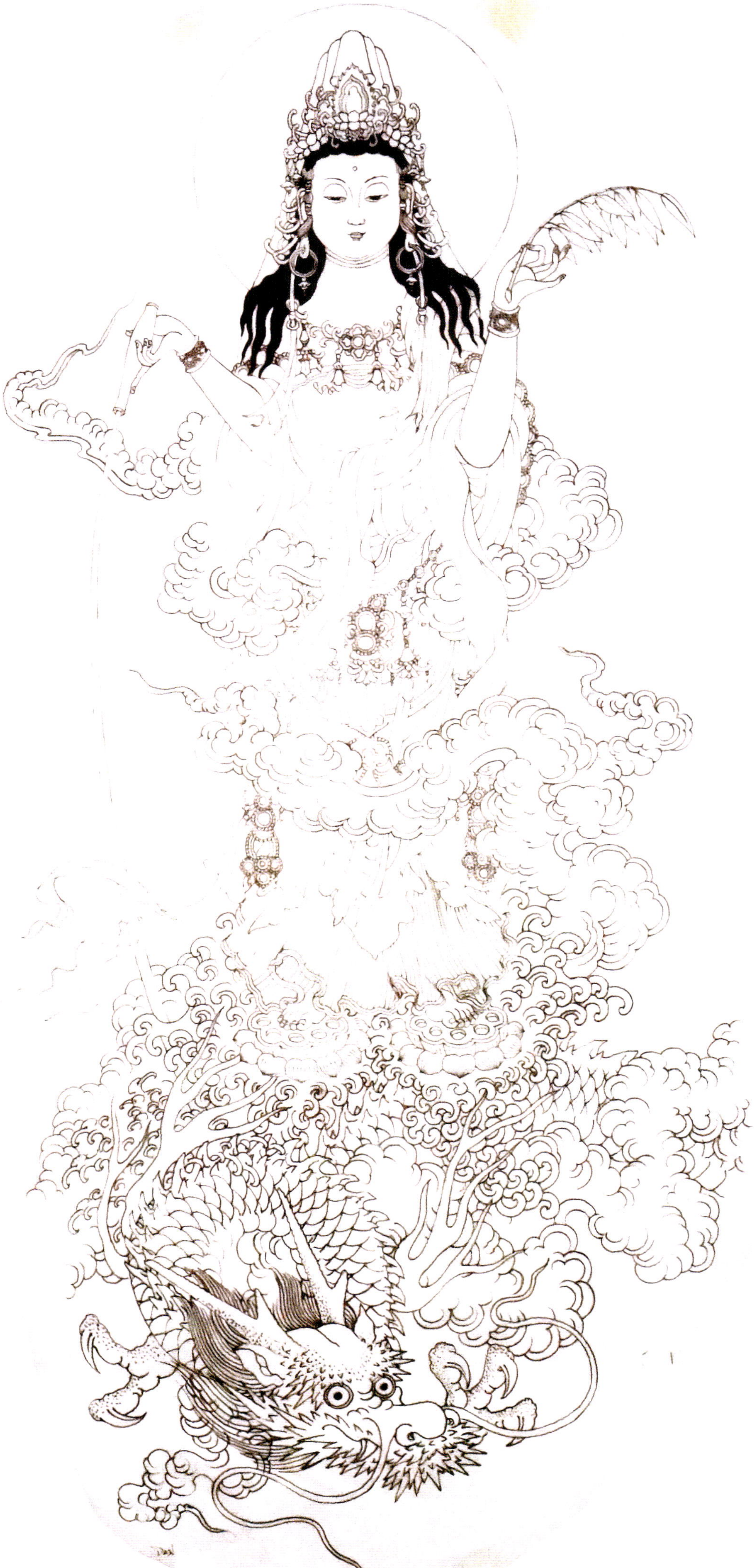

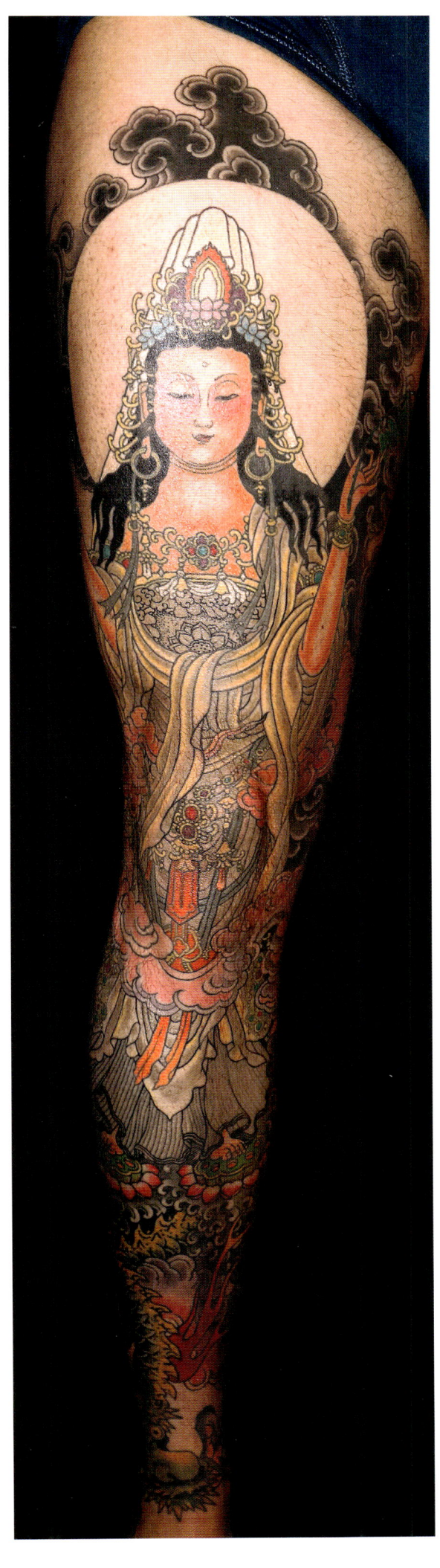

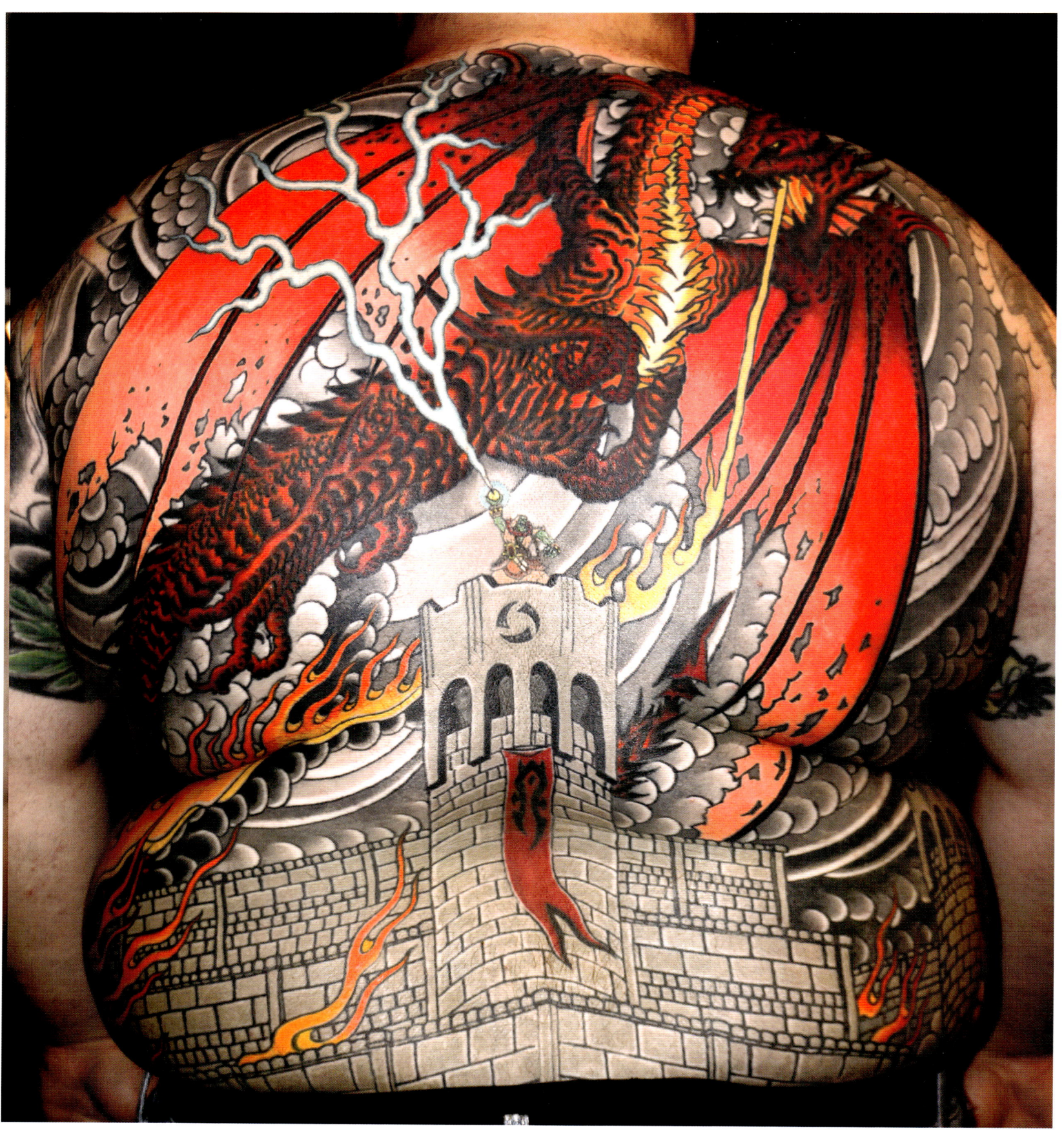

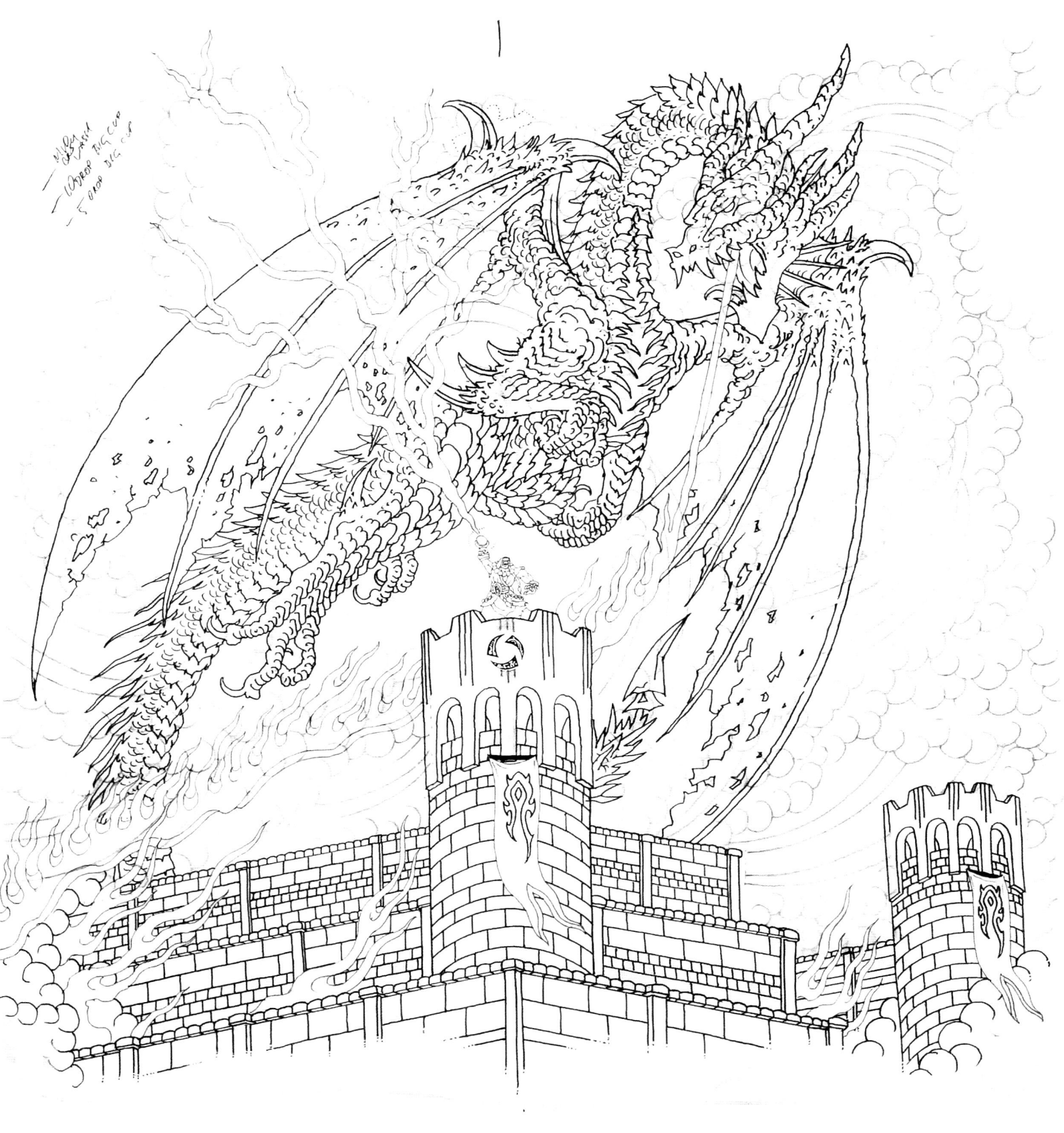

Warcraft
23 x 23

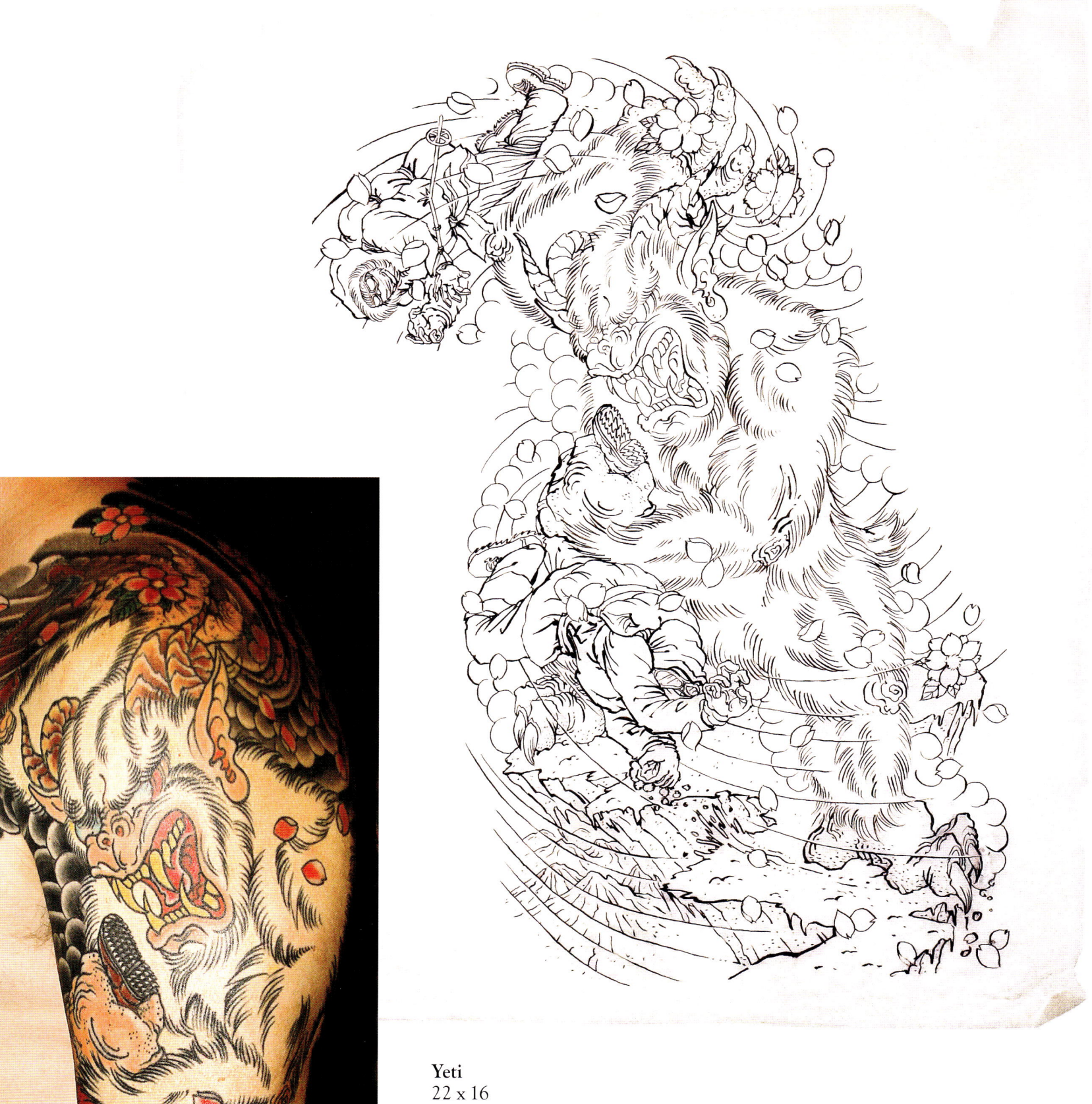

Yeti
22 x 16

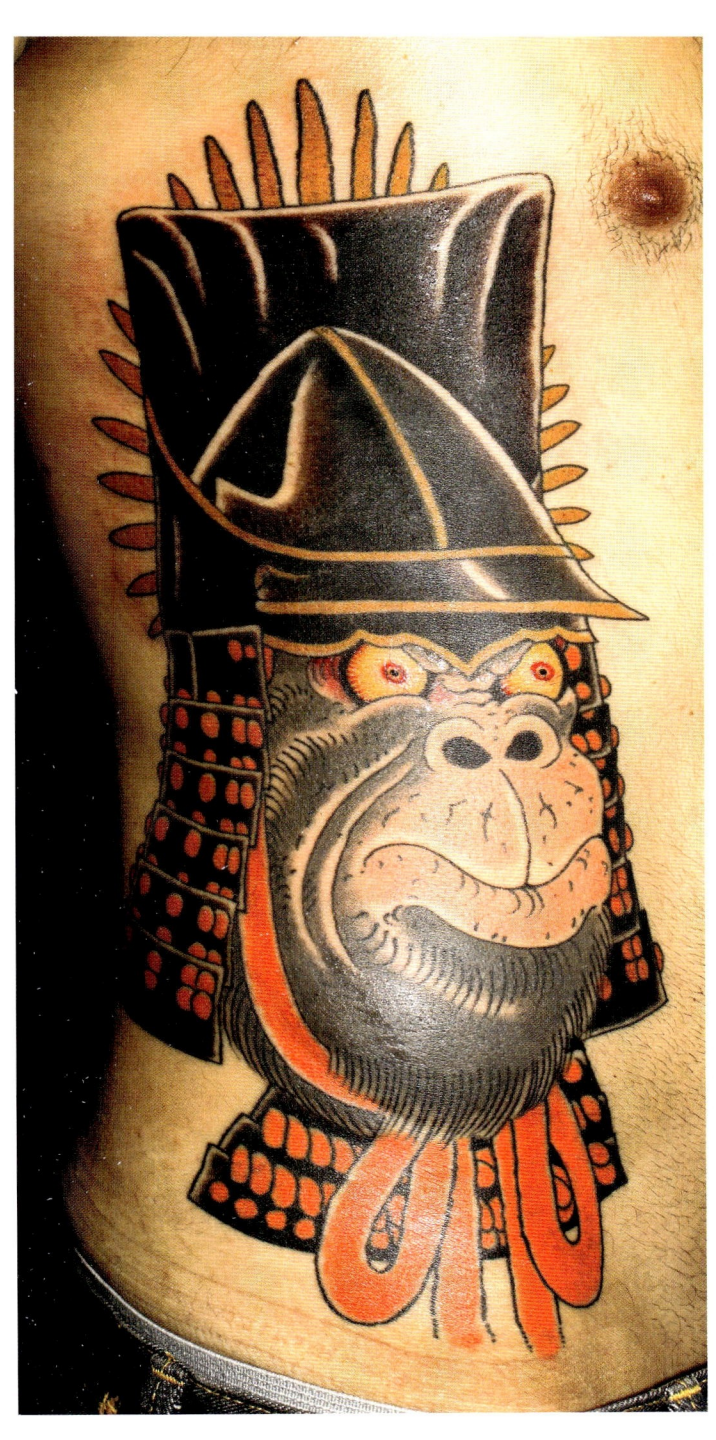

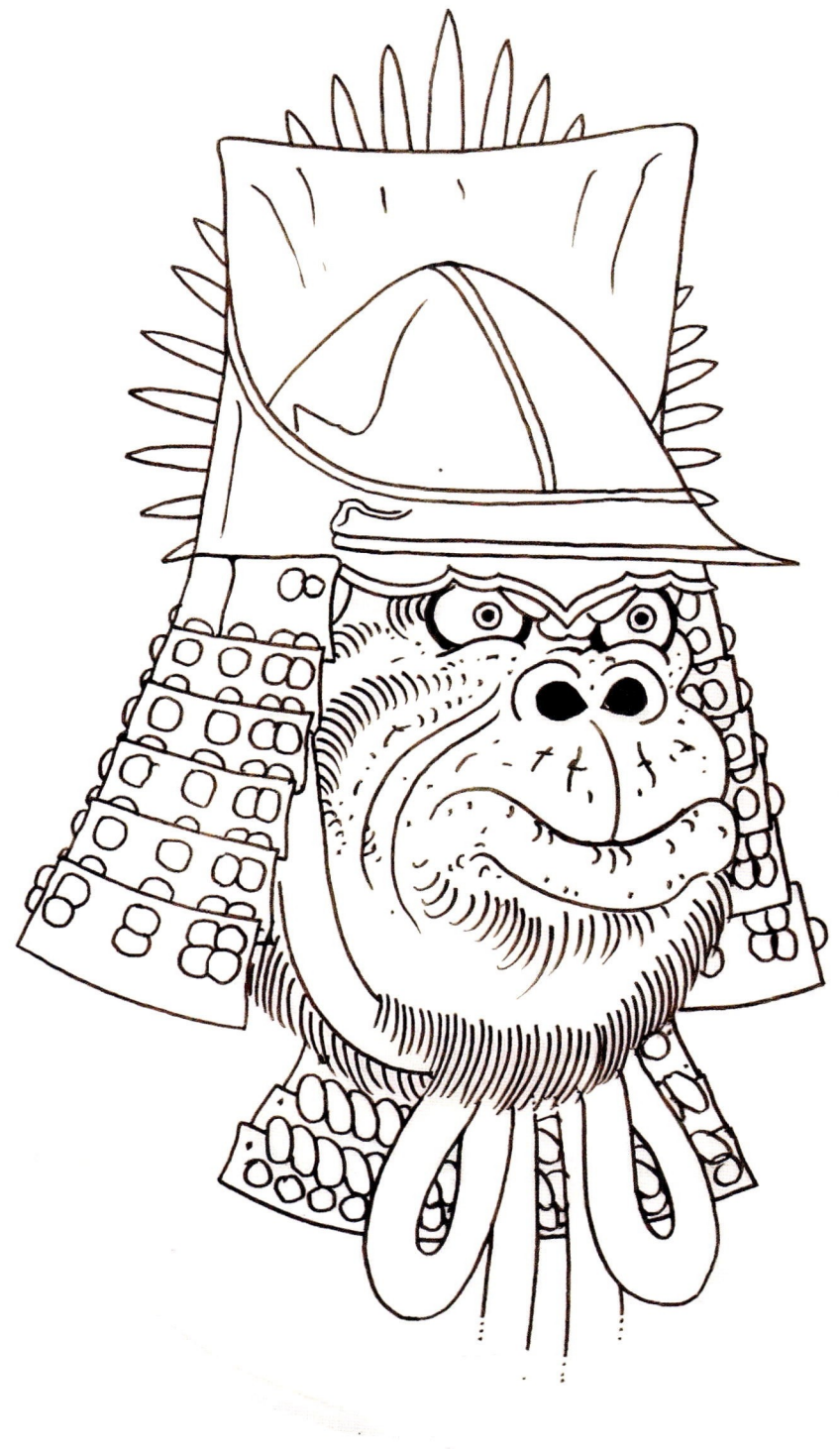

Hideyoshi
14 x 8

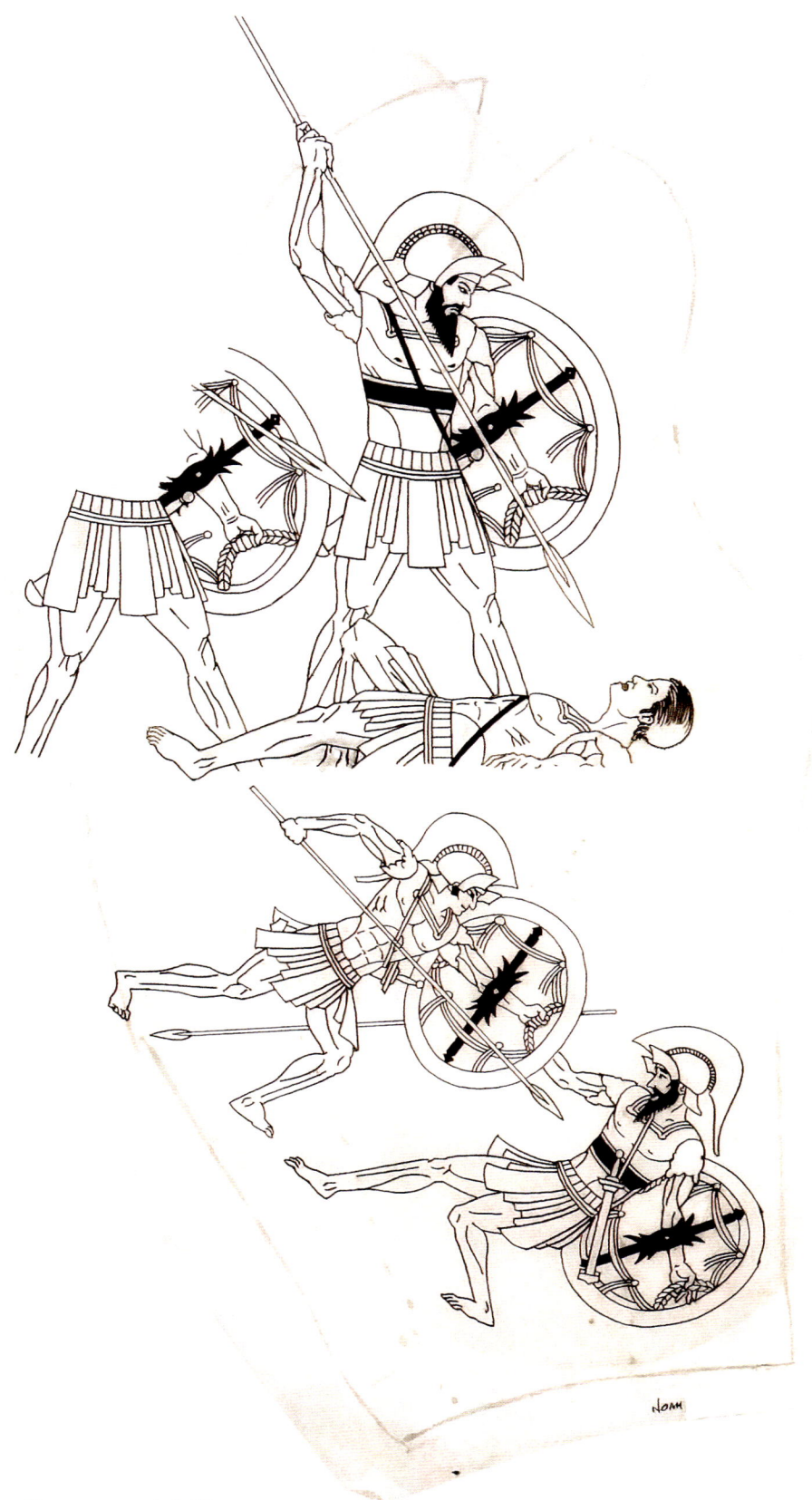

Hector vs. Achilles
23 x 13

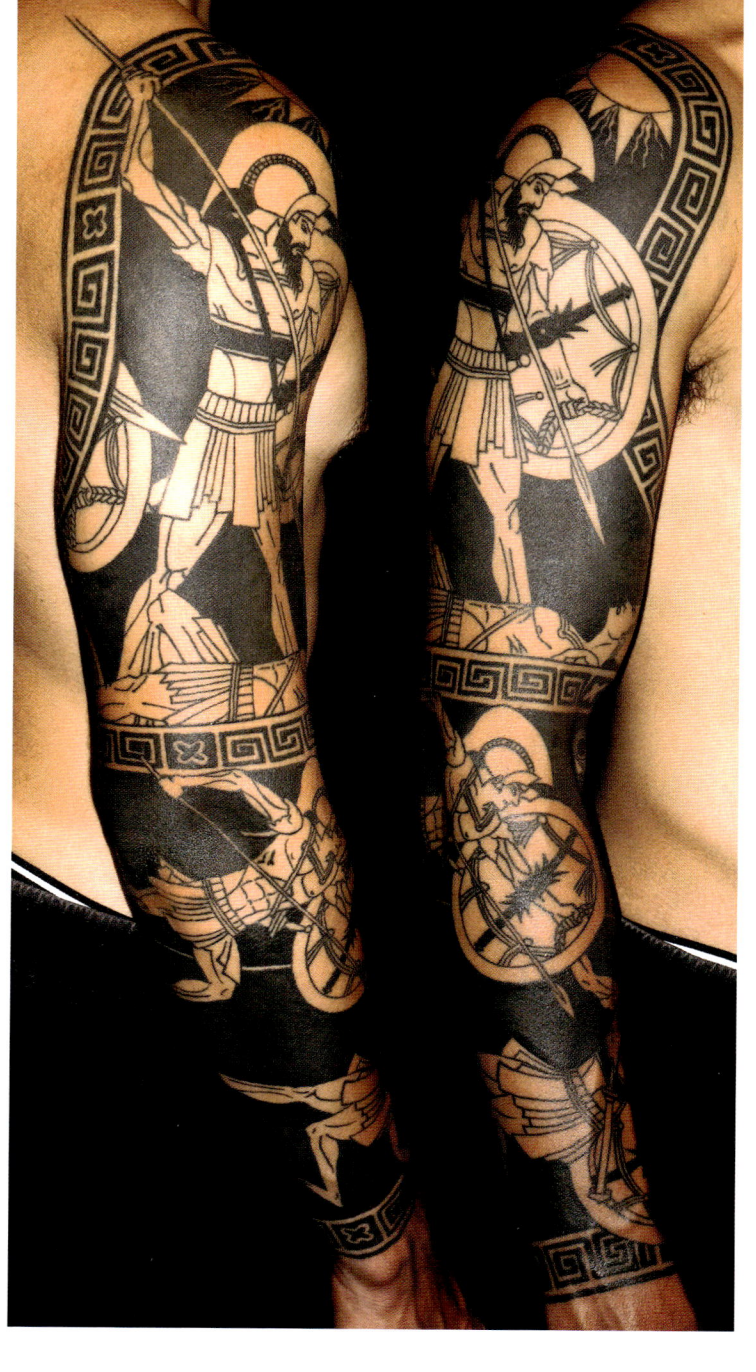

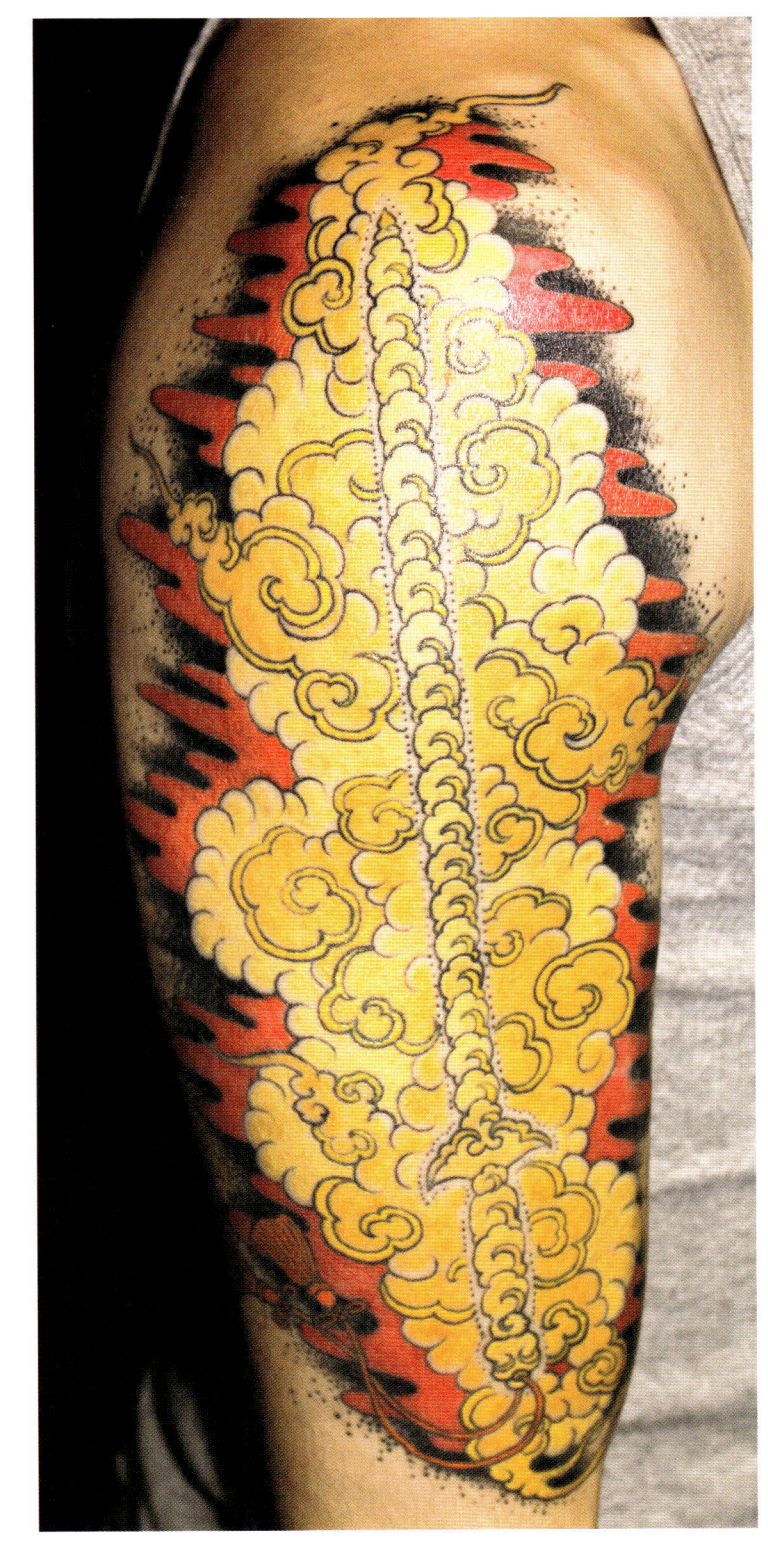

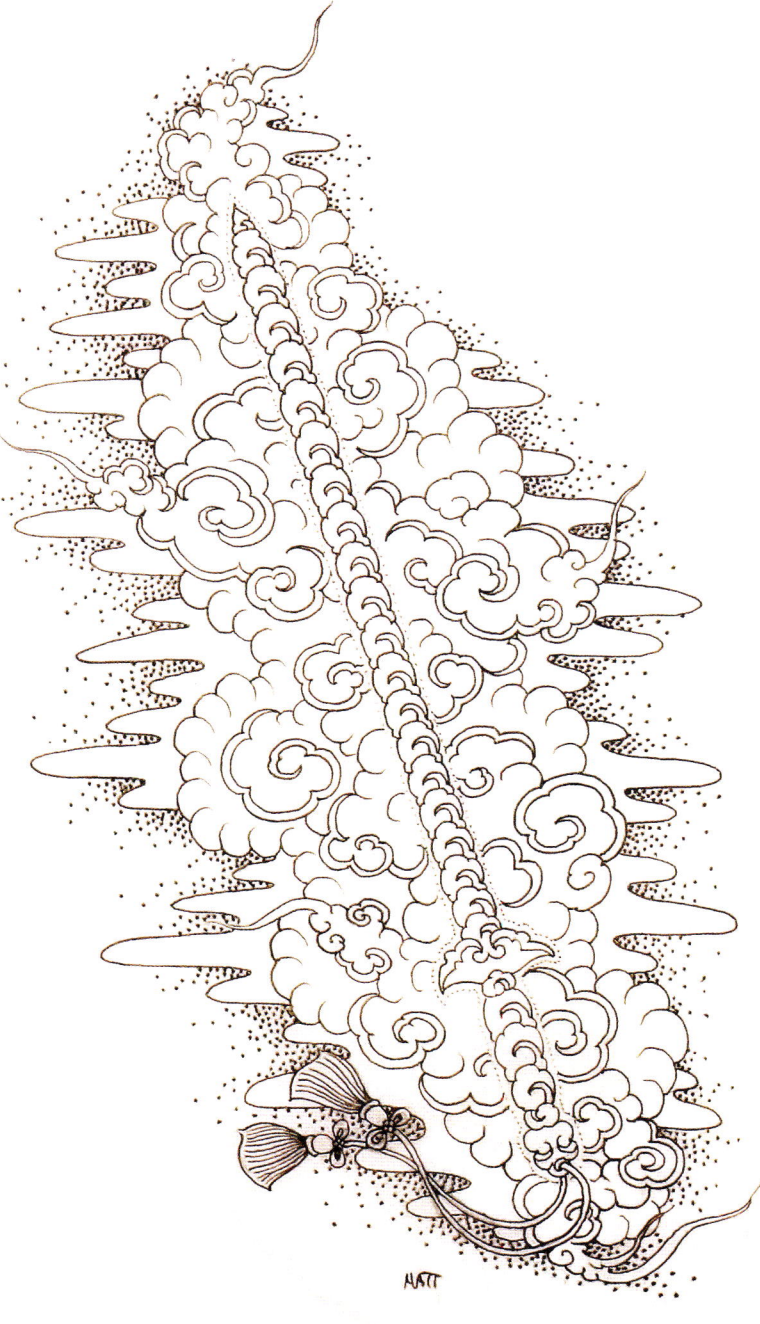

Golden Sword Cloud
12 x 7

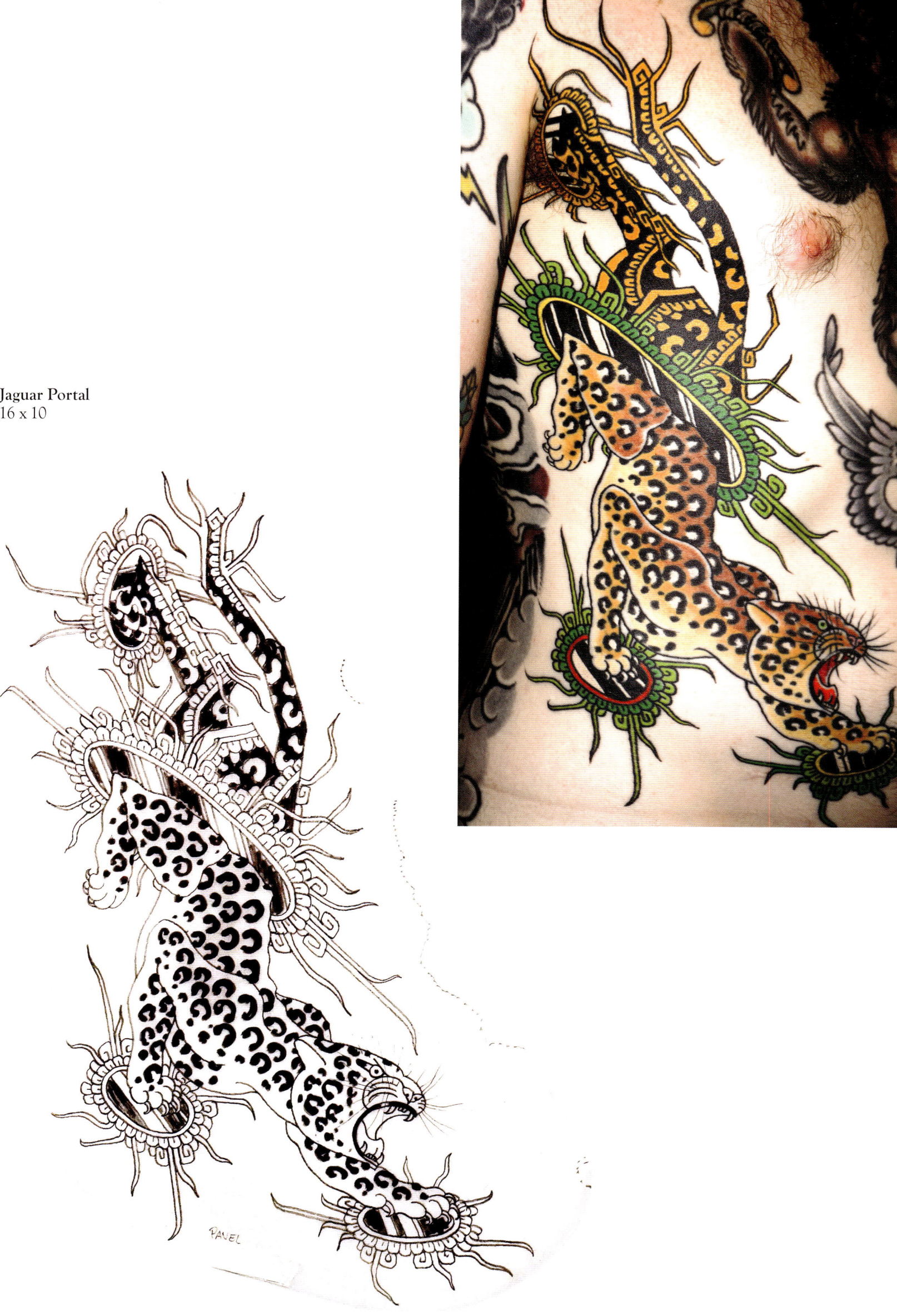

Jaguar Portal
16 x 10

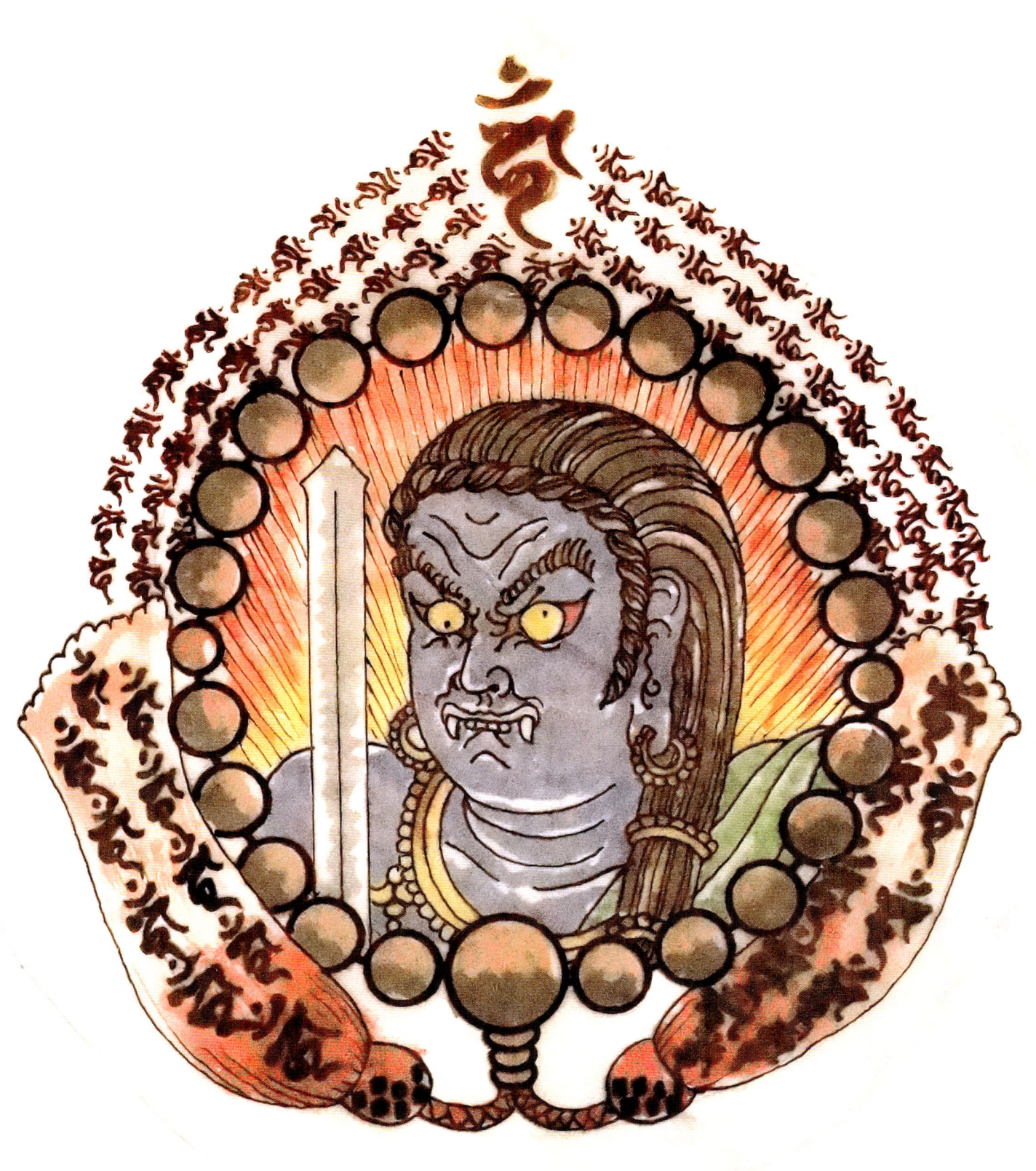

Fudo Juzu
6½ x 5¾

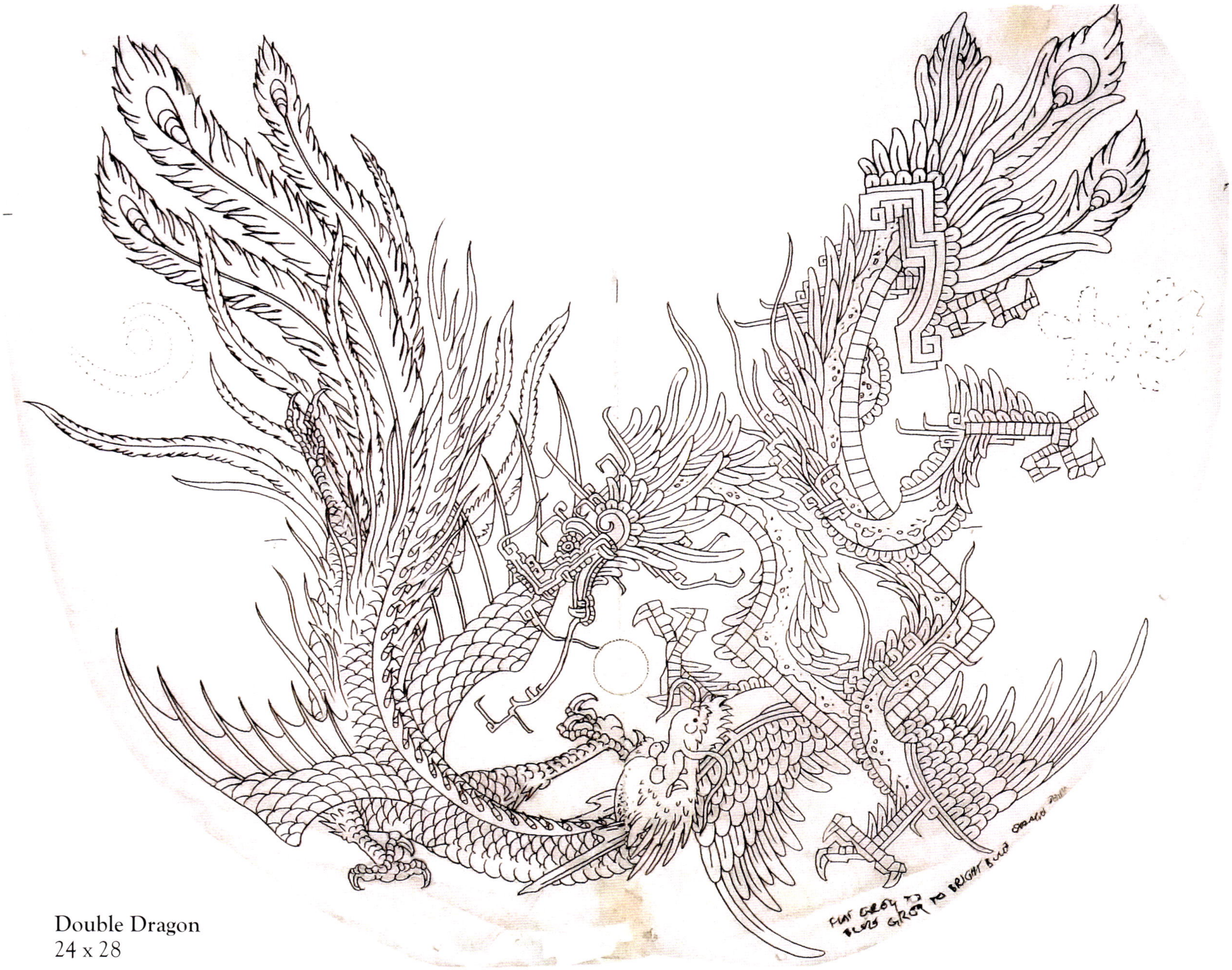

Double Dragon
24 x 28

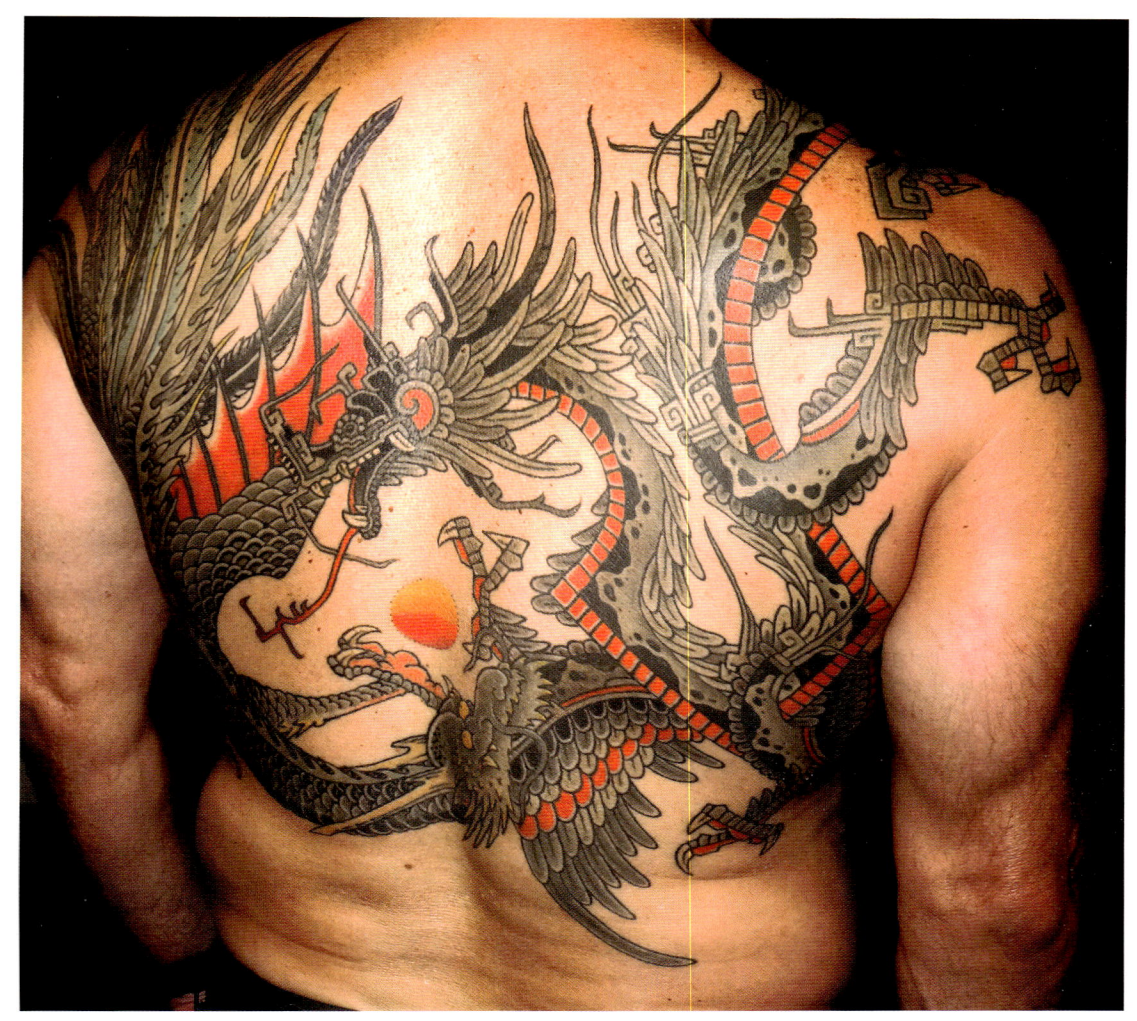

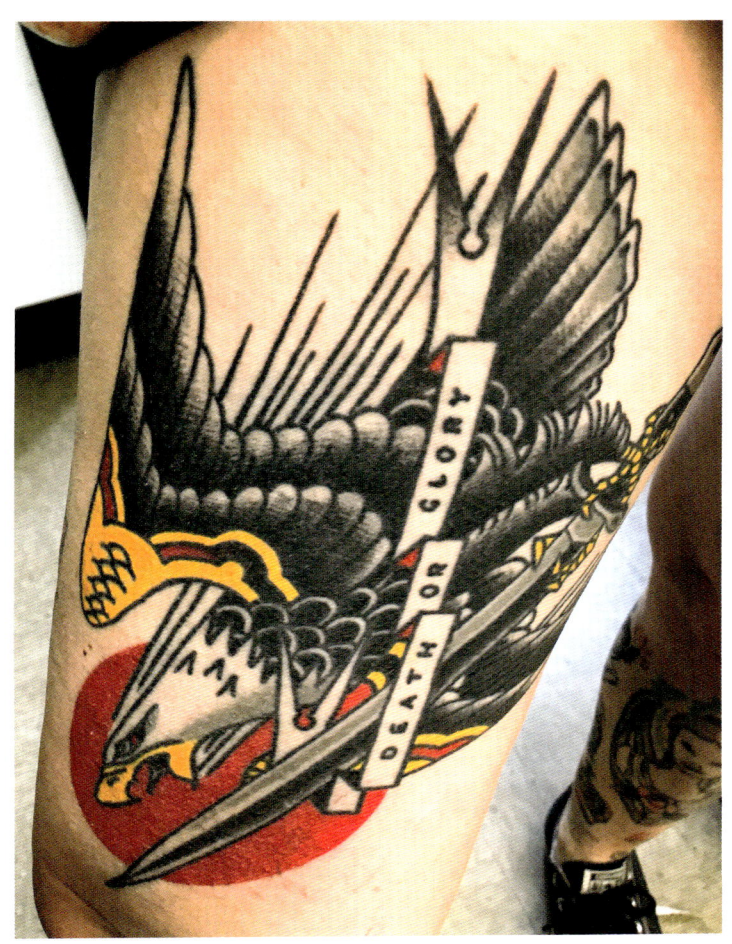

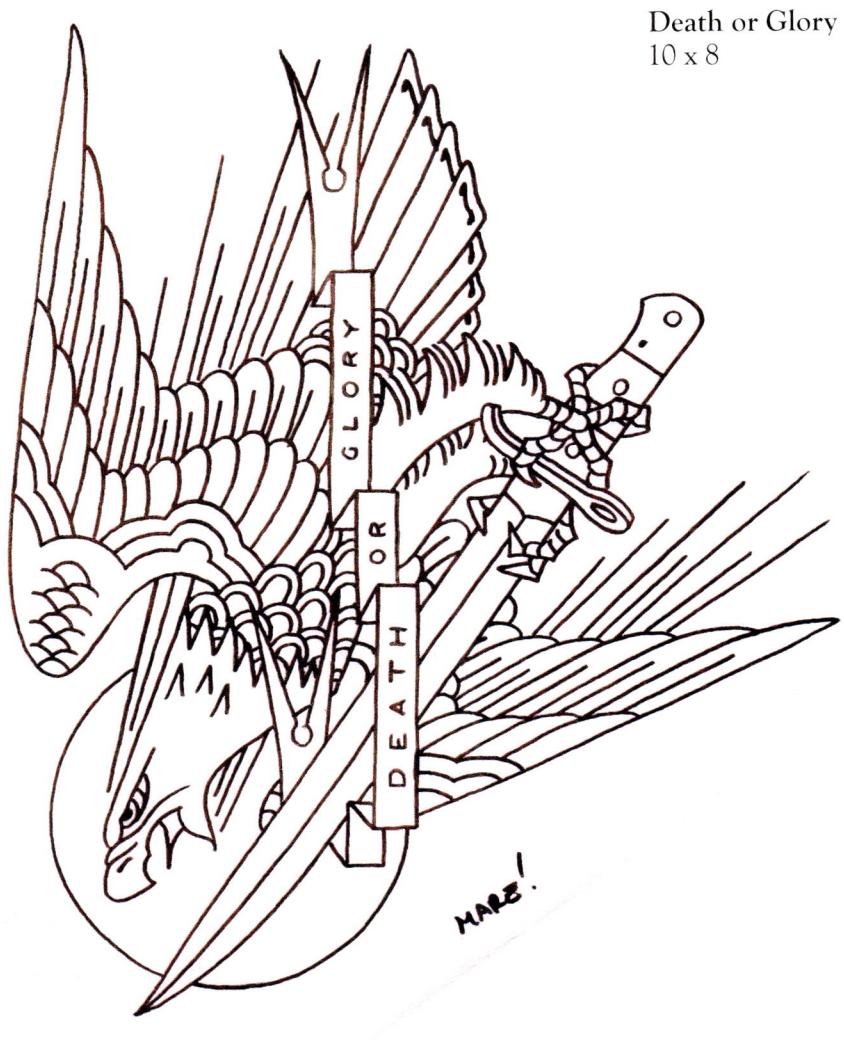

Death or Glory
10 x 8

When leafing through a tattoo magazine in about 2003 I first became aware of Kahlil's work. It instantly riveted me; their power, sophistication and finesse were in a class of their own. Like all art, it's the kind of gut force that cannot be easily put into words. I asked around and found that the perpetrator of this dazzling stuff was currently working in San Francisco. It was at a time when a new artist was needed at Tattoo City. I promptly contacted the shop where he was employed and said I wanted to hire him. This paid off in spades; besides being gifted with a unique and enormous talent, he is a truly nice guy. What he brings to tattooing is enabled with equal amounts of nuanced social skills, born talent as a visual artist, a deep intellect, and relentless inquisitiveness—all honed by an ongoing immersion in literature and history. His work continues to knock me out and it is an honor to showcase it to the world at large.

—Ed Hardy

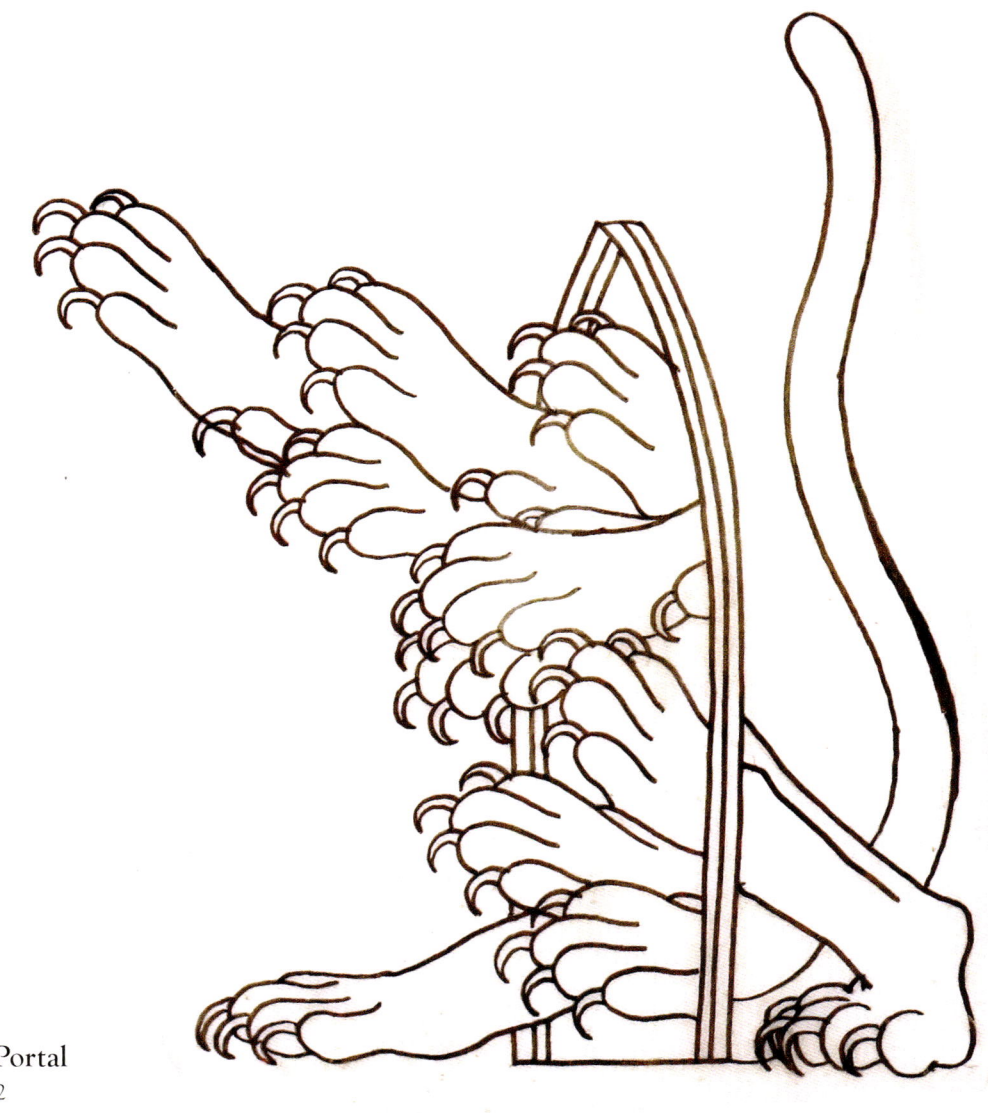

Panther Portal
8½ x 7½

Hardy Marks Publications
700 Lombard Street
San Francisco, CA 94133
hardymarks.com

©2019 Hardy Marks Publications

Library of Congress Cataloguing-in-Publication
Data Available

ISBN #978-0-945367-26-0

Printed and bound by Prolong Press, China
Printed on 157 gsm Matt artpaper
First Edition, 3000 copies

Distributed by SCB Distributors (scb.com)

Text: Kahlil Rintye, D. E. Hardy

Editor: Francesca Passalacqua

Graphic Design: D. E. Hardy
            Craig Okino, Okino Graphics,
            Honolulu, Hawaii

All artworks copyright Hardy Marks Publications